Date Due

de Gruyter Studies in Organization 5

International Business in the Middle East

de Gruyter Studies in Organization

An international series by internationally known authors presenting current fields of research in organization.

Organizing and organizations are substantial pre-requisites for the viability and future developments of society. Their study and comprehension are indispensable to the quality of human life. Therefore, the series aims to:

– offer to the specialist work material in form of the most important and current problems, methods and results;
– give interested readers access to different subject areas;
– provide aids for decisions on contemporary problems and stimulate ideas.

The series will include monographs, collections of contributed papers, and handbooks.

International Business in the Middle East

Editor: Erdener Kaynak

Walter de Gruyter · Berlin · New York 1986

Dr. Erdener Kaynak

Professor of Marketing and Chairman, Department of Business Administration,
Mount Saint Vincent University, Halifax, Nova Scotia, Canada

Dedicated to my wife Glynis
for everything she has done for me

Library of Congress Cataloging in Publication Data

International business in the Middle East.

(De Gruyter studies in organization ; 5)
Bibliography: p.
Includes index.
1. International business enterprises – Near East – Addresses, essays,
lectures. 2. Corporations, Foreign – Near East – Addresses, essays, lectures.
3. Industrial management – Near East – Addresses, essays, lectures. 4. Mar-
keting – Near East – Addresses, essays, lectures. I. Kaynak, Erdener.
II. Series.
HD2891.9.I56 1985   658'.049'0956   85–20437
ISBN 0–89925–021–1 (U.S.)

CIP-Kurztitelaufnahme der Deutschen Bibliothek

International business in the Middle East / ed.: Erdener Kaynak. – Berlin ;
New York : de Gruyter, 1985.
(De Gruyter studies in organization ; 5)
ISBN 3-11-010321-4
NE: Kaynak, Erdener [Hrsg.]; GT

Foreword

Western businessmen who contemplate the prospect of doing business in the Arab countries are cognizant of a number of factors and variables that may impact the success of their endeavors. They often lack, however, a systematic frame of reference that may be helpful in approaching their clients, assessing their prospects for success, and maintaining their relationship with the host country.

The proposed framework for international business relationships encompasses five major components as illustrated in Exhibit 1. These components are:

1. Environment. The economic, competitive, physical, technological, social, and cultural environment of the Arab host country must be analyzed and its essence should be reflected in the business decisions and daily social conduct of the home country managers. Functioning within the environmental context of the host country is the first step towards successful operating management in an Arab host country.

2. Management Processes. The approach and methodology used by host country executives to plan, organize, staff, coordinate, communicate, and control a business organization must be studied, analyzed, and understood. Bridging the managerial gap between home country and host country managment requires the skill of seasoned executives well versed in international business and political aspects of doing business.

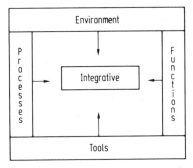

Exhibit 1: A Frame of reference for understanding host country management

3. Business Functions. The content, dominance, and performance of the various business functions including personnel, marketing, logistics, operations, materials, and financial management in the host country must be accounted for and counterbalanced through organizational designs architected to achieve desired performance goals in each and every functional area.

4. Management Tools. Managerial decision making and the daily operation of a business requires the development of a number of tools including economic analysis, accounting, financial analysis, quantitative analysis, and behavioral analysis of consumers, users, and competitors. The nature of the tools used by host country management and the extent and consistency of their application must be communicated by staff assistants in order to prepare management reports comprehensible to all concerned parties.

5. Strategy. The integrative force of the environment, management processes, business functions, and managerial tools is the process of strategy and policy formulation and implementation. Strategy is a way-of-thinking impeded in the managerial culture and influenced by the experience and outlook of the individual manager. Some cultures and experiences encourage and force holistic strategic thinking while others foster operative and tactical orientations.

I was delighted to receive Professor Kaynak's call for papers to develop this excellent volume on *International Business in the Middle East.* The introductory chapter of the book ably presents the design and plan of the text. The components of the environment, management processes, business functions, managerial tools, and business strategy are addressed throughout the text. The emphasis on marketing in this text is warranted as it has been the most neglected business function in the Middle East and in Arab countries in particular.

I congratulate Erdener Kaynak for the successful completion of this project and its potential contribution to improving international business operations in the Middle East.

Adel I. El-Ansary

Professor and Chairman of Business Administration
The George Washington University Washington, D. C. 20052

Preface

Arab countries of the Middle East are of substantial global importance, especially to trade-dependent nations of North America and West Europe. Western business community are in a position to probe the new opportunities for trade links and joint ventures in the Middle Eastern countries, especially those that are rapidly industrializing. Fruitful trading relationships with the Middle East are contingent upon how the Western businessmen deal with the Arabs, which, in turn, depends on the type of knowledge and perception he has about the Arabs' value systems, customs, traditions, expectations, sensitivities, and perceptions of themselves and of the world around them (Almaney, 1982: 11).

Two of the most common errors made by Western businessmen are: a) not investing enough effort in understanding the Arab culture and associated, ways of doing business, b) not being flexible enough in adjusting goals, expectations and operating procedures to allow effective adaptation to the Middle Eastern environment.

This so called Arab Middle Eastern countries are heterogenous in nature, which present more differences than similarities. Some like Libya, Kuwait are very rich. Some others like Egypt and Saudi Arabia are in the process of industrialization and others like Algeria, Syria and Iraq have a highly developed public sector, but many in the region are belong to "have nots" group have neither income nor industry or infrastructure. The region as a whole is enjoying a tremendous growth and this will continue in the forseeable future.

This pioneering book looks at the management and marketing systems of Arab countries of the Middle East – fastest growing markets between Europe and Japan. It is estimated that Arab Middle East's share in world trade will grow at real rates of 5–15 per cent per annum during 1980s. In the same period, the growth of world trade will not exceed 3 percent. The structure as well as the magnitude of Arab trade is going to change rapidly. It is expected that the emphasis on trade commodities will shift from basic socio-economic and infrastructure products to industrial and capital goods to build up manufacturing empires. As well, in light of the changing needs and expectations of consumers as well as their increased purchasing power will trigger intense demand for sophisticated consumer goods.

Part I of this book deals with international business concepts in the Middle East. It particularly looks at the cultural, socio-economic and political context of business operations in the region. Part II examines the indigenous management practices of local companies. As well, managerial approaches for Western firms wishing to enter and operate in the Middle East is presented through a number of country case studies. Part III attempts to evaluate the state of marketing development in the Middle East, and tries to delineate the factors as well as circumstances hindering or enhancing marketing development. Marketing practices of firms in the region in this part are systematically related to the prevalent socio-economic, cultural, governmental and technological factors. The final part of the book concludes with a consideration of the future of international business in the Middle East. In particular, it looks at the types of business relationships we will see taking place in the region.

During the preparation of this volume, I have had the cooperation and assistance of too many individuals difficult to name one by one. I would, first of all, extend my sincere appreciation and thanks to contributors to this volume. Among their busy time schedule, they allocated time and energy for a project they deemed important. Most of the contributors, if not all, coming from the region, they attributed a special importance to the completion of this anthology of readings. Over the past seven years, I have had the pleasure and benefit of working with first class scholars and practitioners of the Middle East whose reservoir of knowledge has widened my horizon and understanding of marketing and management practices of countries, firms and public institutions of the region.

I would like to take this opportunity to thank the publishers of this volume – Walter de Gruyter of Berlin and New York – for their foresight and intelligent decision to take on this project. This volume is part of their international series prepared by internationally known authors presenting current research in organizations from an international perspective. In particular, I would offer my heartfelt thanks and appreciation to the publishing director Werner Schuder who has helped and assisted me throughout the completion of this project. I am positive that without his help it would have been far more difficult to complete this assignment on time.

A project of this type necessitates the help and assistance of a number of people who are so vital for a fruitful completion. I was, indeed, very fortunate being able to receive the support of some very able individuals who have dedicated their scarce time resources in the way of helping me. I would like to acknowledge the help of Dr. Ben Issa Hudanah of Garyounis University, Libya, who read some of the most strategic chapters of the book and made very useful and insightful comments. His thought provoking ideas and wise and gentle suggestions have helped me immensely. At the faculty level Dr. Susan Drain and Musetta Thwaites have reviewed a number of chapters and made very useful style changes. Their professional advice has also improved the literary style of the book. I extend my thanks and appreciation to Mrs. Brenda Nicholson who did a superb job of typing a number of chapters and met my rigid deadlines calmly and efficiently. Secretarial pool of Mount Saint Vincent University assisted me in preparing references by wordprocessing for which I am very thankful and appreciative. My secretary – Mrs. Debbie Smicer, assisted me in corresponding with the contributors and other national and international organizations for which she deserves a praise.

During the completion of this project, I lost a dear friend, great intellect and outstanding scholar – Dr. Metin N. Gürol of Saint Joseph's University, Philadelphia at the peak of his career. I had the pleasure of working with Metin on a number of research projects related to the Middle East. We have a joint chapter in this volume and he was very excited about it. He would have really liked to see the publication of this volume as he had been rightly concerned about the lack of reading material on marketing and management in the Middle East. We will all dearly miss you Metin.

My wife Glynis, my daughters Öykü Hacer, Övgü Ilke and Elif Sevgi were a constant source of encouragement. Their understanding, appreciation and long lasting support is greatly appreciated. I spent endless weekends in the library reviewing material, typing late at nights and crystallizing my thoughts at times when I should have spent more time with them. Beyond a call of duty, they all supported me tirelessly. I really appreciated their kind and thoughtful support which increased my productivity immensely. Their loving care and endless attention put me in the right frame of mind and gave me the much needed extra strength.

Although I have received tremendous help and assistance from many individuals, any faults or errors are the responsibility of the author. I kindly offer this volume to the use of students, scholars, public policy makers and businesspersons who have an interest in marketing and management issues related to Arab Middle East.

Halifax, Nova Scotia, Canada   *Erdener Kaynak*
November 1985

Contents

Chapter 4. Political Risk Assessment by Multinationals in the Middle East: Past Research, Current Methods, and a New Framework
Attila Yaprak

Chapter 5. International Diversification and Investments in the Middle East
Yashar M. Geyikdagi and Necla Geyikdagi

Chapter 6. International Technology Transfer in the Middle East
Asim Erdilek

Part Two
Management Practices

Chapter 7. International Business and the Middle East: Recent Developments and Prospects
Riad A. Ajami

Chapter 8. Managerial Practices in the Middle East
Ugur Yücelt

Chapter 9. The Arabian American Oil Company (ARAMCO) and Saudi Society: A Study in Interaction
Riad A. Ajami

Chapter 10. The Relationship Between Managerial Decision Styles and Work Satisfaction in Saudi Arabia
Abbas Ali and Paul Swiercz

Chapter 11. Cultural Marginality in the Arab World: Implications for Western Marketers
Nabil Y. Razzouk and Lance A. Masters

Part Three
Marketing Practices

Chapter 12. Consumer Market Environment in the Middle East
Lyn S. Amine and S. Tamer Cavusgil

Chapter 13. An Analysis of the Current Status of Marketing in the Middle East

Awad B. El-Haddad

Chapter 14. An Export Marketing Model for Developing Middle Eastern Countries: What Lessons Countries of the Region Learn from Each Other

Erdener Kaynak and Metin N. Gürol

Chapter 15. The Prospects for Export Marketing to Egypt

Gillian Rice and Essam Mahmoud

Part Four
The Future of International Business in the Middle East

Chapter 16. Future Directions for Marketing and Management in the
Middle East
Erdener Kaynak

Part One
International Business Concepts
in the Middle East

Chapter 1
International Business in the Middle East

Erdener Kaynak

1.1 Introduction

In recent years, the importance of Middle Eastern countries as trading partners has grown drastically. The reason for this apparent trend can be attributable to a number of interrelated factors, namely: a) the so-called "Islamic revival", b) the volatile political situation in many of the countries, and c) the growing importance of countries of the region as markets for Western companies (Elbashier and Nicholls 1983: 68). In addition to these, in most of these countries incomes are fast rising, level of infrastructure is developing, sophistication of consumers and their purchasing power are increasing. These coupled with expanding intellectual horizons of consumers and easing market entry conditions have created a current and future market opportunities of considerable magnitude.

As a result of this increased activity, total imports by Arab countries of the Middle East increased from 15,000 million dollars in 1973 to over 78,000 million dollars by 1978 and to 108,000 million dollars in 1981. It is expected that the region's share of import will increase even further in the future. In 1980, of the 27 major Third World importers five of the Arab countries of the Middle East accounted for 11.1 percent of the total imports which, in that year, amounted to 60,546 million dollars (Sinclair 1982: 12).

1.2 Socio-Economic and Government Profile of the Region

There are enormous differences among Arab countries of the Middle East. Some are socialist, some monarchies, some republics. Some take their legal heritage from the Napoleonic Code, some from the Ottoman Empire, and some from the British common law; and all are influenced by Islam (Levitt 1983: 97).

A number of distinctive cultural features give the region a unity and justify the use of the term Arab Middle East. In general, these take the form of similar constellations of subcultures across the area consisting of urban networks with their agrarian and pastoral hinterlands (Cook 1979). The Middle East is not a homogeneous area either in terms of oil wealth (and thus, public and private purchasing power) or government policies (which can greatly influence market conditions) or consumer preferences. Marketing to the Middle East as a result is multifaceted – depending on the individual market, product, and other socio-economic and cultural factors. Environmental conditions in the region are dynamic. Although development and industrialization programs of the countries of the region call for massive influx of imported goods and services, consumer habits and government preferences are changing fast in light of the changing structure of the market place. As Coca-Cola's Senior Vice-President Sam Ayoub noted, "Arabs are much more capable of making distinctions between cultural and religious purposes on the one hand and economic realities on the other than is generally assumed. Islam is compatible with science and modern times." (Kaynak 1983)

The governments of all Arab countries of the Middle East are active in economic decision making. The extent of this role varies from considerable government ownership (e. g.: in Iraq, Kuwait, Libya, Syria and Egypt) to the private enterprise-oriented economies (e. g.: Saudi Arabia and the United Arab Emirates). Because of the differences in trading orientations of countries, selling to the "nationalized economies" can be very different from selling to the free market economies. For instance, 90 percent of Iraqi and 70 percent of Syrian imports are conducted by public sector and there is a rigid state agency control. (Schwartz 1977: 17).

Exhibit 1/1: GNP Per Capita, Various Developing Regions, 1978

Regions	GNP Per Capita $U.S.	GNP Billion $U.S.	Population Million
Middle East	3,120	144	46
South America	1,470	344	233
Central America	1,260	144	115
Africa	560	253	450
Asia excluding Japan	280	600	2,152
World	2,110	8,793	4,160

Source: Adapted from Stuart Sinclair, Third World Economic Handbook, Euromonitor Publications Limited, London (1982:5)

For the most part, the Middle Eastern countries are rich and determined to modernize quickly. Gross National Product (GNP) for the region went from $ 50 billion in 1973 to $ 144 billion in 1978 and reached to $ 361 billion in 1981. The Middle East, as a region with North Africa is one of the highest growth regions of the world. The only other geographical region to match this rapid rate of economic growth was East Asia and Pacific. But in terms of total per capita consumption, the Middle East and North Africa surpassed East Asia and Pacific region quite considerably (World Tables 1980). Exhibit 1/1 indicates comparison of GNP and total population among major regions of the world. As can be seen from this exhibit per capita GNP in the Middle East region is highest among the regions of the world, whereas shear size of the total population of the region is lowest in the world.

1.3 Economic Development Plans

Most Arab states have relatively recent experience in planning their economic development. The key to marketing products and services to the Middle East is to understand the phases of economic development that Arab countries of the region pass through; and of the impact that each phase has upon demand for various classes of products (Copulsky 1959). These countries want products which are appropriate to their own situation and needs (Terpstra 1981: 3). Appropriateness has four dimensions for these countries (IBRD 1976: 19). These are summarized as follows:

a) Appropriateness for goals: Does the technology support the goals of socio-economic development policy of a particular Arab country?

b) Appropriateness of product/service: Is the final product or service delivered by Western companies useful, acceptable and affordable to the intended users be it government or final consumers of a Middle Eastern country?

c) Appropriateness for process: Does the production process inherent in the Western technology make efficient and productive use of inputs?

d) Cultural and environmental appropriateness: Are the production processes and technologies, the products delivered and the institutional arrangements compatible with the local environment and cultural setting of the region?

The economic development plans used by most Arab countries of the Middle East not only determine the appropriateness of products and technology and they are also used for the allocation of countries' expenditures. However, all countries of the region have been searching for infrastructure projects to modernize their communication, transportation and other services. Most countries of the region having established their infrastructure in 1970s are now trying to improve their manufacturing and processing sectors of their economies.

To this end, most North American and West European companies are well placed to assist Arab states of the Middle East in utilizing computers, satellite monitoring, and breeding techniques to improve the region's food supply; in adapting microelectronic technology to decentralize production so that new manufacturing techniques can be integrated into rural societies, in dividing limited resources between telecommunications and transport which would enable villages and small industries to derive more benefits from new developments in communications technology. The Canadian private sector, with expertise, technology and capital at its disposal can play a vital role in economic development of Arab states of the Middle East (Roche 1980: 9).

1.4 International Business Concepts in the Middle East

The Middle East as a region presents a national grouping of the relatively tightly knit countries with one cultural heritage, common moral and religious standards, and generally uniform modes of life (Klat 1976: 41). Despite the prevailing cohesive forces that bind them together, Arab countries of the Middle East and surrounding nations still differ widely in their physical and union endowments, in their social, technological and political structures, as well as in their stage of economic development.

These varied, distinct economic and political differences among Middle Eastern countries must be considered. For instance, it would be difficult to consider techniques to penetrate the affluent, oil rich, relatively free market of Kuwait that at the same time would be equally effective in Iraq. Although relatively affluent from oil wealth, Iraq is totally nationalistic in its commercial sector and has a strict, governmentally-protected purchasing policy (Upshaw 1976: 46). Similarly, there are vast differences among poor

Somalia, oil-rich Algeria and well-financed Lebanon in the way of economic and political environments as well as their prevailing business systems.

As such, the Middle East market is neither so monolithic and easy to penetrate nor so mysterious and costly to enter. But the nature of the business opportunities available there and how to locate and maximize them is not much known to Western businessmen (Shilling 1977: 68). The lack of knowledge about Arab markets arises in part from the fact that the Middle East as a whole has changed drastically since 1973. Lack of knowledge about the Middle East market partly arises from the dearth of up-to-date background data and information. As well, there is poor channels to communicate it to the West from reliable sources at a time when market patterns, preferences, opportunities and obstacles are constantly in a state of rapid change and development.

The Middle East market taken over-all presents major opportunities for marketing of capital and consumer goods as well as a wide range of services. Firms of the West have got to take certain important caveat into consideration before contemplating an entry into this lucrative market. These are summarized as follows (Shilling 1977):

a) There is no single market. Rather, there are a number of individual markets within the Middle East, each of which must be approached and planned for separately in large part.

b) Buyers be it public or private differ in each market of the Middle East, by development philosophies, population base, current level of infrastructure completion, availability of disposable funds and preferences in implementing development plans. Markets range in structure, affluence, aims and absorptive capacity.

c) Usually, market development in the Middle East takes time. Continuing personal relationships and a local presence are prerequisite to establishing a successful market position in the Middle East.

d) Consumers in the Middle East are extremely price conscious and, although they want to buy the highest quality they can get for their money, they will not choose quality at the expense of cost in most instances.

e) Consumers in the Middle East generally dislike paying for intangibles. They are not accustomed to paying for intangibles like services, design, innovative approaches to their problems which must be developed.

f) Choice of partners and agents is the most important and irrevocable decision a foreign company can make in entering the Middle East market. The vast majority of consumer products and most industrial products, however, are sold by independent distributors throughout the Middle East (Thomson 1977: 80). This method has proven successful for two reasons: First, few countries in the region and cities in them have enough concentrated population to rationalize setting up a company-owned sales organization. Second, Middle Easterners have ranked among the world's top traders for centuries. As a result, most large companies like Black & Decker, Beecham, Union Carbide, Unilever, Nestlé, Kraft, General Electric and Gillette all rely on independent distributors to sell their products in the Middle East.

Few American executives return home from an overseas assignment without a collection of anecdotes and horror stories about cultural and social gaffes that resulted in bruised egos, frustration, misunderstandings, and – too often – lost business opportunities. The U.S.A. executive overseas operates in an environment of culture shock, especially in developing countries. Appointments are two hours late. Workers stop the assembly line twice a day to pray. Conversations take place at the uncomfortable distance of six inches. For instance, one businessmen's club in Brazil had to reinforce the railings on its terrace because so many Americans fell into the garden as they backed away from approaching nationals (Stessin 1973).

North American and European companies today are spending substantial amounts of money to innoculate employees and their families against culture shock. This is a particular problem when companies are dealing with Arab countries of the Middle East. Typically the programs prepared address the values, traditions, religion, and history of the host culture, provide advice on education, climate, and day-to-day living, and often include language training.

With this much attention paid to preparing American executives to cope with the overseas environment, why then are so many costly mistakes made? Why do so many American firms experience a high rate of failure in securing and implementing contracts or in setting up and operating businesses abroad? The opinion of Adel El-Ansary is that many American executives have not come to grips with how cultural differences affect management approaches in the Middle East. In his experience, American executives bend over backwards to adapt personally and to adjust their own behavior to the host country's culture. But they fail to understand fully how that culture influences and directs management practices and functions. To put it in simple terms Americans working in the Middle East are prone to transfer intact their management philosophy and style to the host country operation. They are often slow to learn that what works at home may not necessarily work – or be understood or appreciated – in the host country. Cultural adaptation alone does not deal with the more difficult management gaps between home and host countries. Cultural analysis stops short of pinpointing managerial solutions to recurring problems.

Chapter 3 provides American executives with a method for diagnosing and finding solutions for potential problems relating to managerial gaps in negotiations, key management processes (planning, organizing, and controlling), and key business functions (production, finance, and marketing). The author draws on his experience in negotiating and assisting U.S. firms in developing countries in the Middle East. The home country reference is the United States. Host country reference includes almost all the developing regions of the world.

With the explosive rise in technological growth rates, growing environmental complexity, and the globalization of markets, political risk assessment for foreign operations has become a paramount decision-making function for multinational firms. Yet, studies suggest that this activity has only recently become operational in such firms. Such assessments are, of course, of particular relevance in politically-turbulant areas such as the Middle East.

As a managerial activity, political risk assessment is conducted in initial investment, on-going operations, and disinvestment contexts. While a variety of assessment procedures have been developed, in-the-main, political risk measurement has been an imprecise exercise. Among these procedures, those that are quantitative in nature and facilitate the incorporation of "in-house" needs have been favored by multinational firms recently. This shift in perspective appears to have been fueled by the recent political rumblings in the Middle East, particularly the Iranian Islamic Revolution.

Recent research has identified a variety of political risk exposure reduction strategies. As each of these techniques possesses inherent advantages and drawbacks, a balanced portfolio of selected techniques appear to be relevant for given disturbances in the Middle Eastern environment. Insurance of exposed assets, negotiating concession agreements with host governments, and structuring the investment so as to modify and to divest from investments as necessary are among the techniques often recommended. It is further clear that, explicit institutionalization of risk assessment within corporate management can greatly enhance managerial actions on investments or marketing activities in the Middle East.

Managerial challenges in such institutionalization include understanding the evolution of the country's political forces in a historical context; integrating financial evaluation systems into the risk planning functions of the firms, constructing an intelligence and communication system; and, developing organizational structures conducive to environmental response.

Chapter 4 by Attila Yaprak develops a model of strategic thinking which appreciates the interrelationships among these challenges and attempts to link the impact of environmental forces with the firm's political risk assessment function. In so doing, the chapter delineates the successive managerial decision-making dimensions to be followed, and, identifies alternative political risk management strategies which may be adopted by multinational firms operating in the Middle Eastern environment. It also references the discussion with area examples to accentuate the points brought forward for discussion.

The purpose of the study in chapter 5 by Geyikdagi and Geyikdagi is twofold. First, a sample of 28 United States multinational and 28 United States domestic firms are compared during the period 1971–1978 in terms of their average systematic risks to see if the degree of interrelationship of world economics could have an influence on risk reduction through international diversification. As the United States economic cycles, after 1974, became more synchronic with those of other major industrialized economies, where the greater part of United States foreign direct investments lie, it could be hypothesized that the possibilities of risk reduction through international diversification should decrease for United States multinational firms. Consequently, multinational systematic risk, as measured by the betas of the capital asset pricing model, should, other things being equal, increase in comparison with those of domestic firms which should not be directly influenced by less opportunities for international diversification. The results of a year by year paired-difference test supported this hypothesis since the betas of the multinational firms became higher than those of the domestic firms after 1974 when the economic cycles of Japan, Canada,

Germany, France, Italy and the United Kingdom converged with those of the United States.

Also, a study of the economic cycles of six selected Middle Eastern countries during the same period showed that they were very different from those of the United States. Consequently, the United States multinational firms could diversify more efficiently by shifting some of their investments from the industrialized countries to the Middle East.

The importance of international technology transfer (ITT) derives from the central role of technology in modern economic growth. The indigineous firms of the Middle East, like those of other less developed regions, are crucially dependent on transfer of technology from abroad for their innovative activities, which still primarily consist of the absorption and adaptation of imported technologies for successful assimilation. Chapter 6 by Asim Erdilek provides a general framework for analyzing the critical but changing dependence of the Middle Eastern countries on foreign technology. This framework is elucidated by empirical references to specific countries of the region in specific industries.

The chapter begins by examining the several broad indicators which suggest that both the speed and the spread of ITT have been increasing rapidly during the last two decades. The scientific study of ITT is prompted by both the policy considerations discussed in the chapter and a desire to better understand the process itself. Only with a clearer formulation of the concept and better measurement of ITT can such a study be successful. The conceptualization and the measurement of ITT are further complicated by the diverse channels through which it can occur.

After its examination of these general issues, the chapter turns to the specific cases of ITT in the Middle East. It emphasizes the essential distinction among the countries of the region in terms of the relative importance of the oil industry in their economies. It then focuses on the ITT activities of the population-poor but oil-rich countries such as Kuwait and Saudi Arabia, for convenience and due to space constraints.

This chapter concludes that the Middle Eastern countries now offer significant potential to foreign investors and technology suppliers in developing their indigenous technology and training local manpower toward further advancement of certain specific industries, e.g. food production, food processing and handling, minerals exploration, water and its environment, and permanent energy sources. Fields such as building materials, processing of data in local languages, health care, security systems and irrigation equipment are found to be especially in need of the technological and managerial expertise of the industrialized countries.

1.5 Management Practices in the Middle East

The Middle East represents a unique and strategic area of management practise. Business in the Middle East is highly personalized, relying more on cultivation of individual customers and government officials than on media advertising and other sales techniques commonly used in the West. Organizational design is highly bureaucratic and over centralized with power and authority resting at the top. There are vague relationships between line and staff. Furthermore, there is an ambiguous and unpredictable organizational environment. In organizations, employees relate to each other tightly and specifically. Chain of command must be followed rigidly. Management methods used are generally old and outmoded.

The purpose of chapter 7 by Ajami is to look at the recent changes and interactions taking place between multinational enterprises and host Arab society. The prospect for Arab industrialization, westernization and modernity is also addressed. Moreover, the inflow of expatriate managers and workers, and the prospect for new and viable modes of engaging the global community is assessed. Ajami in this chapter, assesses the process of interaction between Saudi Arabia and the four American multinational firms, as well as highlights the effect of this process on both the firm and its environment.

The family structure and the relationship between family members, the degree of acceptance of authority in the society, economic conditions and overall standard of living and personal and behavioral characteristics of Middle Eastern managers contribute to differences in their management style. In terms of satisfaction of needs, they rank self actualization as the most important higher need, followed by social need, esteem and autonomy. The greatest managerial dissatisfaction of the Middle Eastern managers, however, is in the areas of autonomy and self-actualization. Authoritarianism is the most typical management style in the Middle East. The managers believe that authority will produce both higher morale and productivity in the work place, while low morale and low productivity will be the result of applying participatory management systems. In addition, Middle Eastern managers believe that subordinates are incompetent and can not be trusted to perform their jobs independently in a satisfactory manner; therefore, they strongly defend centralization of authority and insist that subordinates should be closely supervised and directed at the work place. In chapter 8, Yucelt examines the managerial style in the Middle East by using Turkey as a case example. The reason for focusing on Turkey in the empirical study was that Turkey became industrialized in the 1930s and has an established industrial setting similar to other Middle Eastern nations; therefore, Turkey's past and current experiences may provide the basis for some conclusions about the managerial styles in the Middle East. Responses from 59 Turkish executives indicated that the Turkish managers lean less toward System 1, Exploitative-Authoritarian, and more toward System 4, participative, management style in private organizations, and more toward System 2, Benevolent-Authoritarian, and less toward System 4 management style in traditional state-owned organizations. With these findings in mind, it appears that the decision making of young and well educated Turkish managers tend to have a participatory character rather than an authoritative one. Yücelt contends that in the Middle East, it is necessary to introduce participative managerial systems in classroom and train prospective managers before they assume on-the-job managerial responsibility. This does not suggest that they change their social values, culture, family structure, and individual pride; rather it proposes to narrow the gap between the management styles of Western culture and the Middle East nations. Then the Western businessmen working for multinational in the Middle East may find a more productive and effective work environment.

Work satisfaction is a well-researched organizational variable that has consistently been found to be associated with a number of important work-related outcomes. The chapter by Abbas Ali and Paul Swiercz reports on the relationship between managerial work satisfaction and the decision-making styles of a sample of Saudi Arabian managers. Saudi Arabia was selected as the research site because it is experiencing high levels of Western influence, is developing very rapidly, and is committed to the maintenance of its traditional society. Five hypotheses were proposed and tested as part of the research effort. Results indicate that participative managers tend to be highly satisfied with their work group, in contrast to the low levels for autocratic managers. It was also discovered that a high proportion of Saudi managers prefer consultative styles and that consultative managers tend to be less satisfied with their organizations than participative managers. Interestingly, among the sample of Saudi Arabian managers, a significant portion practiced a pseudo-consultative style – a finding which may provide some insights into the consequences of the conflict between Eastern and Western management traditions.

Recent events in the Middle East have accentuated a problem which has existed in that region since pre-independence colonialism. The problem is "cultural marginality" which denotes a state of belonging to two or more cultures without being able to identify oneself completely with either. The origin of cultural marginality in the Arab world dates back to the military occupation of Egypt by Napolean in 1798. In the post-colonial decades it has intensified in magnitude and broadened in scope. The discovery of oil in the Middle East, the dramatic expansion of both business and holiday travel of Arabs to the West, the return to home of Western educated Arab students, shattered dreams of Arab unity, and the communications revolution are some of the factors contributing to the ever growing marginality among Arabs in the Middle East. The chapter by Razzouk and Masters focuses on Arab ambivalence ... the love/hate relationship resulting from marginality ..., and its impact on international marketing mix decisions. Western marketers seeking to do business in the Middle East must understand the source and direction of Arab ambivalence toward their own culture and the West. Such an understanding may require specific considerations for implementing a marketing mix strategy most suitable for the region. Arabs value familism, sexual modesty, traditional arts, personal relations and hospitality. Therefore, any Western products which are perceived to reaffirm these central values are accepted with no major resistance. On the other hand, products or services which are perceived as a threat to these central values face strong resistance and ultimate rejection.

1.6 Marketing Practices in the Middle East

The first step to penetrate the lucrative markets of the Middle East is to locate the strongest sales and market opportunities for a firm's particular product(s)/service(s). Before marketing to the Middle East, the same basic questions must be answered as for marketing domestically. These questions are: is there a need for the product(s)? Is demand strong enough to result in a profitable effort? Does the firm have the resources, including funds or access to them, to introduce and establish the product(s)? To answer these questions the international businessmen need information on economic, cultural, consumer, political, and other differences. The market must be evaluated, price levels, distribution alternatives, and advertising and sales promotion needs of international businessmen at varying expenditure and involvement levels also need to be identified and evaluated.

North Africa and the Middle East is a vast geographic area embracing many disparate ethnic groups, languages, cultures and political systems. Moving from Morocco at the Western end of the Mediterranean to Iran on the borders of South-East Asia and then north to Turkey, one becomes aware of an immense variety of marketing opportunities within this region. In chapter 12, Amine and Cavusgil focus attention on three geographically distant nations, Morocco, Turkey and Saudi Arabia.

Although far apart in distance, these markets share a number of important commonalities. If marketers are able to identify and evaluate these common features effectively, then they are able to establish some important macro segments both within and between nations. This approach allows more efficient market penetration and results in scale economies for the marketing function. Moreover, this approach is consistent with the current interest in globalized marketing and the search for greater standardization of marketing procedures.

In this chapter, the authors develop two major themes as they explore and evaluate marketing environments. These themes are:

*Environmental Factors – Converging and Diverging Characteristics
*Marketing Commonalities

Through an analysis they demonstrate that despite several evident areas of environmental difference between the three nations, the market commonalities are sufficiently important to justify a standardized marketing approach to specific segments.

The dominant market commonalities which the authors identify in Morocco, Turkey and Saudi Arabia include the following dimensions:

*Drive for modernization

*Demand for products and services
*Consumer buying behavior and retail practices.

Despite evident economic and financial disparities, all three nations share a common goal of modernization in order to improve the quality of life for their people. Thus we see that behind the mystique of these markets exists a number of thriving consumer market segments. For example the authors identify the new elite segment; the young and upwardly mobile segment; and the traditional mass market of the poor who, despite their low income, still aspire to enjoy the benefits of modern marketing. In many ways the first two segments are not only similar from one country to the next, but also are very little different from consumer segments in developed countries, insofar as demand for products and services is concerned.

It is in the area of consumer buying behavior and retail practices that some major differences from the Westernized model appear. This being the case, marketers must develop a clear understanding of what is possible and acceptable in these markets, rather than simply assuming that "what works here will work there".

Thus, the analysis of the three boundary nations of the region identifies several relatively homogeneous growth segments which span national boundaries. Knowledge of these segments is essential to global corporations interested in the region. Clearly, effective market segmentation is a prerequisite to developing successful marketing programs. The presumption that each country is different and therefore requires tailored products and marketing strategies is likely to result in much wasted effort and many lost opportunities.

The chapter by El-Haddad deals with the current status of marketing in one Middle Eastern country, Egypt. The analysis, based on an examination of the industrial sector of the Egyptian economy, evaluates the Egyptian environment for marketing.

The discussion focusses upon selected environmental factors that have been shown to have a significant impact upon the development of marketing in the Middle Eastern nations. A summary of the degree of marketing orientation and the performance of the marketing-mix variables in Egypt and their implications for international managers and businessmen is presented. The factors impeding marketing development are thought to be: the dominance of a Sellers' market where demand exceeds supply in most industries; relative lack of competition; shortage of able professional marketing staff; inappropriateness of Western marketing concepts and practices to the Middle East Socio-cultural environment; and the business-government relationship which does not provide enough incentive for businessmen to adopt and implement the marketing. The problems are probably typical of those encountered in all developing countries although the importance of the different aspects of a company's external environment (Social, economic, technological and so on) will vary according to different national markets. The implication for the Western businessmen is that they should develop an awareness of local conditions. Their success will be measured by the ability to appreciate environmental differences and to adopt geocentric attitudes.

Less-developed countries (LDCs) rely heavily on export marketing to obtain the foreign currencies necessary for their economic development. Several new developments in the theory of international trade have been incorporated to form general guidelines for an export marketing model for LDCs. The model also incorporates some of the features of the successful Japanese export strategy. Its usefulness is illustrated by applying it to Turkey, an LDC which could greatly benefit from an increase in export marketing. In chapter 14, the export marketing model developed for Turkey provides general guidelines which other Middle Eastern countries could purposefully use.

The chapter by Rice and Mahmoud evaluates the prospects of marketing to Egypt. It discusses opportunities, selected problems and recommended marketing strategies. The focus is on economic conditions, bureaucratic issues, the marketing infrastructure and socio-cultural factors. Economic problems include the presence of a dual economy in Egypt, economic policies relating to trade and price control and government planning procedures. In particular, the chapter discusses the problem of the Egyptian bureaucracy and how this can affect the international marketer. For example, the government actions often do not follow published plans because of ministerial changes. There is a lack of coordination between various government agencies and an apparent inability to honor important undertakings. The marketing infrastructure in Egypt is considerably underdeveloped. Problems exist in the physical infrastructure such as the telecommunications system, although several improvements are occurring. The number of independent agencies offering professional research service in Egypt is small. While secondary data are available, they are usually published in Arabic and not conceptually useful for marketing. The retail trade is fragmented and control over the distribution system is difficult to achieve without a local, trustworthy partner. Advertising problems arise from the limited media available, the high illiteracy level and cultural differences.

Chapter 2
Comparative Study of Marketing and Management Systems in the Middle East

Erdener Kaynak

2.1 Introduction

Many businessmen, business scholars and public policy makers new to the Middle East tend to view the region as a monolithic, homogeneous mass market (Exhibit 2/1). Of course this is not a true picture of the region and its people. The Middle East market is generally full of ambiguities, beginning with the definition of the area itself, and every country is different in its political philosophy and state of economic development (Upshaw 1976). At one extreme is Saudi Arabia with a small population base but with tremendous oil wealth. It has a small but growing base for an industrial society. The country has enormous currency reserves but is virtually unable to absorb them in her own socio-economic development. Saudi Arabia is, however, willing and able to spend funds for development and provide a relatively free enterprise system, allowing the private businessman to freely expand and grow. At the other extreme is Egypt which has growing economic potential, 42 million people, a trained workforce, the Suez Canal, but no oil wealth. Egypt has enormous potential to provide manpower, and management resources to help to develop an industrial Arab Middle East. Given the right capital resources and a stable environment, Egypt might evolve as a prominent industrial base in the Middle East. Between these two extremes are numerous variants; for instance, Kuwait with a relatively free market but requiring different selling techniques compared to nationalistic Iraq with its government purchasing policy (New Encyclopaedia Brittanica 1974). At another point is the Sudan, half African and half Arab; a compromise between the nationalistic commercial environment of Egypt and the free enterprise environment of Saudi Arabia. The Sudan is trying to pave the way to grow out of poverty into prosperity by completing the missing ingredient of their development-capital. This chapter is a comparative study of managerial and marketing systems in the Arab states of the Middle East and neighbouring countries of North Africa.

Exhibit 2/1: The Arabs 1984/85
Source: John C. Kimball: Atlas and Almanac, The American Educational Trust (1984).
Front Cover which was illustrated by Rosemary G. Kimball

To understand marketing and management systems of the Middle East, it is important to examine its resources and handicaps, revenues, the nature of its development, social customs, climatic factors, and trade and trading systems. The Middle East region includes the North of Africa, Egypt, Sudan, and the Asian Middle East. Desert, uplands, and plains and plateaus characterize the region, and aridity is the primary problem (Exhibit 2/2). The population is expected to reach the 200 million level by the mid-1980's, but there is a shortage of manpower. Some of the countries of the region are among the first few oil producers in the world. The rapidity at which changes shaped this region has meant that there had to be almost a complete reliance on the outside for management expertise, but the notion of managerial self-sufficiency is growing (Jain 1980 and Cook 1979).

The oil producing states of the Middle East rank at the top of most development scales in terms of per capita income and similar consumer indicators. Their capacity to produce industrial products is very low. Unless the members of such societies become psychologically involved in the development process, the use of oil revenues to purchase projects and services will result in the transformation of their population into a leisure class of sophisticated consumers increasingly dependent upon foreign labor and technology. (Nimir and Palmer 1982: 94).

A striking feature common to nearly all Arab oil economies with the exception of Kuwait is the highly-skewed internal distribution of oil induced economic and social benefits. Income and consumption continue to rise, but only for small segments of the population. Signs of modernization and urbanization increase rapidly; yet their impact only affects limited sections of the country. Major segments of the population still lead a subsistence existence. In the absence of fundamental structural transformations of the Arab economies, the absorptive capacities of these countries are likely to remain rather limited (Sherbiny 1975: 104–5).

2.2 Socio-Economic Profile of the Region

The population of the Arab region was estimated at 185 million in mid 1984, or about 4 percent of world population in that year. The Arab region has had one of the highest population growth rates in the entire world over the period 1970–77: 2.7 percent compared with 1.8 percent for the world as a whole. The only other geographical region to match this rapid rate of population growth was Latin America and the African continent south of the Sahara (Exhibit 2/3).

The Arab states have also differed in their annual rates of population growth during the period 1975–1980. For example, very high growth rates occurred in the United Arab Emirates (7.7 percent), Kuwait (6.4 percent), Qatar (6.5 percent) and Somalia (7.9 percent), followed by Saudi Arabia (4.2 percent). Most of these are oil-rich states with relatively small populations and attractive employment opportunities. In contrast, lower rates of population growth were experienced in the Yemen Arab Republic (1.9 percent), the Sudan (2.5 percent), Tunisia (2.6 percent), and Mauritania (2.8 percent). In Egypt, where there is the greatest concentration of population, the rate of population growth is estimated at about 2.7 percent annually, which is considerably lower than the average of 3.8 percent for the Arab region as a whole.

The GNP of the Arab region was estimated at about $ 361 billion at market prices in 1981. This amounted to approximately two percent of the total GNP of the world in that year. The average per capita GNP for the Arab region was estimated at about $ 2,170 in 1977. This is somewhat higher than that for Asia, which was $ 780, excluding Indonesia and the Arab Asian

Exhibit 2/2: Land Profile of the Region

	Area (sq. mi.)	Desert, waste, or urban (%)	Cultiv'd (%)	Pasture, meadow (%)	Desert sq. mi.	Principal Cities	City Popul'n	Significant features
Algeria	918,500	80	3	16	735,000	Algiers* Oran	2,200,000 633,000	Fertile coastal plain between Atlas Mountains and Mediterranean. Oil and gas deposits.
Bahrain	230	95	5	–	215	Manama*	90,000	Archipelago with fresh-water springs. Temperate in winter, hot and humid in summer.
Djibouti	9,000	89	1	1	8,000	Djibouti*	135,000	Coastal desert; hot and dry.
Egypt	386,900	96	2.8[2]	–	375,000	Cairo* Alexandria	8,400,000 2,500,000	Nile creates green thread in rainless desert, widening to fertile delta near Mediterranean.
Iraq	167,925	68	18	10	114,000	Baghdad* Basra	3,800,000 –	Tigris and Euphrates River Valleys heavily cultivated. Mountains in north, deserts in south. Oil deposits.
Jordan	37,738	88	11[3]	–	33,000	Amman	648,000	Agriculture is mostly in Jordan River Valley; Israelis occupy West Bank. Temperate climate.
Kuwait	6,200	100	–	–	6,200	Kuwait*	1,000,000	Much oil under sand; summers intensely hot; winters pleasant.
Lebanon	3,950	64	27[3]	–	2,500	Beirut*	1,000,000	Temperate seacoast and snow-capped mountains, Bekka Valley cool and fertile.
Libya	679,362	93	6[3]	–	631,000	Tripoli* Benghazi	280,000 132,000	Scattered oases; no permanent rivers. Extensive oil deposits.
Mauritania	419,229	90	1	10	377,000	Nouakchott*	250,000	Hot and dry, except for verdant area along Senegal River in south.
Morocco	172,415	51	32[3]	–	87,000	Rabat* Casablanca	600,000 1,753,000	Country divided between temperate Mediterranean and desert climates. Snow-capped mountains.
Oman	115,800	99	1	–	114,000	Muscat* Matrah	7,000 20,000	Mostly dry, stony plateau with narrow, coastal plain. Some rain in mountains.
Qatar	4,000	99	1	–	3,960	Doha*	150,000	Mostly flat, barren and gravelly. Desert peninsula; extensive gas and oil deposits.
Saudi Arabia	873,000[1]	98	1[3]	–	856,000	Riyadh* Jidda	750,000 615,000	Mountains, arid plateaus, and deserts; vast oil deposits.
Somalia	246,155	41	0.3	32	100,000	Mogadishu*	400,000	1,700-mile coastline is Africa's horn; hilly in north.
Sudan	967,500	33	3	15	122,000	Khartoum*	300,000	Desert in north; grass, trees, and swamps in south; farms along Nile.
Syria	71,500	21	35	29	14,000	Damascus*	2,000,000	Mountains in west; desert in east. Euphrates River Valley heavily cultivated.

	Area				Population	Capital	Capital pop.	Remarks
Tunisia	63,378	43	28	–	27,000	Tunis*	1,000,000	Atlas Mountains divide fruitful Mediterranean area from desert.
Un. Arab. Emir.	32,300	100	0.5	–	32,000	Abu Dhabi*	300,000	Coastal sand dunes, but some agriculture using rain from mountains.
Yemen (Aden)	112,000	99	1	–	100,000	Aden*	250,000	Flat, sandy coast, mountainous interior; Summer: 130 degree Farenheit.
Yemen (Sanaa)	75,300	79	7	13	59,000	Sanaa* *capital	250,000	40-mile coastal plain, 12,000-ft. mountains with good rain for farm terraces.
Totals:	**5,362,382**				**3,800,000**			
Averages:	260,000 sq mi	71%	4.8%					
For comparison: U.S.A.	3,618,469	22%	19%	27%	800,000	New York	11,000,000	

* Capital   [1] Approximate: some boundaries are undefined.   [2] Mostly irrigated by Nile: 70% multiple cropped.   [3] Includes pasture.

Source: John C. Kimball: The Arabs (1984/85); Atlas and Almanac, The American Educational Trust (1984:16-17).

Exhibit 2/3: Developing Countries By Region: Economic and Demographic Comparisons

Regions of the World	Growth Rates (1970–77)		GDP Per Capita	Total Per Capita Consumption Index, 1977 (1970 = 100)
	Population	GDP		
Africa South of Sahara	2.7	3.7	0.9	111.4
Middle East and North Africa	2.7	7.1	4.3	160.4
East Asia and Pacific	2.2	8.0	5.7	138.9
South Asia	2.2	3.2	1.0	102.9
Latin America and Caribbean	2.7	6.2	3.4	125.0
Southern Europe	1.5	5.3	3.8	131.2

Source: *World Tables*, The Second Edition, The World Bank, Washington D.C. (1980)

states, and for Africa, which was $ 560, excluding the Arab African states. The Arab region as a whole attained one of the highest annual rates of growth of GNP and per capita GNP in comparison with other geographical regions in the same period (Sinclair 1982). One word of caution here is that a considerable part of the increase in the rates of growth of GNP and per capita income of the Arab region was accounted for by the rise in GNP of some oil-producing states of the region. For instance, the overall Middle Eastern Arab Gross National Product (GNP) has grown at 11 percent during 1976–1980 which is far less than Middle Eastern oil countries and higher than poor Middle Eastern countries. As specific examples, oil countries with less than 10 percent population in the region enjoy 57% of the overall GNP and other countries with 71% of the overall population receive 23% of the GNP in the area (El Naggar 1980: 72).

The Arab states generally were at a relative disadvantage in relation to the distribution of income in East Asia and the Pacific in 1977. While the share of the Arab region in world population was 3.7 percent, its share of the world GNP was six percent. This discrepancy reflects the relatively high levels of average investment and consumption in the Arab region. The per capita GNP also varies greatly among the Arab states. Per capita GNP of Kuwait which is normally the highest among Arab states, for example, was

68 times that of Mauritania and about 171 times that of Somalia which had the lowest per capita GNP of the region that year (Exhibits 2/4 a and b).

The increase in oil prices since 1973 has enabled several Arab states to accumulate substantial capital reserves because of a dramatic increase in revenues and the limited absorptive capacity of their domestic economies. Four nations, Saudi Arabia, Kuwait, the United Arab Emirates, and Qatar, account for nearly all the surplus. The mobilization of Arab capital surplus for development finance in the Middle East has, so far, been subject to the fundamental constraint resulting from the lack of appropriate economic and financial institutions within the Arab states themselves. However, since 1973, Arab capital has undergone an important degree of institutionalization and these newly created institutions constitute an emerging, but incomplete, framework for financing Middle Eastern development, a framework which is being constructed at present on three basic levels: a) within the capital-surplus states, b) within the capital-deficit states, and c) at the transnational level. Some of these institutions for the transfer of surplus capital include development funds, such as the Kuwait Fund and the Abu Dubai Fund. Further, there are institutions of commercial investment and finance such as the Kuwait Foreign Trading Contracting and Investment Company and the Kuwait Real Estate Investment Consortium. At the transnational level are: a) the Arab Monetary Fund, b) multi-national development funds, and c) investment banks and companies. Deficit states' institutions seem to be the weakest link in the levels (Salacuse 1980). One can conclude here by saying that countries rich in oil and capital and short of manpower will need a different business strategy than the strategy suitable for Arab countries which are short of capital and oil but rich in people or land.

In light of the above market overview, Arab states cannot be considered as one homogeneous market, but as twenty-one separate distinctive markets that share a cultural heritage, language, moral and religious standards, and over-all goals for socio-economic development (Elbashier and Nicholls 1983). What is required is an overall creative strategy – an umbrella – under which as many individual market distinctions as necessary are accommodated and developed (Thomson 1983).

Another important aspect of the region is that most Arab states do not use a market economy but rely on planning for economic development. Plans are made to help determine the allocation of expenditures. Development plans

Exhibit 2/4a: Demographic Profile of Arab Countries of the Middle East and North Africa

Arab States of the Middle East and North Africa	Population Mid 1984 (000)	%	Average Increase % per year		Projected Population (Millions)		Urban Population	
			1975–80	1980–2000	1990	2000	% of Total Population 1980	% Annual Growth Rate 1970–80
Algeria	21,000	11.4	3.4	2.9	26	34	44	5.7
Bahrain	400	0.02	5.2	–	–	–	–	–
Djibouti	325	0.01	–	–	–	–	–	–
Egypt	47,000	25.4	2.7	2.1	50	60	45	2.8
Iraq	15,000	8.0	3.5	2.8	18	23	72	5.4
Jordan	3,500*	1.9	3.2	2.9	4	6	56	4.7
Kuwait	1,700	0.9	6.4	2.7	2	2.6	88	7.4
Lebanon	2,700	1.5	-0.8	2.0	3	4	76	2.8
Libyan Arab Republic	3,600	1.9	4.1	2.8	4	5	52	8.3
Mauritania	1,600	0.8	2.8	3.1	2	3	23	8.4
Morocco	24,000	13.0	3.0	2.8	27	36	41	4.6
Oman	1,000	0.5	3.1	2.0	1.7	2	–	–
Qatar	250	0.01	6.5	–	–	–	–	–
Saudi Arabia	9,000	4.9	4.2	2.6	12	15	67	7.6
Somalia	5,000	2.7	7.9	2.6	5	7	30	5.0
Sudan	21,000	11.4	2.5	3.0	25	34	25	7.1
Syrian Arab Republic	10,000	5.4	3.8	3.0	12	16	50	5.1
Tunisia	7,000	3.8	2.6	1.9	8	10	52	3.9
United Arab Emirates	1,150	0.6	7.7	1.7	1.2	1.5	72	15.5
Yemen Arab Republic (Aden)	2,100	1.1	1.9	2.5	2.5	3	37	3.8
Yemen Peoples Democratic Republic (Sanaa)	7,500	4.1			9	11	10	8.3
Regional Total	184,825	100.0	3.8 (Average)	2.5 (Average)	212.2	272	46 (Average)	5.5 (Average)
U.S.A.	235,000		1.0 (Average)	0.7	245	259		(Average)

* Includes West Bank of Jordan

Source: *Statistical Yearbook 1979–1980*, United Nations, New York (1981:69–71); *World Tables*, The Second Edition, The World Bank, Washington D.C. (1980:32–227); *The Europa Year Book 1983; A World Survey*, Vol. I, London (1983); John C. Kimball, *The Arabs* (1984/85:24, 28)

Exhibit 2/4b: Economic Profile of Arab Countries of the Middle East and North Africa

	GDP ($Million)		Average annual growth rate (%) 1970–80					1981 GNP ($Million)	1981 defense budget ($Million)	Defense Budget As % of GNP	Value added in manufacturing (Millions of 1975 dollars)		Gross Manufacturing output per capita (1975 dollars)	
	1960	1981	GDP	Agri-culture	Industry	Manu-facturing	Services	1981			1970	1980	1970	1980
Algeria	2,740	41,000	7.0	3.1	7.9	11.4	6.3	41,000	914	2.2	967	3,030	–	–
Bahrain	–	4,000	–	–	–	–	–	1,800	135	7.5	–	–	–	–
Djibouti	–	160	–	–	–	–	–	265	–	–	–	–	–	–
Egypt	3,880	23,000	7.4	2.7	6.8	8.0	11.0	23,400	2,170	9.2	1,835	4,204	208	–
Iraq	1,580	31,000	12.1	–	–	–	–	35,000	2,700	7.7	522	1,422	124	–
Jordan*	–	2,550	9.6	7.4	13.6	–	6.8	3,400	420	12.3	–	191	–	120
Kuwait	–	24,300	2.5	7.4	–1.8	9.2	10.0	27,000	1,100	4.1	367	915	685	966
Lebanon	830	4,000	–	–	–	–	–	–	253	–	–	–	–	–
Libya	310	25,000	2.2	11.1	–2.3	18.9	17.2	24,500	448	1.8	154	632	165	–
Mauritania	70	630	1.7	–1.1	–	0.2	6.8	689	–	–	30	30	–	–
Morocco	2,040	15,000	5.6	0.8	6.6	5.8	6.6	16,100	1,200	7.4	1,138	1,960	–	–
Oman	–	5,300	–	–	–	–	–	5,200	900	17.3	–	–	–	–
Qatar	–	6,700	–	–	–	–	–	5,000	60	1.2	–	–	–	–
Saudi Arabia	–	145,000	1.6	5.3	10.2	6.5	12.2	115,000	27,000	23.5	1,726	3,378	–	–
Somalia	160	1,230	3.4	3.0	–2.6	–3.8	6.9	420	100	23.8	42	32	22	22
Sudan	1,160	7,540	4.4	2.6	3.1	1.3	6.4	5,600	250	4.5	266	284	54	–
Syria	890	15,240	10.0	8.2	9.6	7.9	10.8	12,900	2,390	18.5	575	1,318	282	421
Tunisia	770	7,100	7.5	4.9	9.0	11.2	7.8	8,500	262	3.1	222	540	174	330
Un. Arab Emir.	–	30,070	–	–	–	–	–	30,000	750	2.5	–	–	–	–
Yemen (Aden)	–	600	–	–	–	–	–	792	127	16.0	–	–	–	–
Yemen (Sanaa)	–	2,800	9.2	3.7	14.7	12.2	12.5	3,800	212	5.6	25	83	–	–
Totals:	14,430	392,220						360,366	41,391	11.5	7,869	16,535	1,714	1,859
For comparison: U.S.A.	506,700	2,893,330	3.0	1.2	1.2	2.9	3.2	3,000,000	180,000	6.0	331,522	436,900	3,401	4,616

* Includes West Bank of Jordan

Source: *Statistical Yearbook 1979–1980*, United Nations, New York (1981:69–71); *World Tables*, The Second Edition, The World Bank, Washington D.C. (1980:32–227); *The Europa Year Book 1983: A World Survey*, Vol. I, London (1983); John C. Kimball, The Arabs (1984/85:37, 52, 54, 55).

prepared by most Arab states comprise mainly of the following elements which are worthy of discussion here (United Nations 1976): a) strategy for industrial development; b) specific objectives and targets of the plan, particularly those concerning national product and employment; c) an investment program for the government and public sectors (showing the allocations of developmental expenditures among the principal sectors); d) forecasts of planned investments in the private sector, and an indication of the policies adopted by the Government for orienting and steering these investments into the desired fields through appropriate measures governing fiscal policy, foreign trade, foreign exchange and foreign investments; e) a financial budget giving the resources and expenditures of the governmental, public and private sectors, and of both domestic and foreign exchange; f) a detailed account of sectoral development programs giving the planned projects in every sector and some basic information about every project; g) a statement of basic policies and measures of implementation that will be carried out in order to effect changes favorable for development in the economic, social and administrative spheres, such as labor legislation, agrarian reform, education and training programmes.

As a result of economic development priorities, much of the region's oil revenue will be spent on infrastructure and industrial programs over the next decade. This creates vast opportunities for the sale of Western technology and services, which are regarded highly by business people as well as ultimate consumers throughout the Middle East.

2.3 The Cultural and Political Context of Business Operations in the Middle East

Some years ago cultural empathy (Almaney 1981) was declared as the single most important prerequisite for the successful conduct of business in the Middle East (Arbose 1979). West European and North American managers of multinational companies, as a result, must understand various aspects of Arab culture to improve their management strategies. In the Middle East, personal status depends on family position and social contacts. A Middle Easterner is usually content with the status quo and is always ready to state his opinion. The individual is very tied to his family and dominated by the father. Group-wise, cooperation is generally absent, group leaders tend to have overpowering personalities, and group membership is dominated by social standing. Organizationally, the structure of groups is molded to the executive's desires, loyalty to executives counts more than ability, and subordinates are held accountable to superiors (Pezeshkpur 1978 and Lauter 1970).

In most of the countries of the region, the predominant type of religion is Islam. Islamic values and traditions influence behavioral attitudes toward the conduct of business and attendant management practices (Anastos, Bedos and Seaman 1980). As a result, on an individual level, the Arab's main focus is religion – Islam – and all his actions are controlled by God. He prays that his personal aspirations will be met rather than acting to fulfill them (Looney 1982). In order to carry out business in the Arab market effectively it is of paramount importance to learn and understand central islamic values and influences. These are: a) the emphasis on high ethical standards, b) the principle of egalitarianism, and c) the Muslim's belief in God's control over personal events in his life. Moslems approach their religion as a total system containing its own political-legal, economic-technological, and socio-cultural subsystems. Expatriate managers from the U.S. and Western Europe can expect certain difficulties if they attempt to operate in their Islamic host environment without adapting to the cultural differences they find. Attitudinal differences were noted in areas of: a) personnel, b) organizational perception, c) authority and accountability, d) specialization, e) corporate planning, and f) the role of top managers (Wright 1981).

As a result, Arab managers favor a traditional managerial style influenced by their culture, history and socio-economic characteristics. Managerial characteristics of Middle Eastern managers is depicted in Exhibit 2/5. Generally, Mideastern managers are highly authoritarian with fewer focussed at the top. Business in the Mideast is highly personalized; they like to deal with the man who makes the decisions. High priority is put on concepts such as time, space, body language, and non-verbal cues, and more emphasis is placed on personal contact and less on procedures. An understanding of these elements is essential for Westerners dealing with Mideastern executives (Badawy 1980).

The production or technical function is typically regarded as the major activity of management. Engineering is a high status occupation and is the usual training ground for top management. (Boyd et al 1961: 80). Histori-

Exhibit 2/5: Characterisitics of Arab Management of the Middle East and North Africa

Managerial Function	Middle Eastern and North African Stereotype
Organizational Design	Highly bureaucratic, overcentralized with power and authority at the top. Vague relationships. Ambiguous and unpredictable organization environment.
Patterns of Decision Making	Ad Hoc planning, decisions made at the highest level of management. Unwillingness to take high risk inherent in decision making.
Performance Evaluation and Control	Informal control mechanisms, routine checks on performance evaluation systems.
Manpower Policies	Heavy reliance on personal contacts and getting individuals from the "right social origin" to fill major positions.
Leadership	Highly authoritarian tone, rigid instructions. Too many management directives.
Communication	The tone depends on the communicants. Social position, power, and family influence are ever present factors. Chain of command must be followed rigidly. People relate to each other tightly and specifically. Friendships are intense and binding.
Management Methods	Generally old and outmoded.

Source: M. K. Badaway: Styles of Mideastern Managers, *California Management Review* (Vol. 22, No. 2, Spring 1980:57)

cally, management has concerned itself almost exclusively with production and has delegated the sales function to the wholesaler. With these attitudes, Middle Eastern managers have little regard for marketing, and most marketing jobs are performed by minorities.

The government plays a significant role in doing business in the Middle East and North Africa. In considering the business climate of Arab markets, the following governmental factors need to be taken into consideration by foreign businessmen: a) in the Arab countries, there is a high degree of integration of religious and political leadership; b) most Arab governments are either ruled by a monarch or by certain influential families who hold power in government; and c) as in the socialist countries of East Europe, there is tremendous public sector procurement. Those planning to do business with the Arab world should take these political and government limitations into consideration (Harbon 1980).

The Arab boycott of Israel is a potent factor in international business in the Middle East. It actually began in the late 1940s and early 1950s. The boycott bans direct trade between Arab countries and Israel, pressures foreign companies not to deal with Israel, prohibits Arabs from dealing with black-listed companies, and voluntarily asks foreign firms to boycott Israel. Multinational companies have either complied with it, defied it, repented from dealing with Israel to get off the blacklist, partially repented to the Arab governments but not severed business ties with Israel, or have evaded the boycott by setting up dummy corporations (Kaikati 1978).

As well, cultural and technological differences can become major obstacles in the path of success of international business in the Middle East. The following factors must be considered when working in the region: a) big profits cannot be made without a major investment in time, money and energy, b) business must be conducted at high levels – Middle East businessmen want to deal with their corporate counterparts, not lower level executives, c) day-to-day follow-up is mandatory, so local permanent representatives are necessary, d) a lack of modern management systems will be encountered, e) time concepts in the Middle East have different mean-ings than Westerners have come to expect (Arbose 1979).

2.4 The Potential of Arab Markets for Western Firms

Governments of Arab countries are faced with the need to satisfy ever increasing expectations of their rapidly growing populations, to accelerate socio-economic development, and improve living standards. They regard modernization of their economies as a key public policy goal. During the process of development and modernization labor is shifted from subsis-tence agriculture to more productive jobs in industry. As a result, agricul-tural productivity is improved and industry is diversified. To carry out all of these projects, Arab states are badly in need of equipment, machinery, parts and technical assistance. Most of these products, if not all, are imported from technologically advanced countries of the West (Dobson 1979).

Despite this tremendous market potential for Western products, very few companies assess the market potential of these countries. This limitation is due to the existence of certain constraints: lack of data, non-comparability

Exhibit 2/6: Purchasing Differences Between Private and Public Customers in the Middle East

	Traditional economic market	Government-financed development projects markets
Product ideas	The seller initiates product ideas and determines their technical and economic feasibilities.	The buyer (a government agency) initiates product suggestions and very often requests specific sellers to develop the item.
Demand estimates and resource financing	The seller evaluates potential demand and finances the acquisition of resources and production facilities.	The buyer specifies the number of units desired (very often subject to change) and typically provides funds for the acquisition of resources and production facilities through a system of progress payments. In the extreme case, the government may pay for and retain ownership of the seller's facilities and equipment.
Pricing	The seller determines product prices and institutes marketing strategies to sell the items.	Price is determined by a bargaining process between buyer and seller and consists of a target cost and a percentage of that cost to provide profit incentives – a target fee. Price may be adjusted periodically (in either direction) as the buyer modifies product specifications to adapt to governmental pressures, alternative projects and/or up-dated intelligence estimates of the intentions and capabilities of other nations.
Time of purchase	Buyer chooses to purchase or not to purchase the products after they are produced.	The buyer makes the purchase decision before the product is designed, developed or assembled. This decision may be reversed at any time by the buyer.
Profitability	The producer's profits or losses depend largely upon consumer reactions.	Profits or losses depend upon the target cost and target fee negotiated, the agreed-upon share ratio, contractor performance, contract modifications, and the evaluations of governmental agencies who have the legal power to redetermine contractor profits.
Competition	Prices are kept reasonable because of competition among sellers of the same or substitutable products and because of the fact that excessive profits attract additional sellers which tends to	Since only one firm or one coalition of firms produces the system, competitive pressures do not exist to insure fair prices. The government attempts to achieve these through financial incentives and by exercising administrative control over the product and its costs. The longer

Traditional economic market	Government-financed development projects markets
bring profits and prices back to a competitive level.	a firm produces a system, the more difficult it is for other companies to enter into product competition. In a real sense, the market is characterized by a monopsonist and a monopolist.

Source: Adapted from Walter J. Hill, "Government Contracts – Poison in the Pie of Plenty," *European Business* (No. 23, Spring 1971:63)

of the existing data, and the presence of unfamiliar factors (Samli 1972). Lack of data forces companies to use new approaches for estimating market potential in Arab countries. Given the paucity of information and its relative unreliability, marketers are faced with the problems of estimating customer markets from aggregate data sources. As a result, it takes much preparation to properly identify local needs and to figure out how to appeal to basic motivations (Alghanim 1976: 20).

Purchasing differences are evident between private and public customers in two different types of Middle Eastern markets. These are traditional economic market and government-financed development projects markets which are shown in Exhibit 2/6. In making national estimates regarding market potential, regional and cultural differences exist within the Arab world should be taken into consideration. Most companies use two basic approaches; assessment of the size of the existing markets, and forecasts of the size of future markets.

Western business people's ability to compete successfully in the fast growing, lucrative market created by the economic development programs in the oil-producing Arab countries depends on such business people's ability to deal with the Arabs; this ability, in turn, depends upon knowledge of the Arabs' value systems, customs, expectations, sensitivities, and perceptions of themselves and the world around them. One crucial aspect of the Arabs' behavior is their perception of the West, and the factors which have conditioned this perception. The Arabs' mixed feelings of admiration and resentment toward the West tend to lean strongly toward resentment and suspicion (Almaney 1982) which negatively affects their trading relationships with the West.

In doing business with the Middle East, primary responsibility must rest with corporate management. Rapid delivery is vital to business success in the Middle East, as some Islamic countries view such breaches of promise as behavior that cannot be forgiven. The ingredients for marketing in the Middle East require picking one or two target markets and backing sales resources with high-quality service (Corcoran 1979).

2.5 Stages of Market Development

There are socio-economic, governmental, and technological differences among the countries of the Middle East. The emergence of these countries in the region at vastly different stages of market development calls for a new organizational arrangement. Due to this apparent trend developed country firms should be reorganized to respond to the most important dimensions of the Middle East environment.

One approach which may prove to be useful is organization by stages of market development. A stages-of-market development organization assemble the countries of the region into groups which reflect similar market conditions (Schwartz 1977).

First group of countries are producing oil but have few other resources. These are small, sparsely-populated oil-rich countries. These countries will be labelled as Advanced Stage Middle Eastern Arab States. The second cluster includes populous but rich countries. They are not so endowed. These countries will be labelled as Intermediate Stage countries. Finally predominantly agricultural countries which posses natural resources other than oil as well as those countries endowed with poor resources of any description where the pattern of life style has changed very little. These are labelled as Growing Stage Countries (Schwartz 1977: 4–8).

ADVANCED STAGE COUNTRIES: These countries import the best money can buy and are limited only by their absorptive capacity. These countries are wide open to foreign marketers and discriminate only according to speed of delivery, quality, after-sales service, and price (e. g. Kuwait, and other Gulf States, and Saudi Arabia). Private sector plays a predominant role in trading orientation of countries in this group.

INTERMEDIATE STAGE COUNTRIES: Although rich in oil and natural gas, these countries give their first priority over private consumer
spending to industrial development, infrastructural needs, development of
an agricultural base, and defense procurements. Import quotas are set and
competitive bids invited for large equipment and many consumer goods.
This governmental involvement predisposes them to dealing with state-
trading countries, and much trade has been with the Soviet Block. (e.g.:
Iraq and Syria). Public sector plays an important role in these economies.
As well, state agencies control exporting and importing of commodities.

GROWING STAGE COUNTRIES: In these countries there are import
restrictions of some kind. These restrictions are imposed more from economic necessity than ideology. The countries in this group receive aid from
oil-rich countries of the region, for agricultural or industrial production
(e.g.: Egypt, Yemen and Jordan).

An example of the categories and country assignments that a businessman
and/or public policy maker might utilize is shown in Exhibit 2/7. The
advantage of the stage of market development organization is its ability to
focus the efforts of the decision makers upon strategic problems and
opportunities associated with the most significant dimensions of today's
Arab market.

Organization by stages of market development would encourage organizational efforts by focusing organizational efforts on market needs. It would
also encourage product development, pricing, and communications strategies tailored to Arab-country-market needs. The important question for a
decision maker considering a market stages organizational structure is
whether or not the scale of company operations in the Middle East markets
at different stages of development is sufficient to justify the creation of
separate organizational units. Exhibit 2/8 depicts conceptually diffusion of
new product ideas in different Middle Eastern countries. Because of the
apparent socio-economic and technological differences among different
countries of the region, there will be some time lag in the diffusion of new
products. As well, acceptance of new products and their penetration in the
market place will again necessitate different marketing efforts depending
upon how developed is a particular Middle Eastern country.

Arab countries of the Middle East will not pay foreign companies new to
them to develop any type of product, service or technology. They will

Exhibit 2/7: Hypothetical Grouping of Arab Markets of the Middle East

Stage of Market Development	Country Typologies	Country Examples	Marketing Policy Implications	Allocation of Expenditures	Market Prospects
ADVANCED STAGE COUNTRIES	The Small Sparsely Populated Oil-Rich Countries	Kuwait Saudi Arabia Oman Bahrain Qatar United Arab Emirates	Import luxury products. Limited absorptive capacity because of low population. Wide open to foreign firms. Competitive advantage can be obtained through speed of delivery, quality after sales service and price.	Industrialization, manpower training, agricultural development, housing water desalination, power projects, telecommunication equipments and services, road paving.	Food production, poultry production, fishing industry, agriculture products, machinery and food processing equipment port development, hospital equipment and health care products, petroleum, natural gas equipment, aircraft and parts. Consumer goods.
INTER-MEDIATE STAGE COUNTRIES	The Populous But Rich Countries	Iraq Syria	Although rich in oil and natural gas, these countries give priority over private consumer spending to industrial development, infrastructural needs, development of an agricultural base, and defense procurements. Import quotas are set and competitive bids invited for large equipment and many consumer goods.	Irrigation systems, grain storage facilities, date growing and processing equipment, education, housing, public building programs, petrochemical industry, transportation facilities, infrastructure mineral resource development and communication.	Livestock and poultry production, port development, Hotel tourism industry supplies and equipment. Petroleum, natural gas equipment. Petro-chemicals, energy systems. Consumer goods.
GROWING STAGE COUNTRIES	Countries With Import Restrictions of Some Kind	Egypt Jordan Democratic Yemen Yemen	They receive aid from oilrich countries earmarked generally, for arms expenditure, agricultural or industrial production.	Infrastructure, industrialization, agricultural projects. Meat and dairy projects. Port, harbour and railroad construction oil shares and other energy sources development. Mineral production, hydroelectric plant development.	Food processing, hotel tourism industry supplies and equipment. Industrial equipment, hospital equipment and health care products. Textile machinery and consumer goods.

Source: Erdener Kaynak, "Marketing in the Middle East and North Africa", *Management Decision*, Vol. 22, No. 1, 1984, p. 26.

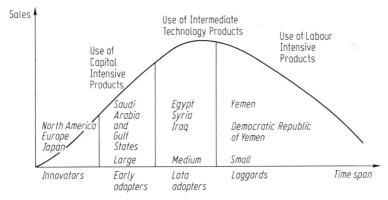

Exhibit 2/8: Diffusion of New Products in the Middle East

rather go with existing technology where the final outcome is certain, rather than pay for R & D where results may be uncertain or costs unclear. In cases what they need is not available, occasionally they will ask a company known to them, an architectural and engineering firm with a long history of completed projects in that country, to produce what they need.

In a study investigating the sensitivity of marketing mix to cultural differences, ten British companies exporting to Arab nations were interviewed and profiled. Generally, export managers of the companies surveyed agreed that cultural factors play a key role in international marketing, but not necessarily a greater role than economic and political factors. As a rule, the companies did not analyze cultural differences systematically. Instead, they depended on observation and experience. Export managers regarded Arab consumers as less rational, price-conscious buyers who tend to be conservative and to prefer foreign goods. Exporters responded to cultural problems by: a) adapting advertising and products, b) consulting with local distributors, c) employing local or culturally sensitive personnel, and d) monitoring cultural surroundings with personal observation (Elbashier and Nicholls 1983).

There are a variety of commercial conditions in the Middle East in both the capital and consumers goods segments, most of which might be considered alien to the foreign businessmen attempting to penetrate these markets. In Saudi Arabia, for example, the brand preference syndrome has evolved to the extent that tissues are Kleenex and Kool-Aid is Kleenex Juice due to an innovative mechandising scheme that included a package of Kool-Aid in each box of Kleenex. There is also no Coca-Cola in Saudi Arabia, but there is a drink called Kaki-Cola, in a very familiar bottle with a very familiar taste (Upshaw 1976: 47). Is it Arab boycott, contract clause or merchandising strategy?

2.6 Segmenting the Arab Market

Arab country markets can be segmented in a two-step process. First, the "macro" segment composed of individual or groups of countries can be identified, based on national market characteristics. Then, within each macro segment, the market can be further subdivided, based on customer characteristics. Through this approach an initial screening of countries and selection of certain countries on the basis of national market characteristics can be undertaken. Two bases for segmentation can be used: general characteristics and situation-specific characteristics. General characteristics do not vary across purchase situations. They include at the customer level, demographic, socio-economic and psychological (personality and life-style) characteristics. Situation-specific characteristics are those that vary with the individual purchase situation or particular product such as brand loyalty, frequency of purchase and attitude toward the given brand (Douglas and Dubois 1977).

Classification of countries on the basis of country characteristics appears to provide only weak indicators of marketing behavior in Arab countries. That is the season why further investigation of both general and situation-specific customer characteristics within each Arab country is required to identify relevant target segments. The design, and implementation, of appropriate strategies for marketing products and services to a target Arab market requires a more detailed empirical investigation of customer behavior within a target country. Consumer market opportunities in Arab countries of the Middle East and North Africa is shown in Exhibit 2/9. The opportunities for marketing Western products and services in the Middle East markets, and tools for successful marketing in these areas are very promising. The need for capital and industrial goods is rising constantly, and demand for packaged goods and food products is growing at a faster rate.

Exhibit 2/9: Consumer Market Opportunities in Arab Countries of the Middle East

Product Categories Considered	Current Demand[a]	Potential Demand[b]
Electrical Appliances	*	
Home Furnishings and Decorative Pieces		*
Household Furniture	*	
Modified Kitchen Utensils	*	
Appliances, Gadgetry, and Basic Tools	*	
Western Clothing for Men and Women	*	
Shoes	*	
Perfumed Toiletries	*	
Automobiles with Maximum Options	*	
Home Care Products (furniture polish, wax)		*
Health Products and Vitamins		*
Novelty Gift Items	*	
Hobbies and Leisure Games (video games)	*	
Hobbies and Leisure Games for Outdoors		*
Nonfood Baby Items	*	
Processed Foods		*
Geriatric Products		*
Make-up and Cosmetics		*
Retirement Homes		*
Frozen and Fast Foods		*
Labour Saving Devices		*
National Market Characteristics	Affected by Situational-Specific Characteristics	Affected by General Characteristics

a Currend demand means a reasonably good sized market presently exists for these products.
b Potential demand means that changes in attitudes or awareness levels will have to be developed before demand increases sufficiently to justify a market base.
Source: Adapted from Mushtaq Luqmani, A. Z. Quraeshi and L. Delene, Marketing in Islamic Countries: A Viewpoint, *MSU Business Topics* (Vol. 28, No. 3, Summer 1980: 22). Also the author's additions of a number of product categories to the list.

In the mid-1970s, the problem was satisfying a demand that seemed insatiable. The challange in 1980s is entering the Middle East market and maintaining market share. Coping with this dilemma requires a grasp of packaging, advertising, distribution and market research problems peculiar to this region (Kaynak 1984). While international marketers to the Middle East formerly misapplied North American and West European commercial concepts directly to the Arabic world, the new approach has been to tailor product exposure to the Arabic consumer, for instance, Arab consumers of the Middle East will not appreciate bucolic, green European scenes in a milk advertisement. A Dutch powdered milk manufacturer produced a television commercial that showed a bucolic scene on a misty morning with cows grazing peacefully in a pasture. This advertisement failed because the customers lived in the desert, that they would not relate to a lush, green country side and that very few of them had ever seen a farm. At a later stage, the manufacturer ran a simple newspaper advertisement which read: "Milk – gives you strength and vitality." The brand name appeared at the bottom of the advertisement. This advertisement created a lot of sales for the company (Abuljobain 1981: 61).

The consumers may not be familiar with the use of a toilet bowl cleanser or a liquid baby bath, so detailed instructions should be advertised. Arab preferences for stronger scents in perfume or shampoo, or for the ostentatious, must be reckoned with. Market research must often be conducted to find out what Arab consumers expect from products. As a result, Johnson- & Johnson found out that when introducing a new product into the Middle East, one of the most important things is to explain clearly how the product should be used (Arbose 1981).

Arab consumers are also becoming more discriminating and less capricious. This pronounced consumer sophistication – whether individual, coporate or governmental – is a result of the sharply increased exposure Arabs have had during the 1970s and thus far into the 1980s to the ways of the West. It is also a result, of course, of a slowdown in oil income. As a result, in the marketing of consumer or capital goods in the Arab world, each country, each market, in fact, each transaction must be evaluated on its merits. But frequently the conditions change and the business approach must be re-thought, the strategy re-developed, and the tactics altered. Once a product establishes itself, sales can be boosted by refinements that make it more acceptable to the Middle Eastern customers. For example, the U. K.-based Beecham Group Ltd. more than doubled sales of its Silvikrin range of shampoos in some Middle Eastern countries when it re-launched the product. It featured a new bottle with a brighter label and a higher viscosity formula, all in line with Arab consumer preferences.

2.7 Implications

Before entering into the Arab Middle East and North Africa one should study the prevailing business environment very carefully and try to match company resources with the realities of the market place (Kaynak 1982). At present, most countries of the Middle East and North Africa are at a lower level of development stage compared to Western countries. Western companies trying to enter or penetrate into the region should be more market oriented. To this end, firms should mass their organizations' marketing and technical resources around the prevailing environmental differences apparent in the region. These differences are essential dimensions of response of Western companies whose products a) serve a different function, b) fill a different need, and c) are used under significantly different socio-economic, cultural, governmental and technological conditions of the region.

To be able to become successful in the Middle East and North Africa, the nature and intensity of both current and potential demand in each country of the area as well as the regional demand variations need to be assessed empirically. In this process, the primary task is the selection of a distribution system through which particular markets can be tapped. To effectively operate in the Middle East, multinational corporations must hire native agents or distributors who are overseen by travelling sales managers. In free-market economies, agents are paid commissions by suppliers and then use distributors who sell the products at a markup. In state-regulated economies, foreign suppliers sell to state-owned companies and then hire private sales forces to sell their products to end users (Dunn 1979). As well, international marketers selling to Kuwait, Bahrain and the United Arab Emirates should be familiar with the laws on the use of local agents in these countries. For instance; a) protection is directed towards the exclusion of foreign agents in these countries, b) agents are entitled to special compensation at the end of their agency relationship, c) no differentiation is made between agents and distributors under the laws, d) many rules concerning agents are considered to be of a "public order" character (Vukmir 1983).

To this end, Western companies should attempt to find out if their products have a current and potential demand in particular Arab markets. Should there be markets, what is the size and extent of the demand? What characteristics and specifications Western company products must have in order to be acceptable in the Middle East. As well, the nature of the pricing and commission structure existing for Western products in the region need to be delineated.

In addition to the above, Western firms operating in the Middle East should establish channel strategies and find, motivate, and support local distributors on a continuous basis (Slater 1977). Nothing will generate a Western company's sales success in the area more than an effective distribution system. By taking a systematic approach to international distribution management, a firm can reduce the problem and risks so often encountered in the Arab countries.

In the Middle East, in order to make the sale, distribution is critical, but it is only half the battle. Service is a key competitive weapon. The vast majority of consumer products and most industrial products are sold by independent distributors throughout the Middle East. Each trading company typically is controlled by one family that has built it up over the years. International marketers work with distributors differently in the Middle East. Rolls Royce cars are represented throughout the Arabian Gulf States by one trading company. Union Carbide takes a more independent approach by associating with the best trading group they can find in each country. General Electric Company relies on distributors for sales and on itself for product service. In addition to company controlled servicing, Black & Decker makes a strong point with distributors and purchasers of its large warehousing operation, based in Dubai, United Arab Emirates, for the Arabian Gulf (Thomson 1977).

The analysis of the Middle East marketing and management system reveals that it is a very lucrative market for multinational marketers who are contemplating an entry. At the same time, Middle Eastern business is facing certain challanges which are worthy of mention here (El Naggar 1980: 83): a) business and industrial democracies versus the need for centralized management control; b) long range economic development versus short-term development in different Arab countries of the Middle East; c) foreign direct investment of oil surpluses versus national investments to diversify sources of GNP; d) business monopolies limited to Arab nationals versus business competition open for all Arab nationals; and finally e) slow growth due to unwillingness to hire expatriates in order to avoid social and cultural problems or to run such social and political risks.

Chapter 3
Managerial Gap Analysis: A Frame of Reference for Improving International Business Relations with the Middle East

Adel I. El-Ansary

3.1 Introduction

Much has been said and written on the significance of international markets and marketing for U.S.A. businesses with particular reference to securing large project contracts in developing countries of the Middle East. Despite the entrepreneurial spirit of many American businessmen and their willingness to actively engage in business with Middle Eastern countries, they experience a high rate of failure in securing and implementing contracts for large industrial and agro-business projects.

The reason for such failure is attributed to the social, economic, political and cultural differences that underlie business practices at home (U.S.A.) and in the host countries (Middle East). While helpful in diagnosing failure, cultural analysis stops short of pinpointing managerial solutions to these recurrent problems. Executives understand, now better than before, that they have to adjust and adapt to the cultural norms and mores of the host country. Keys to adapting to local ways include: (a) abiding by local business rules, (b) being open-minded, and (c) providing the services that were promised. For instance, all foreign companies operating in Saudi Arabia must have a 50-50 partnership with a Saudi national (Telephone Engineer and Management 1982). Cultural adaptation, however, does not deal with the more difficult managerial gaps prevalent between home and host countries.

This chapter provides American executives with a frame of reference to diagnose potential problems relating to key management processes, i.e., negotiations, planning, organization, decision-making, and communication, and key business functions, i.e., production, financing and marketing. Besides using the international business literature, the author draws on his experience in negotiating and assisting American firms in promoting business relations with developing countries in the Middle East. While the home country reference is the U.S.A. specifically, host country reference can be extended to include other regions of the world. Contrary to the differences in management styles among developed countries, similarities exist among developing countries.

3.2 Managerial Gaps

The frame of reference espoused in this chapter enumerates a number of gaps between home and host countries relating to management processes and business functions. These gaps and related diagnoses are summarized in Exhibit 3/1. The remainder of this chapter is devoted to an examination of these gaps with references to case histories encountered in agro-business and industrial projects. The thesis, recommendation, and essence of the message is: when the U.S.A. executives embark on business relations with Middle Eastern countries their approach should be one of problem-solving, their strategy should be to bridge gaps; their overall attitude should be host-country management education, and their posture should be one of patience and persistence.

Exhibit 3/1: Managerial Gaps: Developing Countries and the United States

Management Processes	The Developing (Host) Countries of the Middle East	The United States (Home Country)
• Negotiations		
– Parties	Governmental	Corporate
– Credentials	Political	Banking/Financial
– Time Frame	Long and Drawn	Short and Brief
– Need	Continuous	Contractual
– Concessions	High Significance	Less Significant
– Legal Emphasis	Weak	Strong
– Legal Representation	All Parties	Hiring Party
– Legal Participation	Contracting Phase	All Phases
• Planning		
– Objectives	Inconsistent	Profitability and Market Share, etc.
– Concept	Production	Strategic (Financial/Marketing)
– Time	Annual is Long Range	5 to 10 Years in Long Range

Management Processes	The Developing (Host) Countries of the Middle East	The United States (Home Country)
• Organization		
– Orientation	The Individual	The System
– Structure	Functional	Program and Matrix
– Authority	Centralized	Decentralized
– Management	Owners	Managers
– Accountability	Informal	Formal
– Performance Indicators	Adherence to Procedures	Results
• Decision Making		
– Nature	Incremental	Strategic
– Participants	Government/ Public Sector	Private Sector
– Information Base	Weak and Spotty	Strong and Well Balanced
– Psychology	Emotional/Personal	Rational/Corporate
• Communication		
– Direction	Top Down	Multiple
– Frequency	Infrequent	Frequent
– Urgency	Urgent	Routine
– Primary Purpose	Orders	Informs
– Orientation	Reactive	Interactive Open/Clear
– Channels	Obscured/Hidden	

Business Functions	The Developing (Host) Countries of the Middle East	The United States (Home Country)
• Production		
– Dominance	Higher	Lower
– Orientation	Quantity	Quality
– Capacity	Physical	Marketing
• Marketing		
– Orientation	Products	Markets
– Concept	Void	Marketing Mix
– Emphasis	Warehousing	Distribution Management
• Financing		
– Magnitude	Millions	Billions
– Sources	Limited International	Consortium International Conventional Terms
– Terms	Soft Loans	Feasibility Studies Cash Flow, Pay-Back, and
– Security	Government Guarantees	Return on Investment
– Criteria	Funding	

3.3 Negotiations

Negotiations is a way of life in the Middle East. As such it is the first and most difficult step in establishing international business relations. At this stage, a number of gaps exist in reference to parties involved, establishing credentials, time frame (Young 1977), need for negotiations, and the need for concessions.

While most American executives deal with the U.S.A. government as a regulator, in overseas projects they are confronted with foreign governments as a customer. Large-scale overseas projects are government sponsored. Unless the U.S.A. corporation boasts an internationally established name, such as Ralph Parson, Exxon, General Electric, it has to establish credentials in the host country. Because many foreign governments trust other governments more than businesses, political credentials are more important than business credentials.

> A U.S.A. agribusiness conglomerate headquartered in Arizona, with no track record in the Middle East, had to secure letters of reference and introductions from a Senator and the White House envoy to the Middle East prior to commencing any talks to undertake an agribusiness joint venture in Egypt. When top management officials of the U.S.A. company paid visits to Egyptian officials in the highest offices the focus was on their prior accomplishments, ties, and track record with other governments in developing countries.

Dealing with government officials in Middle Eastern nations is a difficult proposition requiring both an understanding of the personalities and leadership dynamics in these governments and enormous time investment (Wright 1981: 37).

> The agribusiness development corporation seeking the joint venture in Egypt had to deal with the President's advisor on Food Security, the minister of Land Reclamation, New Communities and Desert Development, Agriculture, and Irrigation and Water Resources. Political rivalries existed between the occupants of these top offices and little coordination existed among them. Top management representatives of the U.S. business were assigned to deal with these top government officials. Occupied by other business interests in the U.S.A., top management officers could only spend a maximum of one week at a

time on any particular venture. Because they were unable to call on Egyptian government officials with the desired frequency, the result was failure at the negotiations stage.

Negotiations with developing countries is a time-consuming proposition. While the U.S.A. businessmen view negotiations as a short term process to achieve a contractual arrangement, officials and businessmen in the Middle Eastern nations see negotiations as a continuous process. To prove their efficiency and demonstrate their negotiations skills, government officials look for concessions and good deals. Haggling over prices and terms is not at all unusual even after draft agreements have been initialled off by the parties involved (Khuri 1968). Negotiations are viewed by some government officials as an end rather than means to an end. Their egos are boosted when dealing with executives from numerous top corporations. To them this phase is part of the all indispensable "psychic income" syndrome as well as a demonstration of their clout.

Legal frames of reference are important during the course of negotiations and during subsequent stages of a business relationship. The U.S.A. businessmen strongly believe in establishing business relations on a contractual basis while Middle Eastern countries look for foundations of mutual trust to strengthen these relationships. The mere presence of lawyers in the early stages of negotiations establishes an atmosphere of mistrust in the minds of the Middle Eastern country officials. Lawyers in most Middle Eastern nations are trained to be professionally responsive to all parties, not just to the organization for which they are working. Businessmen in these nations are annoyed, threatened and disturbed by the presence of American lawyers representing the sole interest of their employer. Once a contract is prepared they see no need for retaining legal representation.

3.4 Planning

Although many Middle Eastern countries have central planning ministries or units in charge of the preparation of national plans, these plans are neither followed nor carried out within their established time frames. Oftentimes, national plans are overly ambitious and unrealistic and in most cases prepared by bureaucrats who do not know much about the market realities. The objectives and focus of national goals are frequently shifted.

Therefore, the U.S.A. businessmen who interpret projects in the national plan as absolute opportunities are in for a shock.

Drought conditions in many North African countries exacerbated existing food shortages. Under these circumstances, governments are quick to shift funds allocated for development projects to importing food stuffs. The experience of these governments, as in the cases of Algeria, Morocco and Egypt, dictates such action not only for humanitarian reasons, but also to maintain whatever political stability they may have.

Ailing infrastructure and industrial machinery acquired in the 1960's by many Middle Eastern countries needs frequent and unexpected repairs. There is an urgency and temptation to divert funding from new development projects to support ailing ones.

National development plans are based on production figures in the different sectors of the economy. Therefore, the entire planning effort in government and business units can be safely characterized as production-oriented. When project planning or feasibility studies are underway, officials in Middle Eastern countries are preoccupied with production planning (Jain 1980). Meanwhile, their U.S.A. counterparts are hopelessly trying to ascertain the feasibility of markets and financing prior to any discussion of production planning.

Despite all good intentions and labeling national development plans as five-year or seven-year plans, such time frames are forgotten once the fiscal year is underway. Short-lived tenure of ministers and other top government appointees precludes long term implementation modes. The U.S.A. consultants and businessmen are quick to attest that day-to-day survival or tactical responses to emergencies is the modus operandi in Middle Eastern countries. Survival in this environment requires adaptation of long range planning to fit annual planning frames and placing more emphasis on tactical planning for day-to-day survival.

3.5 Organization

The orientation, structure, authority, management profile, and accountability in organizations of Middle Eastern countries vary significantly from those of the U.S.A. Individuals, personalities, and personal goals are supreme considerations in these countries. Organizations tend to adapt themselves to dominant "personalities" (Wright 1981). Coordination is sacrificed when personalities clash. This emphasis on personalities and occupants of position translates into suboptimal performance of the entire system. This is probably the single most important cause for the failure of large scale projects to achieve their goals.

> "12,000 shiny new 1981 Chevrolet Malibus, built for the desert but gathering snow in Canadian parking grounds ... are part of an estimated $ 200 million (Canadian) deal between GM Canada and Iraq ... The Iraq Automobile State Enterprise, a government agency, ordered the cars for use of military personnel ... GM and Iraq disagree over what engines and accessories were to come with the Malibus, and to complicate matters more, the Iraq agency that negotiated the deal has since changed staff. The new person isn't sure he wants the Malibus or not ..." (Wall Street Journal 1982: 37).

Large scale projects require a great deal of coordination, thus lending themselves to matrix and project-type organizational structures. U.S. businesses accustomed at home to project management utilizing a matrix organizational structure attempt to implement such organizations in Middle Eastern countries which are accustomed to functionally-oriented organizations requiring significantly less coordination. Sooner or later they find themselves in a trap. When matrix organizational structure is combined with the supremacy of the individual over the system (typical in the Middle East), it literally becomes a time bomb for a project under implementation.

Cultural anthropologists and sociologists acknowledge the father as the authority in the tradition-oriented societies of the Middle East. Therefore, centralization of authority should not come as a surprise to the U.S.A. businessmen. In these countries, middle managers unaccustomed to the increased authority inherent in decentralized American management, often times do not exercise their newly delegated authority. As a result the entire organization becomes paralyzed through delegation and decentralization of authority.

When the U.S.A. businessmen deal with the private sector in Middle Eastern countries they have to deal with owners. Most thriving private sector firms are family-owned. Even when professional managers are hired to staff lower top management positions, final business decisions rest with the "family" (upper top management).

> The executive vice-president of a large Swiss international manufacturer of appliances flew to Cairo, Egypt to introduce his company's product line to a leading distributor. The managing director of the distributor's organization was the owner. Both the title and arrangement are typical of most privately held companies in Egypt. Unfortunately, the managing director had to be admitted to a hospital for a surgical procedure the day before the scheduled appointment. His twenty year old daughter, a special assistant, represented him. The vice-president of the firm, a professional manager, second in command to the owner was also present. The daughter led the discussion and concluded the meeting with no deference to the age or expertise of the professional manager.

All the above organizational orientations and conditions confound the notion of accountability. After all, said a government official in a Middle Eastern country, "We are underpaid by any standards, and we are operating in a very tough environment. This is enough punishment." Because the accountability is lacking or at best weak, there is a tendency to manage and evaluate performance by adherence to procedures instead of results achieved.

3.6 Decision Making

The nature of decision-making varies between the U.S.A. and Middle Eastern countries. Because of emphasis on corporate planning in the U.S.A., executives are trained for strategic decision making. Meanwhile, the day-to-day operational and tactical emphasis in Middle Eastern countries encourages managers to make incremental decisions. The largest impact is encountered in the financial management area. Since there is a tendency in these countries to undercapitalize projects, it becomes necessary to apply for incremental funding. Tension mounts and the confidence of foreign bank officers erodes as the frequency and amount of requests increase.

The decision makers in Middle Eastern countries are mostly government bureaucrats. When dealing with the U.S.A. private sector executives, they are quick to realize that the U.S.A. executives have strong and balanced information bases for their decisions. In contrast, Middle Eastern countries have fragmentary and weak information about the project and the companies they negotiate with. Such imbalance in information bases fuels mistrust between the parties involved. As the government bureaucrats encounter new information, the need for continuous negotiations is established.

The supremacy of the individual over the system in Middle Eastern countries renders management decision making emotional and personal. For example, rejections of budgets submitted may be interpreted as an expression of dislike and personal animosity. The weak and spotty information bases for decision making increases reliance on personal trust and contacts in getting positive decisions, thus, increasing the personal and emotional components of the process. This tendency frustrates U.S. executives who are accustomed to rational corporate-oriented decisions.

In the Middle East, agenda for meetings must be very carefully set, but because local officials do not want to lose face, they have been known to make agreements they have no power to make. For instance, at one city the Port Director agreed that additional facilities would be made available if the visiting consultants could prove a definite volume of future use. Cautiously checking further, the Americans found a Port Commission existed to whom the Port Director reported. Moreover, the Port Commission's decisions in turn were submitted to the local sheik. The sheik had the final say – in fact, he could decide matters on his own, reversing the Port Commission or not, then advising his port officials of the new policy (Rand 1976: 50).

3.7 Communication

Communication can be safely characterized as the most underdeveloped and abused management process in Middle Eastern countries. Because of the authority concentrated at the top management level, most communication flows downward in the form of executive orders and manifestos. Such communication is highly urgent, though infrequent, except for when the big bosses are under fire from the bigger bosses. Rarely do subordinates gather the courage to initiate communications, their communication is reactive, not interactive. There is much more of a communication gap between the Middle East and the U.S.A. Americans in the Arab markets often do not have the patience, unless they are with a very big company, to stay in there long enough. Japanese are patient and they receive more government backing. They also normally compete as an industry, and that gives them a lot of clout (Advertising Age 1977).

Information is an important source of power in organizations. In the absence of other sources of power at the middle and lower management levels in Middle Eastern countries, the temptation to hide information is great. Sharing information is akin to losing power. Hardest hit are communications necessary for horizontal interorganizational coordination, e. g., between different units and divisions and interorganizationally, e. g., between ministries. The centralization creates major communication breakdowns due to the long and rigid formal reporting procedures and the unavoidable companion problem of unavailability of timely information for decision making. This highly bureaucratic atmosphere leads to apathy, indifference and lack of initiative among employees at various management levels (Arbose 1979: 22).

In 1979 Coca-Cola concluded agreements with the Government of Egypt to undertake a desert land reclamation project for agribusiness development. When work commenced on location in the desert, workers found themselves one morning under a barrage of artillery fire. Fortunately, there was no loss of life or extensive damage of equipment. The incident was later explained as an oversight. The land under reclamation had been assigned earlier for army training and military maneuvers. The communique issued by the Ministry of Land Reclamation to reassign this parcel to Coca-Cola for reclamation did not reach the appropriate office in the Ministry of Defense (Business Week 1979: 48).

Accustomed to quick responses from the U.S.A. businesses, top management officials in Middle Eastern countries issue requests for proposals and bids with a very short lead time. To meet these stringent deadlines the U.S.A. management resorts to developing standard and modular off-the-shelf proposals that can be quickly adapted to specific requests. Additionally, some firms appoint local representatives and retain professional consultants and legal talent to enable them to obtain requests for proposals and bids well in advance of their formal release.

Thus far our discussion has focused on gaps related to management processes. Similar gaps exist in management philosophy, orientation, and modus operandi in the performance of the key business functions, namely, production, marketing and financing.

3.8 Production

The production function is viewed in Middle Eastern countries as the most important business function and consequently engineers are viewed as the most critical personnel (Saddik 1973). Presidents and chairmen of large industrial concerns come from engineering backgrounds and the vice-presidents for production or manufacturing are the second in command and heirs-apparent to the management throne. Engineers in these countries have minimal or no exposure to business management as a field of study. While some attend management development programs, the majority receive their management training on the job. The technical-engineering orientation of top management filters through the entire organization rendering marketing, finance, and other business functions and their personnel second-class constituents.

The production-orientation of management in Middle Eastern countries results in defining capacity as plant or production capacity rather than in terms of marketing, which includes the capacity of the market to absorb quantities produced. In addition, when management performance is judged by output, quality is often sacrificed. When warehouses are flooded, goods are haphazardly stored in open spaces throughout the plant location fully exposed to weather elements. Visitors to factories in Middle Eastern countries bare witness to this fact.

3.9 Marketing

Marketing is the most neglected function in the business enterprises of Middle Eastern countries. The production-orientation focuses management efforts on the products with very little or no consideration to consumer needs in the market place. Accustomed to chronic shortages of goods, management often believe that once produced, goods "sell themselves". Simply put, there is no need for marketing. Management thinking in these countries is practically devoid of marketing concepts. In these countries seller's market conditons still prevail.

"Commercial Managers", an often used title in the Middle East, are usually in charge of buying and selling functions. A good deal of their time and effort is devoted to purchasing production supplies and dealing with inventory problems. Distribution or logistics management is a foreign term to them in both concept and practice.

The absence of domestic marketing transcends national boundaries to the international market place. Therefore, the failure to sell overseas spells disaster for the balance of trade and payments of Middle Eastern countries. Adding insult to injury, it is the rule rather than the exception that raw materials and some other production supplies are imported.

3.10 Financing

Project financing is the greatest stumbling block in conducting business with Middle Eastern nations. Inflation and technological advancements have shifted project financing requirements from the realm of millions into billions of dollars. This is particularly shocking to Middle Eastern country officials in the agricultural sector. The notion that the cost of one lazer-box-equipped tractor can reach the quarter-of-a-million dollar mark staggers their imagination. Accustomed to labor-intensive agriculture, it is equally difficult to convince them that agribusiness is capital intensive.

The high risk involved in project financing in Middle Eastern countries dictates broad participation by a consortium of international banks representing in some cases ten or fifteen countries. Financial syndication and international consortia development represent an international banking conspiracy in the minds of some officials of Middle Eastern nations. They are "spoiled" by "soft loans" providing for up to 50 year repayment terms at interest rates ranging from ¾% to 3% by the U.S.A. Agency for International Development and the World Bank. They view soft loans as the rule rather than the exception and are quick to reject conventional loans at current international financial market rates.

Despite the good intentions of bilateral and multilateral organizations in providing soft loans to Middle Eastern nations, such loans reinforce antiquated perceptions of the international financial markets and endorse inefficient business management. The staggering international debts of these nations combined with frequent debt refinancing to avoid default, attest to the failure of these strategies. In countries where successful project financing means securing the funds rather than managing cash flows and exercising control through payback and return on investments, the U.S.A. businesses should look for market guarantees rather than government guarantees of loans.

3.11 Conclusions

The conventional wisdom of the much touted cultural analysis approach to international business relations guides the U.S.A. businessmen to adapt to the cultures of host countries. On the other hand, the managerial gap analysis approach uncovers the breadth and depth of the gaps in managerial practices between American and Middle Eastern country managers and provides the basis for adapting their practices, which are in obvious need of change, rather than those of the U.S.A. businesses which have been proven successful time and time again.

A good example of this approach is the case of the Japanese multinationals who frequently engage in business with Middle Eastern countries. Management thinkers who ascribe the success of the Japanese multinationals to their willingness to adapt cannot be more wrong. The Japanese culture is rigid and their managerial thinking is disciplined. Their success is achieved as a result of first recognizing and understanding the gaps thoroughly and then exercising patience in the educating and training process which results in transforming managerial practice in Middle Eastern countries to fit the Japanese mold. As a result, the Japanese have an edge over their major competitors and they are the most successful marketers in Saudi Arabia. For instance, one Japanese company ships a load of construction vehicles unsold to Jeddah's harbor. They call on a government minister responsible for buying that product, who, after expressing an interest but not a buying decision, asks when they could be delivered. The answer: "Today". The sale was made on the spot (Owen 1977: 98).

There are many lessons yet to be learned in order to improve the U.S.A. business relations with Middle Eastern countries, but before we can cross the threshold into more complicated – more sophisticated areas we must acquire and exercise the ability to deal with Middle Eastern countries in a managerially acceptable manner. Cultural analysis, sensitivity, and adaptation on the part of overseas American business endeavors are invaluable tools in devising managerial change strategies and packaging managerial change in acceptable frames of reference. These strategies, applied with abundant patience throughout their implementation will go far toward achieving success.

Chapter 4
Political Risk Assessment by Multinationals in the Middle East: Past Research, Current Methods, and a New Framework

Attila Yaprak

4.1 Introduction

The explosive growth in international business activity and increasing environmental complexity in the last few decades have elevated environmental analysis to an important decision platform for multinational firms. Among the many domains of the environment spectrum which have gained significance (e. g. technological, competitive, etc.), continued global political turbulence has propelled political risk assessment to the forefront of environmental analysis. Political discontinuities in Chile and Iran, persistent instability in the Middle East and Central America, and the internal unrest in Poland are recent examples of political currents which have affected international operations.

During this period, sovereign governments' political intervention in international business has also increased substantially. Scrutiny of proposed and existing investments has increased leading to disinvestment codes in some countries. Investment requirements demanded in value added, export generation, local sourcing, financing, and content are now greater than ever before. Increased regulations and controls on pricing; repatriation of capital and earnings; job security; and, exchange restrictions now supplement the traditional risks associated with expropriation of profits and property. Systematic evaluations of the social costs vs. benefits of an investment now complement economic assessments such as the efficiency in utilizing domestic resources, effects on government revenues, income distribution, and the balance of payments (Wells 1975).

Yet, past research shows that systematized approaches to country risk analysis have been only an emerging function in multinational firms. Neubauer and Solomon (1977) and Fahey and King (1977), for example, have argued that significant gaps exist between the conventional assumptions concerning environmental analysis and its implementation in multinational corporations. Further, a recent Conference Board study (Kobrin et. al. 1980) has revealed that, only half of the firms surveyed had established formal political risk assessment responsibility. Even in these firms, formalized procedures had been reactive rather than proactive; rigor and system had been more the exception than the rule.

Current studies, however, paint a more encouraging picture. They suggest that political risk analysis may be on the threshold of rapid diffusion into corporate planning (Simon 1982). To enhance this diffusion process, it is clear that, frameworks for identifying and anticipating different types of political risks must be developed, and these must be effectively integrated into the corporate functions of multinational firms. The purpose of this article is therefore threefold: to present a cohesive overview of past research findings; to comment on the current methods of practice; and, to present a general framework which may lead to affective political risk management by multinational firms, particularly those operating in the Middle East.

4.2 Political Risk Research

An evolutionary overview of the political risk literature posits that political risks can be viewed as governmental or societal actions and policies originating either within or outside the host country, and negatively (or positively) affecting either a select group of, or the majority of foreign business operations and/or investments (Simon 1982; See Exhibit 4/1). As such, political risks are viewed to arise from the uncertainty of political events which affect business, rather than with the events themselves. Where change is gradual and progressive, reflecting continuity in government policies and political forces, political risk is considered to be low. When discontinuities occur in the business environment as a result of unanticipated political change or action however, political risk is considered to be high (Robock and Simmonds 1983).

Studies have also contended that political risk need not deter investment, but be weighed against prospective gains. For example, dramatic changes in the People's Republic of China which resulted in investment opportunities there exemplify how changes in political currents may result in potential gains. Further, some products or industries may receive favorable political attention from governments relative to others in terms of protection, reduced tax rates, exemption from quotas, control of competition, and other concessions (Cateora 1983: 159). The Sudan's attempts to encourage investment in high-priority or target industries by exemptions from corporate taxes, from customs duties and surcharges, giving priorities in financing from local banking institutions, and protecting them from foreign competition through quotas or increased duties on imported goods illustrate this point (Cateora 1983: 159).

4.3 Macro and Micro Risks

Robock (1971) and Simon (1982) have distinguished between *macro* and *micro* political risks. Macro risks are said to arise from policies directed at all foreign enterprises in a host-country while micro risks are associated with actions aimed at selected industries or firms. Political risks can also be distinguished by origin – public or government originated – and by orientation – internally or externally directed (Simon 1982).

Revolutions, civil wars and other types of internal violence such as nationwide strikes, work slowdowns, and boycotts symbolize internal, public-initiated macro risks, while restrictions on the repatriation of capital and earnings are examples of internal, government-initiated macro risks. Public-initiated macro risks can also originate outside the host country: cross-national guerilla warfare observed in Latin America, Southeast Asia, and Southern Africa are among examples of this type of risk. Repatriation restrictions, leadership struggles, alliance shifts, international boycotts and embargoes, factional, ethnic or religious conflicts, and high levels of external debt (currently experienced by many developing countries) are other examples of macro political risks encountered by multinational firms.

Direct, and (relatively) permanent, takeovers of private foreign enterprise such as those in Cuba in 1959–60; communist expropriations in Eastern Europe and China following World War II; and, expropriation actions in Algeria, Egypt, Ghana, Indonesia, Chile, Uganda, Libya, and Iran during the last two decades all exemplify other macro political risks encountered by multinational businesses. In this context, Bradley (1977) has found that

Exhibit 4/1: An Overview of Political Risk Literature

Analyst/ Organization	Definition of Political Risk	Type of Analysis	Data Base	Key Variables Discassed/Analyzed
Root	Attitudes and policies of host governments, rival political parties, labor unions and nationalist groups that threaten foreign investments	Descriptive and conceptual	Survey of business executives	War, revolution, expropriation, transfer operational, ownership/control uncertainties, import restrictions
Stobaugh	General conditions that affect the investment climate in the host country	Descriptive and quantitative	Survey of business executives	Nationalization, inflation, devaluation
Robock	Unanticipated discontinuities in the business environment that result from political change and affect the profit and goals of a particular enterprise	Conceptual	N/A	Competing political philosophies, social unrest and disorders, confiscation, expropriation, discriminatory taxes
Boddewyn and Cracco	Host government adoption of nationalistic policies that promote and control socioeconomic development	Conceptual	N/A	National interest, national sovereignty, national identity
Green	Negative orientation towards foreign investment due to radical political change	Conceptual	N/A	Types of political systems (instrumental-adaptive, instrumental-nonadaptive, military dictatorships, modernizing autocracies)
Knudsen	Expropriation of foreign business due to high levels of national frustration	Conceptual and quantitative	Public secondary sources	Environmental variables, degree of urbanization and unionization, percent change in per capita GNP
Rummel and Heenan	Objective measurement of a political environment, resulting in a probability estimate of the risks involved in a foreign investment	Descriptive and quantitative	Prior contract research; discussions with business executives	Riots, purges, war, inflation, external debt levels

Analyst/ Organization	Definition of Political Risk	Type of Analysis	Data Base	Key Variables Discussed/Analyzed
Van Agtmael	Business loss due to political instability, nationalization, or external political change	Conceptual	N/A	War, revolution, coup d'etats, nationalization, external political change
Kobrin	Significant changes in host government policy towards foreign direct investment	Quantitative	Public secondary sources	Expropriation, partial divestment, price controls, remittance restrictions
Bradly	Risk viewed as essentially due to nonpolitical factors	Quantitative	Harvard Business School's Multinational Enterprise study; State Department data	Expropriation, ownership, technology, vertical integration, size of firm

Source: Jeffrey D. Simon: Political Risk Assessment: Past Trends and Future Prospects, *Columbia Journal of World Business*, (Vol. 17, No. 3, Fall 1982:67)

between 1960 and 1976, Latin American countries accounted for 49 percent of all expropriations followed by the Middle Eastern countries with 27 percent. Similarly, a study by the United Nations of foreign firm takeovers between 1960 and 1974 reported that two-thirds of all takeovers were accounted for by just ten nations including Middle Eastern countries like Algeria, Libya, and Iraq (United Nations 1978). Various Arab countries' political boycott of companies that have branches in Israel, that trade with Israeli concerns, or that have licensing or technical assistance agreements with Israeli affiliates are other examples of macro political risks encountered in the Middle East.

Micro risks are more difficult to identify and forecast. Further, these risks have been found to vary according to the sector of the investment: the extractive and service sectors, for example, have experienced a larger number of political actions than the manufacturing sector. In a Canadian study ranking sector vulnerability, technologically dynamic industries importing new technology were found to have a low degree of political risk. In contrast, natural resource projects (particularly petroleum and mining), and the financial sector were found to experience a high degree of political risk (Information Canada 1970).

Micro risks associated with government action also include pressure for joint venture operations, local content legislations, imposition of discriminatory taxes and industry-specific regulations, price controls, and the subsidizing of local competition. Deteriorating diplomatic relations between the host and the home countries leading to loss of investment opportunities is also considered a form of micro risk. Selective strikes and protests are among the internal, public-initiated micro risks, while the influence of activist groups, selective international terrorism, and the international boycott of a firm's products (such as in the case of Nestlé) are examples of external, public-initiated micro risks.

Simon (1982) has argued that political risks are likely to be more *micro* than macro. That is, risks are likely to be firm- or even project-specific, and are likely to result from the interaction of organizational strategy with the environment rather than from political events that effect all foreign firms in a given country. Kobrin has corroborated this view with his study where he concluded that managerial perceptions of the political environment and the uncertainty about the likely impacts of changes within it on the firm's operations were the major areas of concern. That is, political risks were increasingly taking the form of constraints on operations, rather than on ownership of assets (Kobrin 1982).

4.4 Political Risk Assessment

Political risk assessment is primarily conducted in investment decision contexts. It is an attempt to forecast political instability and thus alter the rules-of-the-game in market entry decisions (Cateora 1983: 161). It may be associated with proposals for capital expenditure in a new venture, in the update of the firm's long-range investment/disinvestment plans, or in the firm's attempt to formulate a global operations strategy. For example, when asked where political risk assessment was routinely utilized, 80% of the respondents to a recent survey cited initial investment; 71% cited strategic planning; 67% reinvestment; 48% disinvestment; and 26% day-to-day monitoring of operations (Kobrin 1982). In this context, Jain (1984: 238) has contended that political risk assessment may be useful in three areas:

(a) to identify countries which turn out to be the Irans of tomorrow (so that the firm can minimize its exposure); (b) to identify countries unnecessarily discounted as politically unsound (for example, Angola and Zimbabwe) and those where political risks have improved (for example, Egypt); and, (c) to identify countries that may be politically risky, but not as risky as to be automatically ruled-out (for example, many Middle Eastern countries).

While traditionally the role of political risk assessment has been most important in the earlier stages of the foreign investment process, recent research has favored the later stages of the project's life cycle such as in disinvestment considerations and in day-to-day monitoring of operations. It is apparent that many multinationals are now developing extensive analysis systems to monitor the country's social fabric and political development, the quality of its economic management, its industrial relations, exchange controls, patent laws, tax regime, and even the likelihood of changes in production sharing agreements. These firms are also becoming aware of the host country's evaluation of the social benefits vs. costs expected from the investment, and, are developing intelligence systems to monitor changing political conditions in the host-country on an on-going basis (Micallef 1981). It is therefore clear that, political risk assessment is becoming an integral component of multinational corporate planning within *all* phases of the investment decision process: in pre-investment (in conjunction with marketing, finance, logistics, and ownership plans); in on-going operations (to guide, protect, and nurture existing operations); and in disinvestment (to achieve an effective withdrawal from the investment).

4.5 Approaches to Political Risk Assessment

While considerable progress has been made in developing methodologies for operationalizing the political risk assessment function, current research shows that the state of the art remains greatly underdeveloped. Kennedy (1981), for example, has revealed that only two of the 10 models utilized in his study offered reasonably accurate assessments of the 1978 Iranian revolution and the resulting expropriations of foreign assets in that country.

Further, there seems to be no concensus in the literature as to what constitutes political risk, nor is there an accepted methodology available for assessing overseas developments (Simon 1982). Kobrin (1982) and Simon

(1982) have both argued that the integration of political risk assessment into investment decision-making has, for the most part, been a subjective process rather than a formalized, systematic one. Kobrin (1982) found that even in the "institutionalized" firms utilized in his study, the output of assessment units was used only as background data, not as the basis for investment or operational decisions. In addition, the problems of processing, filtering, and transmitting environmental information were found to be exacerbated by the extended network of the multinational firm, often limiting the effective diffusion and application of such data.

These findings suggest that political risk assessment by multinational firms has been an imprecise exercise. A variety of political risk assessment procedures, however, have nevertheless been applied in various contexts by multinational firms. These models can be fitted into three categories: qualitative, quantitative, and firm-specific approaches.

Until recently, multinational firms have preferred the use of qualitative models whose application involved a panel of experts from various academic disciplines, nationalities, ideologies, and geographic locations expressing their judgments about the likelihood of alternative political scenarios in selected countries. This traditional Delphi approach seems to be changing, however; research suggests a shift toward the use of relatively more quantitative procedures, and "in-house" models. Among the more frequently used quantitative procedures are Haner's Business Environmental Risk Index (BERI), Business International's Index of Environmental Risk (BI), and Frost and Sullivan's World Political Risk Forecast (WPRF) (Exhibit 4/2).

While their use has been somewhat extensive, these procedures have not been very successful in providing the day-to-day intelligence that companies need to deal effectively with immediate changes in their environment (Fairlamb and Sender 1983). Critics argue that they paint so broad a picture of likely developments that their assessments are of limited practical use. It is further documented that they often disagree widely in their assessments of a particular country, and their evaluations sometimes differ from the financial market's perceptions. Their over-reliance on econometric models, their treatment of countries with a predetermined view to fit them into a certain category, and, their projection of a country's past behavior into the future without giving due consideration to sudden changes in government policy are viewed to be other difficulties associated with their application.

Exhibit 4/2: Selected Approaches to Political Risk Assessment

Analyst/Organization	Definition of Political Risk	Key Variables Discussed/Analyzed
Business Environmental Risk Index (BERI)	Political processes that negatively affect foreign business.	Bureaucratic delays, nationalization, currency convertability, political stability.
Business International's Country Assessment Service (BI)	Governmental attitudes and actions, and social unrest that negatively affects foreign business activity.	Internal factions, size, and influence of middle class, government attitudes toward private sector.
World Political Risk Forecasts (WPRF)	Political and economic conditions that produce general concerns for all business operating within a country, and economic conditions that present more specific risks to fewer enterprises.	Regime change, political turmoil, expropriation, repatriation restrictions.
Political System Stability Index (PSSI)	Probability of political events occurring that will change the prospects for profitability of a given investment.	Demonstrations, guerrilla warfare, ethnolinguistic fractionalization GNP growth per capita.
Institutional Investor's Country Credit Rating	Political, economic and social conditions that affect a country's creditworthiness.	Creditworthiness, political, social and economic climate.
Euromoney's Country Risk Index	Viewed from the perspective of trends in international credit markets.	Floating-rate syndicated Euro-loans.

Source: Adapted from Jeffrey D. Simon, Political Risk Assessment: Past Trends and Future Prospects, *Columbia Journal of World Business*, (Vol. 17, No. 3, Fall 1982:67)

Partly in response to these problems, many multinationals have been developing more comprehensive and custom-tailored risk assessment systems that better fit their product, market, and organizational needs and that better account for firm-specific social and political factors. The Bank of America System, for example, relies primarily on a standardized economic stability index, and an external debt-servicing index which are currently adjusted for specific political and social risks to allow for cross-national comparisons. The Marine Midland Bank of New York utilizes a three-phase approach including econometric modeling, country-risk surveys, and specific country studies to arrive at a composite-score ranking of the majority of countries in which it operates. General Motors Corporation utilizes a composite-score analysis developed by the International Economics Group which leads to a risk classification of the countries in which GM operates. In addition, for most major decision, independent assessments are also made by local plant management, the Corporate Worldwide Product Planning Group, the Market Analysis Activity Group, and the Industry-Government Relations Activity. American Can Corporation has developed a specialized Primary Risk Investment Screening Matrix (PRISM) to quantitatively assess the index of economic desirability and the index of risk payback of its subsidiary countries. United Technologies Corporation has designed a complex computerized simulation model to identify desirable/undesirable future involvement areas. G. T. & E., devastated by its unexpected losses in Iran, has since developed a specialized risk assessment methodology to better cope with similar catastrophies in the future. Other multinationals including Exxon, Bechtel, Merck, Xerox, and Chase Manhattan have developed similar inhouse risk assessment procedures (Kraar 1980).

4.6 Operationalization of the Political Risk Assessment Function

Micallef (1981) has argued that political risk assessment should involve three tasks: economic and political forecasting; effective integration of the risk assessment process into the firm's planning activity; and, devising proactive strategies to protect the firm from exposure. Effective management of this function would involve prudent tapping and use of political risk information sources; monitoring of country-wide, as well as project-specific risks; and, effective diffusion of the processed information to the relevant decision-makers.

There is concensus in the literature that no one political risk forecasting technique is applicable for all firms or situations. Further, the forecasting task should not be detached from other forecasting activities of the firm, particularly economic forecasting. For the political risk assessment function to be effective, a parsimonious mix of forecasting procedures, information sources, data patterns, and information diffusion systems ought to be developed. The propensity of the forecasting procedure to blend with qualitative assessments and consultants' risk indices, and, its relative operational flexibility are also desirable features. (Mahmoud and Rice 1983).

Previous research also argues for explicit focus on the association between specific types of governmental instability and resulting political instability in a foreign environment. In a recent study, Brewer (1983a) found for example, that only factional changes such as coalition rearrangements were statistically related to political instability in 115 countries. This was especially true in the industrialized as compared to developing countries. Neither systemic changes (such as a transformation in the basic form of the government including changes in the constitutional basis of the government's authority) nor personnel changes (such as a change in the head of the government) were statistically correlated to political instability in these countries. In monitoring political developments, therefore, it seems imperative to note that different forms of political instability may lead to differential policy consequences: policy instability may be more likely to be associated with some types of political changes than with others.

Recent studies also show that the most important sources of political risk information are internal to the firm; subsidiary and regional managers and corporate headquarters personnel are the most highly tapped resources in assessing foreign environments. Among the more highly rated external sources are the banking community, external consultants (including analysts at other firms), and international organizations (Micallef 1981). Interpersonal contacts with affiliate or local managers and regional subordinates are found to be most frequently utilized in assessing short-run environmental developments while external sources are more frequently tapped for longer-run concerns.

There is growing evidence in the literature also that international money markets' interpretations of political risk in a country (as reflected by the markets' interpretations of foreign exchange or exchange control risks) may be relatively unbiased indicators of "true" risks associated with that country. Brewer (1983b), for example, has argued for attention on political sources of foreign exchange and exchange control risks in monitoring international money markets for political risk assessment purposes. Duran (1983) also showed some statistical correlation between international financial markets' evaluations of political risks in selected countries (measured by the Euromoney index) and chosen political risk models' interpretations of the same risks.

Shapiro (1981) has identified four separate techniques with which a firm can reduce its political risk exposure. These are avoidance, insurance, negotiating the environment, and structuring the investment.

Avoidance, or screening out investments in politically risky countries is viewed to be an unwise strategy since this may ignore the potentially high returns that could be realized under bearable risks. For example, the profit potential up to the time when political risk is expected to be high may be sufficiently attractive to make the project of considerable interest. Inexperienced international managers, sometimes applying ethnocentric standards, may cause the firm to miss otherwise profitable investment opportunities due to their unfamiliarity with the political patterns or styles of a given country rather than due to actual political risks there (Robock and Simmonds 1983).

Insurance of exposed assets, on the other hand, can allow the firm to concentrate more fully on managing, rather than protecting, the investment. Government-subsidized agencies such as the Overseas Private Investment Corporation (OPIC) and the Ex-Im Bank, as well as private insurers such as Lloyds of London, provide a wide range of political risk insurance services to multinational firms. For example, according to OPIC's 1983 annual report, this agency had issued a record volume of nearly $ 3.1 billion in insurance for over 100 American investment projects during fiscal 1982. It had also made direct loans and guaranteed committments worth $ 108.7 million in addition to a $ 1.5 million local currency loan covering 20 projects. Further, changes in OPIC's legislation enacted in 1981 allowed the agency to expand its activities into 15 additional countries including the People's Republic of China bringing the total number of countries in which OPIC operates to 100. This legislation expanded OPIC's program to include civil strife insurance in addition to insurance against war, revolution, terrorism, sabotage and insurrection. During 1982, OPIC made payments on 15 claims including five for expropriations of investments in Iran, and nine inconvertibility claims. Exhibit 4/3 shows some of the coverages available for political risk insurance and some settlements paid to U.S. multinationals for losses due to political risks.

Some multinationals have opted for negotiating concession agreements with the host government prior to undertaking the investment. These agreements which define the rights and responsibilities of both parties have recently been viewed as "blatant exploitation" by developing countries

Exhibit 4/3: Major Coverages Available For Political Risk Insurance

War Damage: Destruction of property resulting from armed conflict between organized political entities and involving use of explosives and other weapons of war.

War Contingencies: Loss excluding physical damage resulting from war, revolution, insurrection or from war involving the Five Great Powers: U.S., U.S.S.R., U.K., France and China.

Expropriation: Host government takeover of ownership or control of a foreign facility without prompt, adequate and effective compensation.

"Creeping" Expropriation: Series of discriminatory measures by host government designed to "ease out" foreign owners of a commercial project. Involves a broad range of possible actions such as limiting export quotas, harassing personnel and many other tactics.

Confiscation: Host government seizure of assets and/or property, without promise of compensation.

Nationalization: Takeover and operation of a foreign-owned facility by the host government.

Deprivation: Host government refusal of permission, or revocation of prior permission, to remove property or equipment brought into the country for temporary use.

Inconvertibility: Inability to convert local currency of host government into a foreign currency, resulting in blockage of fund transfer for royalties, dividends, loan installments or repatriation of capital.

Wrongful Calling of Guarantees: By beneficiary of an On-Demand Bank Guarantee or Performance Bond (often an agency of the host government). Arbitrary and capricious drawing down of posted funds when the contractor is not in default.

Generally excluded (particularly by private carriers) are losses due to:
- devaluations or currency fluctuations
- payoffs, labor disputes or competitive problems
- fraudulent, criminal or dishonest acts
- failure to comply with local laws
- default on, or failure to perform under, contracts
- financial default or insolvency

Source: *Journal of Insurance* (September–October 1981: 18–24)

Exhibit 4/4: Some Settlements Paid by OPIC to U.S. Multinationals for Losses Due to Political Risk (1967–79)

Company	Country	Amount
Chile Copper	Chile	11.90 million
Cabot Corp.	Argentina	1.00 million
GMAC	Dominican Republic	0.05 million
Belbagco, Inc.	Bougladesh	0.90 million
International Dairy Prod.	Vietnam	1.00 million
Celanese Corp.	Peru	0.50 million
Chase International Inv.	Zaire	0.20 million
Union Carbide	Ghand	0.25 million
Bradeu Copper	Chile	66.90 million
Reynolds Metals	Guyana	10.00 million
ITT	Chile	59.50 million
Chase Manhattan	Vietnam	8.00 million

Source: *New York Times* (January 28, 1979)

however; hence, their use has declined sharply in recent years (Shapiro 1981) (See Exhibit 4/4).

Most firms now pursue proactive political risk management activities by structuring the investment. Structuring is undertaken by increasing the firm's political leverage, and by increasing dependence on the firm's operating policies in production, logistics, marketing, and technology transfer. Establishing financial policies which broaden the base of concern beyond the firm involved may be another structuring tool. One example of this risk diversification technique is joint-venture investments with other foreign companies to increase the political "clout" of the firm. Alternatively, joint ventures with local firms, or allowing host country investors to own a sizable portion of the investment while retaining a controlling interest, may allow the firm to transfer a portion of political risk to host country citizens. Expropriation (or other adverse political action) in this case may amount to a tax on the host country stockholders; even if the government were to compensate these stockholders after the action, this would effectively increase the cost of nationalization for the host-government, thus creating an additional deterrant.

Making the local affiliate dependent on the firm for markets and supplies may be another structuring tool. Also, retaining control of the distribution network of the local affiliate's products can serve to increase the firm's political leverage against a host government. Both Chrysler Corporation and Marcona Mining Company have used this strategy effectively in their dealings with the Peruvian government. (Micallef 1981).

Concentrating R & D facilities and proprietary technology in the home country or in "off-shore" locations; or alternatively, maintaining the latest technology on site can also help cover political risk exposure. For example, continuous upgrading of operations with new technology, even before the return on investment can justify the new capital outlay, may be considered a form of insurance premium paid to protect the firm from nationalization (Shapiro 1981).

Another method of risk diversification is to develop external financial stakeholders in the venture's success. This involves raising capital for the venture through local borrowing, or from the host and other governments, or even from international financial institutions and customers (with payment to be provided out of production), rather than employing funds supplied solely by the parent company. In addition to spreading risks in this case, an international response can be elicited by an expropriation move or other adverse action by the host government.

4.7 The Need for Institutionalization

It is clear then, that *affective management* of the political risk assessment function necessitates explicit *institutionalization* of it within the corporate organization and corporate culture. Kobrin (1982), for example, has argued convincingly for the formal designation of political risk analysis units to continuously scan the global environment and plot alternative strategic scenarios. The motives behind this "specialist" approach are the desire to improve communication flows through information systems, and, operationalization of the assessment unit as a focal point for political analysis in the firm. It is argued that a specialized unit can facilitate better understanding of the origins and nature of different types of risk; enhance anticipation of their occurrence; lead to creative blending and use of in-house and external assessments; and, foster informed application of the outputs. Others have argued for integration of this activity, as part of a broader environmental scanning function, into the corporate culture of the firm (Thomas 1980). The motives behind this "generalist" approach are to raise corporate awareness about global strategic posturing and to enhance corporate responsiveness to evolving political scenarios worldwide. The proponents of this approach favor the pulsing of political currents trans-nationally, and by *all* functional units of the firm.

4.8 Managerial Challenges

Whichever approach is favored by a chosen firm, it is clear that *proactive* management of the political risk assessment function presents decisionmakers with several challenges. A primary challenge is a thorough understanding of the evolution of a country's political system within its historical context (Nehrt 1970). Robock and Simmonds argue that this would involve continuous monitoring of the paths along which policies, attitudes, and political forces may have been moving; particularly philosophies of those forces which are not shaping policies at present, but are likely to do so in the future (Robock and Simmonds 1983). The 1979 Islamic Revolution in Iran provides a case in point. The Shah's swift modernization programs imposed upon the Iranian people (who were unable to absorb rapid economic development) appears to have blinded Western observers to the dramatic disruptions which followed. Similar catastrophies may also be brewing in neighboring Saudi Arabia where the fundamentally muslim, tribal-nomadic society is seemingly being transformed overnight into a modern, industrial state (Jain 1984: 236). A key variable that must be closely scrutinized in this context is the discrepancy between the aspiration levels and the expectation levels of a country's political forces which can lead to abrupt political changes, placing foreign firms in a "scapegoat" position. The validity of this hypothesis has been proven by Knudsen's (1973) study where he showed that a high correlation existed between the frustration limits and expropriation in Latin America during the 1968–71 period. Nehrt has also argued in his 1970 work that the analysis of past patterns of political behavior, and the evaluation of opinions of (sometime exiled) political forces could have led to improvements in political risk assessment for some firms operating in Tunisia, Algeria, and Morocco. Similarly, Ajami (1979) in the context of the Libyan revolution in 1969; Hawkins, Mintz and Provisiero (1976) in the context of 170 takeovers between 1946 and 1973; and, Bradley (1977) in regard to 114 expropriations between 1960 and 1976 in the Middle East, Africa, Latin America and Asia have confirmed the significance of the historical evolution of political forces in a given country for affective risk assessment.

A second challenge involves the integration of the *financial evaluation procedures* associated with foreign investment projects into the risk planning function of the firm. According to Micallef (1981), two tasks may be paramount in this integration. First, varying hurdle rates for investing under different conditions of political risk might be established. Second, different capital budgeting plans reflecting changes in the level of political risk may be designed. For example, a response to a rise in political risk may be activated by imposing a higher premium on new loans, by increasing premiums on existing loans, or by recalling old loans. Spending gradually declining proportions of capital budgets in the light of increasing risks, or negotiating/renegotiating political risk clauses within tax agreements with host governments may be other examples of meeting this challenge.

A third challenge may involve the construction and implementation of *communications systems* that facilitate more effective diffusion of political risk information throughout the firm's global network. According to Buss (1982), the design and implementation of an effective information filtering mechanism, competent orchestration of the information flow, and prudent acquisition and use of relevant information technology may contribute significantly to a firm's competitive posture in country risk analysis.

Perhaps the ultimate challenge lies in the design and construction of *organizational archetypes* that may more effectively respond to environmental risks in a continuous manner. If the premise that organizational structure is contingent upon environmental dynamics is accepted, innovative skills in organization architecture and behavior may facilitate more proactive political risk management. Organizational archetypes which enhance efficacy in managing the competitive expectations of various political forces within a chosen environment may prove invaluable in affective political risk management.

4.9 Integrating Political Risk Management into the Corporate Planning Function of the Firm

It is clear that affective *management* of political risks is deserving of a central focus in global corporate planning rather than its mere assessment in various country contexts. This is a demanding perspective as it requires formal institutionalization of risk assessment responsibility; innovative architecture and implementation of organization structures including communication systems; efficient utilization of qualitative, quantitative, and in-house assessments; and, effective design and use of continuous, proactive response postures to political discontinuities in the global environment. Successful implementation of such a comprehensive managerial process may enable the multinational firm to manage its environmental analysis function more effectively and economically. Exhibit 4/5 presents a flow diagram which aims to operationalize this perspective.

As this figure illustrates, effective integration of political risk assessment into corporate planning ought to appreciate the interrelationships among the various types of environments considered. Changes and trends in each domain affect, and are affected by, events in others. This could be particu-

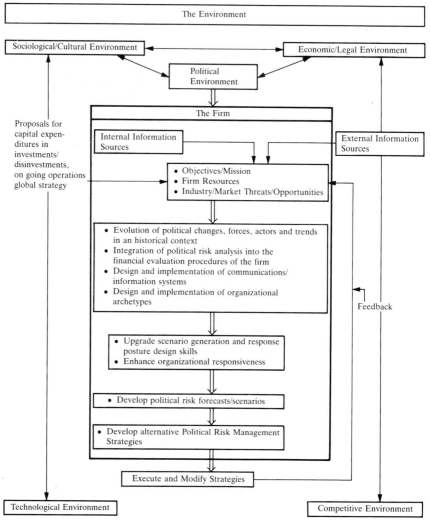

Exhibit 4/5: Integrating Political Risk Management into the Corporate Planning Function of the Firm

larly true for future, as compared to current, developments. The ascending legitimacy of certain sociological forces or shifts in the competitive structure of the firm's industry or even the emergence (or diffusion) of given technological developments may have significant political risk implications in the future. These interrelationships may be incorporated into the political risk assessment process through a structured way of thinking about the relevant trends and corresponding expectations in both the external as well as the internal corporate environment (Neubauer and Solomon 1977). Through the use of internal and external information sources, systematic assessments of the impact of such changes on the firm's mission and objectives, resources, and market opportunities and threats can be more reliably delineated. This process may also facilitate debate on the divergent views on the relevant changes and may help shape more explicit perceptions and expectations about the possible impact of political currents on potential market opportunities.

Such deduction may further facilitate a more comprehensive overview of the evolutionary growth of political forces in an historical context and may help integrate the potential impact of political developments into the financial evaluation procedures of the firm. Creative design and construction of organizational archetypes which facilitate more effective communication flows may then enhance the firm's response posture skills, forecasting abilities, and strategy formulation skills. When strategies formulated through this deductive process are executed and continuously modified in the light of market feedback, the long-term survival and development of the enterprise within a politically uncertain global environment may be considerably enhanced.

4.10 Conclusions

Growing environmental complexity which has characterized the last two decades is likely to increase even further in the future. Systematic evaluation of the environment and the development of flexible strategic response skills are therefore likely to rise in importance within the corporate planning function of the multinational firm. A principal component of this function, political risk assessment, is apparently emerging as an integral dimension. Affective management of political risk analysis, however, appears to be underdeveloped. While it is clear that considerable progress is underway in the identification of the types of political risk; in the utilization of various risk assessment models; and, in the operationalization of the risk assessment function, the integration of political risk management into the corporate strategic planning function appears to be lagging desired progress.

Utilizing past political risk research as its base, this paper has outlined a deductive managerial procedure for integrating effective political risk management into the corporate culture of the multinational firm. In underscoring the concepts brought forward for discussion, the paper highlighted relevant examples from the Middle East. While this procedure may not, necessarily, be applicable within the corporate culture of all multinationals operating in that area, it could have merit in demonstrating the value of systematic strategic thinking, and in developing alternative response postures to evolving political scenarios in the Middle Eastern environment. As the nature of political risks and their interrelationships with other environmental forces are likely to change in this area in the future, deductive strategic approaches may prove valuable in preparing multinationals to more readily anticipate and respond to these developments more affectively. Given the unexpectedly long-lasting Iran-Iraq conflict; the historic rift between Israel and some Arab countries; potentially explosive political currents assumed to brewing in Saudia Arabia, Libya, Egypt and Jordan; and, political uncertainties surrounding succession in Syria and Iran and everything in Lebanon, such systematic approaches to political risk management may be more imperative in the years ahead than ever.

Chapter 5
International Diversification and Investments in the Middle East

Yasar M. Geyikdagi and Necla V. Geyikdagi

5.1 Introduction

The purpose of this study is to examine risk reduction possibilities for United States multinational firms through investments in the Middle East. To this end, we should first try to establish, if indeed, international diversification can play a role in risk reduction. After this, we may try to determine if an increase in the share of investments in the Middle East, at the expense of the six largest industrialized countries (Canada, France, Germany, Italy, Japan and the United Kingdom) outside the United States, could play a positive role in risk reduction for United States multinational firms.

It is hypothesized that synchronic economic cycles among the major economies of the world will lead multinational corporations to have less room for risk reduction through international diversification.

Risk reduction through international diversification has been treated by a rather large number of authors. Elton and Gruber (1981) Rugman (1979) and Stanley (1981), among others, have written on this topic extensively.

The first step of this study is to take a sample of 28 United States multinational firms and compare the average of their systematic risks with those of 28 United States domestic firms during the period of 1971–1978 to see if the degree of interrelationship of world economies could have an influence on risk reduction through international diversification. It could be hypothesized that as the United States economic cycles become more synchronic with those of other major economies, where the majority of United States foreign investments lie, the possibilities for risk reduction through international diversification should decrease for U.S. multinational firms. Consequently, multinational systematic risk, as measured by betas of the capital asset pricing model, should, other things being equal, increase in comparison with those of domestic firms which should not be directly influenced by less opportunities for international diversification.

5.2 Data and Methods

Total risk, which can be defined as deviations from an expected value, is subdivided into unsystematic risk and systematic risk. Investors can diversify their securities to such an extent that the unsystematic risk, which is the risk particular to the share, will be eliminated, and the investors will be left with systematic risk, which is the risk pertaining to the market as a whole. Thus by efficiently diversifying their portfolio of securities, investors can eliminate the unsystematic risk component of the shares and then, they will be left with only systematic risk. The beta is a measure of systematic risk or of the sensitivity of a stock's price to overall market fluctuations

A brief explanation of the steps involved in computing a beta should prove helpful to readers who are unfamiliar with portfolio analysis. First of all, a holding period rate of return has to be calculated. A holding period rate of return measures the total return investors could have realized had they held the asset during the period studied (D'Ambrosio 1976, p. 346). Its formula would be:

$$r_{hp} = \frac{P_t - P_{t-1} + D_t}{P_{t-1}}$$

where r_{hp} is the holding-period rate of return; P_t is the ending price for the period in question; P_{t-1} is the beginning price for the period; and D_t is the cash received during that period.

The holding-period rate of return of both the individual asset and the market index, in which the asset is traded, are calculated.

Then, the characteristic line is computed. This line depicts the relationship between the rate of return on a single asset, the dependent variable, and the rate of return on the market for all assets (the market index), the independent variable. The characteristic line is an ordinary least-square regression line. The beta is the slope of this line. Thus, the beta indicates the extent to which one can expect a change in the rate of return when the market's predicted rate of return is given. The greater the slope of the characteristic line is for a stock, as measured by its beta, the greater its systematic risk will be. The market beta will be equal to one (D'Ambrosio 1976: 334).

The betas used in this study are taken from *Value Line Investment Survey* which started to calculate them in 1971. *Value Line* betas use the New York Stock Exchange Composite Index as the measure of the market index. The individual asset (stock)'s rate of return and the New York Stock Composite Index rate of return are calculated weekly over a period of five years and the beta is derived from a regression analysis.

In this study, any firm which has 35 percent or more of its operations abroad is considered to be a multinational while any firm with 15 percent or less of its operations abroad is accepted to be a domestic firm. Although the minimum difference is 20 percentage points during any year, the average difference is far larger than that since there are multinationals which have more than 50 percent of their operations abroad. The total of 56 industrial firms, consists of 28 multinationals and 28 domestic selected from the *Fortune* list of the largest 500 firms. We were able to find only 56 firms which satisfied the above conditions. This is the same sample as in the study carried out by Geyikdagi (1981) and (1982) and consists of SIC (Standard Industrial Classification System) industry groups, namely, petroleum refining, electrical machinery, non-electrical machinery, chemical and allied products, fabricated metal products, non-ferrous metals and food products. Exhibit 5/1 shows the number of multinational and domestic firms in each industry group.

We used a paired-indifference test to find out statistically significant differences. This method is used to compare pairs of values in small samples using

Exhibit 5/1: Number of Firms in Industry Groups

Industry Group	SIC Code	Multinational	Domestic
Petroleum Refining	291	3	3
Electrical Machinery	3	3	3
Non-electrical Machinery	35	8	3
Chemical & Allied Products	28	7	5
Fabricated Metal Products	34	2	5
Non-Ferrous Metals	333	2	3
Food Products	20	3	6
All groups together		28	28

the Student's t distribution technique. It measures the level of significance of the differences. Rather than taking the average of each of the samples that we want to compare, we pair a value in one of the two samples with a corresponding value in the other sample according to a common denominator. To give an example form this study, the 1972 beta for multinational firms will be repeated for each year during the period under study. The procedure for calculating the paired-difference test will be as follows:

Years	$d_i = B_{M^i} - B_{D^i}$
1	d_1
2	d_2
.	.
.	.
.	.
n	d_n

where n represents the points in time which are years, d_i represents the difference between the variables which are paired, B_{M^i} stands for the multinational beta average during a given year i and B_{D^i} is the beta average of domestic firms during a given year i.

We let d and Sd stand respectively for the average and standard deviation of the n difference measurements. If Md represents the average difference, then

$$H_o: Md = O$$

This means that we want to test the null hypothesis that the average difference is zero. Unsing the relationship

$$t = \frac{\bar{d} - O}{Sd/\sqrt{n}}$$

we find the student's t value. We use a 95 percent confidence interval or a value of $\alpha = .05$ (.025 for each tail) for the difference and n – 1 degrees of freedom. The block design of the paired-difference test increases the amount of information to be obtained. The technique of the paired-difference test has been explained at length by Mendenhall and Reinmuth (1974).

5.3 Empirical Results

Exhibit 5/2 shows the CAPM beta averages for the multinationals and the domestic firms during 1971–1978 while Exh. 5/3 indicates the annual percentage changes in the gross domestic products of the seven major industrialized countries from 1966 to 1977.

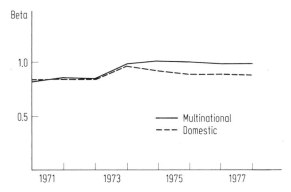

Exhibit 5/2: CAPM Betas (Average of All Groups)

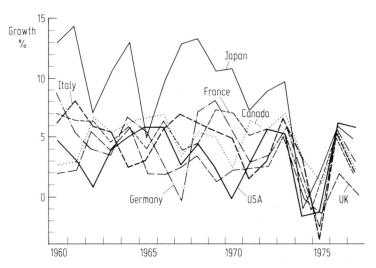

Exhibit 5/3: Gross Domestic Product in Seven Industrialized Countries

Source: Wood and Jianakoplos (1979: 47)

An examination of Exhibit 5/2 shows that the average beta value of all groups for the multinationals goes together with that of the domestics until the end of 1973. After than, the two averages fork out with the multinational betas coming higher in relation to domestic ones. Thus, we see that systematic risk which was about the same for both until 1973 becomes different after that. The explanations of this phenomenon can be sought in the degree of interrelationship of the economies of world countries.

Rugman (1979) looks at the issue through the interrelation of world equity markets which became very strong after 1972. Wood and Jianakoplos (1979) examine the annual percentage change of the gross domestic products of the United States, the United Kingdom, Canada, France, Germany, Italy and Japan. As Exhibit 5/3 indicates, they found that starting from 1973, there has been a greater similarity in rates of growth of output among the major industrialized countries. One can think that this situation left less room for international diversification and hence considerably less possibilities for the reduction of systematic risk. This is a very probable explanation for the increase, relative to that of domestics, in the systematic risk of the multinational firms after the economic recession which began in 1973.

If there were less co-variation of national economies before 1973 than after, then one would expect returns from multinationals before 1973 to exhibit a lower covariance with the U.S. market index than they do afterwards. It may be assumed that domestic returns have the same covariance with the U.S. market index before and after 1973. Hence, the betas of the multinationals should rise in relation to those of the domestics. The formulation for beta should make it more evident:

$$\text{Beta} = \frac{\text{Covariance } (r_m, R_f)}{\sigma_m^2}$$

where r_m, R_f and σ_m^2 respectively denote the market return, the risk-free rate of return and the variance of the market returns.

Other than international diversification, there are product and export diversifications. However, as Pras (1980) explains, the influence of product diversification for large firms such as those in our sample is negligible while that of export diversification is significant. Export diversification was of greater importance for the domestic firms in our sample since they either had no operations overseas or had them on a much lesser scale than the multinationals. A cursory study, based on the reports of a part of the companies together with phone calls for others, seems to indicate that domestics were greater exporters than multinationals, especially after 1974. However, the reader should be cautioned that data could not be obtained for all firms, and when they were obtained, a range of values or simply ordinal rather than cardinal information was often given out. The results of the paired-difference test are summarized in Exhibit 5/4.

Exhibit 5/4: Paired-Difference Test Results

Industry Group	t value	α
Petroleum refining	3.186	.02
Electrical machinery	13.210	.01
Machinery, except electrical	7.890	.01
Chemical & allied products	5.690	.01
Fabricated metal products	4.830	.01
Non-ferrous metals	4.030	.01
Food products	10.820	.01
All groups	3.850	.01

One can see from the t values in Exhibit 5/4 that there is a significant difference between multinational and domestic betas for the overall average of all groups as well as for each group. Thus, the difference between the overall multinational and domestic betas as seen in Exhibit 5/2 is statistically significant.

The results of the test support the hypothesis that synchronic economic cycles among the major economies of the world will cause multinational firms to have less room for risk reduction through international diversification. The test shows that as the major world economies began to have similar cycles in 1973, the systematic risk of United States multinational corporations become higher in comparison to that of United States domestic firms.

Having observed the relationship between the growth of the gross domestic product of the United States and those of the major industrialized countries where the majority of United States investments lie, it would be appropriate to examine the same relationship between the United States and a selected group of Middle Eastern countries (Iraq, Morocco, Saudi Arabia, Syria, Tunisia and Turkey). As Exhibit 5/5 indicates the growth of the gross domestic product of the United States is not synchronic with those of the Middle Eastern countries even after 1973. It can be concluded that, the Middle East offers greater prospects of risk reduction through diversification than the major industrialized countries do. Thus, the multinationals should make it a point to examine the possibilities of increasing their shares of investments in the Middle East and other regions which promise greater prospects of risk reduction.

5.4 Conclusions

Two aspects have been explored in this study. After finding test results which support the hypothesis that there is a negative relationship between synchronic economic cycles and international diversification, we examined the relationship between the cycles of Middle Eastern countries and those of the United States. The marked difference between the two, suggest that the Middle East offers ample room for international diversification for prospective multinational firms from the United States, or for that matter, from the industrialized countries which have economic cycles more or less synchronic with those of the United States.

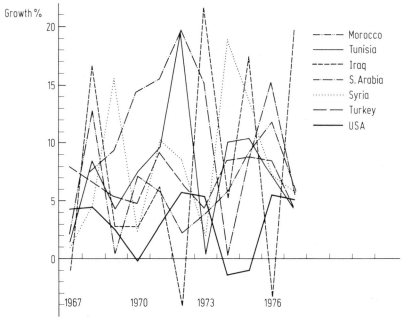

Exhibit 5/5: Gross Domestic Product in Selected Middle Eastern Countries
Source: Yearbook-United Nations (1980: 185; 305)

Chapter 6
International Technology Transfer
in the Middle East*

Asim Erdilek

6.1 Introduction

The importance of international technology transfer (ITT) derives from the central role of technology in modern economic growth (National Research Council 1978: 18–48). The continuing diffusion of successive innovations, whether domestic or foreign in origin, whether product- or process-oriented, is essential to sustained productivity increases in any economy, whether a developed or a less developed one. On the micro level, both price and quality competitiveness of any firm either at home or abroad is ultimately determined by its innovative activities. These innovative activities can be based on either self-generated or acquired technologies. The long-run viability and continued growth of a firm in international competition depend on its progression from a mere purchaser-adapter initially of all technology to a creator-seller eventually of at least some technology.

The indigenous firms of the Middle East, like those of other less developed regions, are crucially dependent on transfer of technology from abroad for their innovative activities, which still primarily consist of the absorption and adaptation of imported technologies for successful assimilation (Erdilek 1982: 64–84). The purpose of this chapter is to provide a general framework for analysing the critical but changing dependence of the Middle Eastern countries on foreign technology. This framework is elucidated by empirical references to specific countries of the region.

* I would like to thank Atif Cezairli for his research assistance.

6.2 The Increasing Importance of International Technology Transfer

International technology transfer (ITT) has been a subject of considerable interest to several diverse groups including government policymakers, international civil servants, business executives and business as well as academic researchers. This broad interest has spawned numerous discussions and studies on various aspects of the subject. Despite all this attention, however, the concept of ITT remains vague, controversial and inadequately operationalised. Moreover, satisfactory measurement of ITT is frequently hindered by the lack of appropriate data and the diversity as well as the complexity of the channels through which technology is transferred.

ITT has been occurring since almost the dawn of civilisation. It has, therefore, evoked considerable interest and discussion for a very long period of time. There is a popular perception, however, that its importance has been increasing substantially more recently. Public officials in many countries express serious concern about the causes and effects of ITT (in terms of either inflows or outflows of technology). Their concerns have led to considerable study and debate, at both the national and international levels, on whether governments, individually or in collaboration, should and can control ITT, in ways that will minimise its negative effects and encourage its positive ones.

There are several broad indicators suggesting that both the speed and the spread of ITT have been increasing rapidly during the last two decades or so. The world appears to have become much more integrated and interdependent as more and more nations have entered the world trading system and as international trade as a percentage of gross national product has risen for many, especially the industrialised countries. Furthermore, direct foreign investment (DFI) activity has increased substantially. Along with the increases in international trade and investment, there has been a remarkable expansion in the stock of knowledge, coupled with vast improvements in global communication and transportation facilities that have permitted knowledge to diffuse more rapidly throughout much of the world.

Higher educational levels and technical capabilities in less developed countries (LDCs) have expanded these countries' capacities to absorb new technology. The greater capability to both transmit and receive information has reduced the costs of transferring technology, leading to the possibility of more and faster transfers. Furthermore, the process of technological development itself has become much more internationalised than ever before with the expansion of DFI, along with the growing role the multinational enterprises (MNEs), as well as the spread of joint R and D ventures, cooperative research arrangements, co-production agreements and the like among different countries.

It is generally accepted that the flow of technology across national boundaries has increased rapidly. Unfortunately, however, our ability to identify and measure the diversified processes that constitute ITT remains rather limited. Therefore, it is difficult to document and substantiate what actually is occurring in this area. International trade indicators point to a growing relative share of trade in high-technology products, at least for the industrial countries. Likewise, DFI-activity indicators show growing shares of MNEs in world manufacturing production and trade. But no equally satisfactory indicators are yet available fot ITT.

Whether or not ITT is growing in importance in some quantitative sense, it is being subjected to intense scrutiny by public policymakers, by those involved in it directly and by those interested in studying its various dimensions. Public officials at both the national and international levels are primarily interested in how ITT affects domestic economic development, international competitiveness and national security. They are concerned about the need for and efficacy of national controls on either outflows or inflows of technology. Besides the many national governments assessing their role in ITT several international institutions, including GATT, UNCTAD, OECD and the United Nations, have set up commissions and study-groups to investigate various aspects of the subject.

The private economic agents, firms as well as individuals, who are directly involved in ITT as either suppliers or recipients of technology are obviously also interested in a better understanding of the subject. Their individual activities concern the selection of technologies as international transferors or transferees, the choice of the channel(s) of transfer, the pricing of the transaction and the choice of the payment mechanism(s). Besides being occupied with ITT itself, they have to keep up and cope with the attempts of national governments to exert increased control over ITT.

The scientific study of ITT is prompted by both the policy considerations that have been discussed above and a desire to better understand the process itself. The aspects of ITT that are of primary interest appear to fall into three broad categories:

(a) understanding the process itself, especially its determinants,

(b) effects on transferors and transferees, and

(c) factors affecting its control.

Although we can debate whether these issues are any more important now than they have been in the past, they are presently receiving considerable attention. A clearer formulation of the concept and better measurement of ITT should help in examining and resolving some of these important issues.

6.3 The Problems in Conceptualising International Technology Transfer

We have already discussed the phenomenon of ITT too long without having attempted to define it. Unfortunately, ITT is not an easy process to define, particularly in an operational manner. Of the three words associated with the process, 'international' is the easiest one to define operationally. Technology transfer across national boundaries is generally accepted as international technology transfer. As long as nation-states are well defined, there is no problem in determining whether a particular technology transfer is international or not. Denoting a particular transfer as international by using this definition, however, does not by itself provide any information about the nationality of either the (original) supplier or the (ultimate) recipient of the technology in question. Such information may be of critical importance with respect to several public-policy issues, particularly those in which the ultimate possession of the technology is an important consideration.

'Technology' is a more complex concept. It generally refers to a class of knowledge about a specific product or production technique. The technical skills necessary to utilise a product or a production technique may also have to be included in the definition of technology. This latter issue arises because technology is usually not a form of knowledge which is easy to either reproduce or use. The recipient of technology must have adequate education or experience to at least recognise that the knowledge being transmitted is useful. The other interesting aspect of technology is its public-good status. When knowledge is made available to another party, that knowledge usually remains available to the transmitting party. However, although one's use of technology does not diminish another's use of it, the benefits derived from using a particular technology can be and are generally affected by the number of parties having access to it.

'Transfer' is the most controversial of the three words. There is considerable debate about the factors that determine whether a transfer of technology has actually occurred (Steward 1979). Some participants in this debate contend that technology is not really transferred unless the knowledge that has been transferred is actually used by the transferee. Others argue that what the transferee does or can do with the knowledge he receives should not be a factor in determining whether a transfer has occurred, although they recognise that the mastery of that knowledge is a critical factor in examining the effects of any given transfer. The fact that technology is knowledge rather than some tangible product makes the concept of transfer a difficult one to define operationally. When a product crosses a national boundary, it is no longer in its original location. Whether or not it is used, it can be said to have been transferred. However, in transferring commercially useful knowledge, the transferor is not giving up the knowledge, but is essentially sharing it with others. If the recipient does not understand what he receives, the knowledge can hardly said to have been transferred.

A firm's absorptive and adaptive capabilities in assimilating outside technology, like its capabilities to create and exploit in-house technology, are cumulative processes. Both sets of capabilities are enhanced by the firm's own R and D activities and skills in production engineering. Therefore, the successful transfer of technology from one firm to another often requires similar levels of technological maturity within the same sector if not product group. That is why ITT has been much greater between developed countries (DCs) than between DCs and less developed countries (LDCs).

Moreover, effective ITT is intimately tied with the recipient country's national policy to stimulate public and private investments in changing and improving its level of indigenous technology (Erdilek 1978). Neither the initial assimilation nor the later diffusion of imported technology is a passive process. Whether the foreign technology is intended to provide operational, duplicative or innovative capabilities (in order of rising sophistication), an active, both public and private, involvement in learning is mandatory for success. This is indeed at least as important as the national regulatory policies in screening technology transfer agreements in order to minimise duplication, restrictive clauses, absolescence and over-payment, and observing closely the conduct of foreign technology suppliers in order to ensure the proper implementation of signed agreements (UNIDO 1977).

6.4 The Channels of International Technology Transfer

The conceptualisation and the measurement of ITT are further complicated by the diverse channels through which it can occur. It can occur through both formal and informal channels. Many of these channels often work in concert. Some channels involve voluntary and intentional ITT, others do not. The principal channels of ITT are:

- licensing
- direct foreign investment
- sale of turnkey plants
- joint ventures, co-operative research arrangements and co-production agreements
- export of high technology products and capital goods
- reverse engineering
- exchange of scientific and technical personnel
- science and technology conferences, trade shows and exhibits
- education and training of foreigners
- commercial visits
- open literature (journals, magazines, technical books and articles)
- industrial espionage
- end-user or third country diversions
- government assistance programs

ITT through most of these channels is very difficult to detect and monitor. Usually, formal channels (the first five above) involve the market mechanism and assign an explicit value to ITT. It is not known whether the bulk of ITT occurs through the formal channels or through the informal ones which are much more difficult to detect and monitor. If actual transfers can not be clearly recognised it is difficult, if not impossible, to determine the more important transfer channels. The critical first step in analysing ITT is to distinguish among its different occurrences. Even for those transfers which can be clearly recognised, it is difficult to place a value on the transaction, especially if the transfer channel is an informal one. Even when an explicit value is available, it may not reflect the 'true' value of the technology being transferred.

ITT is still widely effected through traditional equity interactions, i.e. either wholly-owned subsidiaries or joint ventures, and non-equity interactions, such as licensing agreements between non-affiliated enterprises. We now observe, however, increasingly important new non-equity interactions such as production-sharing agreements, management and marketing contracts, and counter-trading arrangements as additional channels of technology transfer. These new non-equity channels of transfer owe their increasing importance, especially in the Middle East, largely to the fundamental change in the LDC attitudes toward the activities of MNEs in the extractive industries (Penrose 1975; Sayigh 1975; Lenczowski 1976: 9–12; Shwadran 1977, Chapter 6). After the widespreaad nationalisations in the 1970s of especially the petroleum MNES' equity-based operations in LDCs, indigenous public companies were created to take over their ownership and management. For these young and inexperienced companies, it has been necessary to import technical know-how, often from their former foreign parents, for engineering, management and marketing services, through novel non-equity arrangements such as technology-sharing agreements.

In the rest of this chapter, 'technology' refers to industrial technology. It means the accumulated knowledge and know-how required for either manufacturing a final product or processing intermediate inputs. That accumulated knowledge and know-how includes product designs, production techniques and related managerial systems. Technology 'transfer' means the transmission, revision (adaptation) and implantation (absorption) of such accumulated knowledge and know-how that are actually put to productive use. In short, transfer is active, deliberate and effective diffusion engineered by either the transferor or the transferee (but not necessarily by both of them).

This definition of technology stresses its specificity in terms of both its inputs and outputs, as in Pavitt (1983). Furthermore, it is taken to be a primarily private good whose transfer from one production unit to another, even within the same firm, has a real resource cost. In short, technology is a highly specific private good with positive costs of production to its initial

owner (Mansfield 1968), and positive costs of transfer to its transferee and/
or transferor (Teece 1977).

Although technology is a primarily private good, it is not easily priced and
traded through arm's-length transactions in inter-firm markets either domestically or internationally. This is due to the inherent asymmetry in the
distribution of the information about the technology between its owner and
potential buyers, and the well-known fundamental paradox resulting from
its correction (Teece 1981). Much international technology transfer is
'internalised' within MNEs as the owners of technology bypass the external
markets in order to maximise their expected net benefits (quasi-rents) from
the transfer.

6.5 International Technology Transfer in the Middle East

The Middle East consists entirely of LDCs. Despite the fact that it is a
Middle Eastern country, Israel is excluded from the discussion because of
its special status. Although available data on science and technology (S and
T) indicators for the Middle Eastern countries are very scanty, it is
indisputable that the region's indigenous S and T activities are relatively
insignificant. This is true of both the rich oil-producing and the low/middle-
income non-oil-producing countries. In particular, local R and D efforts in
industry are either non-existent or primarily experimental on a limited
scale. Consequently, the Middle Eastern countries are all dependent technologically on the industrialised Western capitalist countries and, to some
extent in certain cases, Soviet-bloc socialist countries. Of course, there are
significant differences among the individual Middle Eastern countries in
their technological dependence on the DCs. Analysing those differences,
however, are largely beyond the scope of this chapter.

The first essential distinction among the Middle Eastern countries has to do
with the relative importance of the oil industry in their economies. Countries that are oil-rich and highly dependent on oil, such as Saudi Arabia, and
countries that are oil-poor and less dependent on oil, such as Egypt, have
had different technological demands and options. The second essential
distinction is in terms of population density. Again Saudi Arabia and Egypt
are opposites as sparsely populated and densely populated countries,
respectively. This distinction, too, has affected crucially their technological

demands and options. Iran, on the other hand, as oil-rich and highly dependent on oil, and also densely populated, has had an altogether different configuration of technological demands and options.

In terms of these distinctions, Bahrain, Kuwait, Libya, Oman, Qatar and the United Arab Emirates resemble Saudi Arabia; Jordan, Lebanon, Sudan, Syria and the Yemens resemble Egypt; and, Iraq resembles Iran. Of course, each of these countries is unique in terms of its factor-endowment and socio-political environment. But for our purposes, we can concentrate on the oil and population characteristics as the most revealing ones for the three groups of countries.

The oil-rich but population-poor countries such as Saudi Arabia have demonstrated primary dependence on imported technologies that are (a) largely capital- and energy-intensive, (b) largely oil- and export-oriented, and (c) accompanied by large numbers of foreign experts for the local absorption and adaptation of those technologies. These countries, as 'low absorbers' have also channelled significant portions of their oil wealth into both portfolio and direct investments in the Western DCs. Those investments have become important means of foreign technology acquisition for these countries in their quest for diversification both at home and abroad out of the oil industry[1].

The oil-poor but population-rich countries such as Egypt have been particularly dependent on imported technologies that are largely (a) labor-intensive, (b) import-substitution-oriented in primarily light manufacturing as well as agriculture, and (c) absorbed and adapted locally without the help of many foreign experts. These countries, without any surplus oil-income and other sources of significant wealth per capita, have not invested abroad but instead have attempted to attract foreign investments from both the DCs and our first group of the Middle Eastern countries. As host countries to DFIs from the DCs, they have gained access to foreign technologies in order to accelerate the development and growth of their economies.

The oil- and population-rich countries, namely Iraq und Iran, as 'high absorbers', showed until 1979, a mixed pattern, as we would expect, in between the first two groups of the Middle Eastern countries, with respect to their imported-technology dependence. Their ambitious development programs entailed importing technologies and creating industries that resi-

1 This phenomenon was anticipated by Loutfi (1975).

sted any straightforward classification. Especially Iran also undertook sizeable DFIs in both Western Europe and the United States. Since going to war against each other in 1979, however, Iraq and Iran not only have had to abandon their quest for economic development, but also have lost many of the past benefits that they had derived from imported non-military technologies. Iraq's oil revenue in early 1984 was one third of what it had been before the war. The war-mandated austerity program has halved imports. Iraq has become an international net borrower and is having difficulty in meeting payments on its outstanding foreign contracts for development projects (The Economist 25 February 1984: 62). Iraq has received at least $ 30 billion in financial aid from the Gulf Cooperation Council countries, primarily Kuwait and Saudi Arabia.

In the rest of this chapter, the author will focus on the technology transfer activities of the first two groups of Middle Eastern countries, especially Kuwait and Saudi Arabia. This special focus, chosen for convenience and due to space constraints, in no way implies that the other countries' technology transfer activities do not deserve to be analysed in detail.

International technology transfer (ITT), based on direct foreign investment (DFI) can occur not only via the transferor country's DFI activities in the recipient country but also via the recipient country's DFI activities in the transferor country. As is well known, several Middle Eastern members of OPEC with high per capita wealth have been diversifying their investment portfolios by putting larger amounts of their surplus oil-revenues into DC-based enterprises by acquiring equity interests. The United States, West Germany and Japan appear to have been the leading host countries for these investments.

Until the mid-1970s, DFI from the wealthy Middle Eastern OPEC countries had been concentrated in the banking and real estate sectors of the DCs. Since then, however, the manufacturing and oil sectors have attracted significant DFI as these OPEC countries have begun to seek products and services, together with the associated technologies, for export to their home markets and industries. Perhaps the best example of this new trend is Santa Fe International, an oil and gas drilling, services and engineering concern, which is the world's single largest investment by an OPEC member and the first US enterprise to be bought entirely by an Arab government (Mufson and Ibrahim 1982: 1). Santa Fe International's parent is Kuwait Petroleum Corporation (KPC), a petrochemicals concern established in 1980, and owned by the Kuwaiti government. The $2.5 billion acquisition of Santa Fe International in 1981 was a key element in the longstanding plan of Kuwait to build KPC into a position of greater global dominance. KPC is a professionally well-managed company, relatively free from political interference by its owner. The Kuwaiti acquisition has proved to be very beneficial for Santa Fe International, which has been expanding and diversifying more rapidly than it did prior to passing into KPC ownership, just before the precipitous world-wide slump in the oil business. Santa Fe International is the most outstanding and thus far the most successful example of the marriage of Kuwaiti oil wealth and American technological know-how, yielding significant mutual benefits.

For Santa Fe International its acquisition by KPC could not have come at a better time. Before the acquisition, it was concerned about its debt, expected layoffs, reduced order-backlogs and cash flow, as the global oil market was about to contract. KPC's ownership has enabled it financially to expand in its existing businesses and also to enter into new ones. It has itself acquired a US oil exploration firm and entered into several joint exploration agreements in both the United States and abroad. Furthermore, it has become involved in several industrial and civil-engineering projects in Kuwait.

It should be noted that, more than any other OPEC member, Kuwait, which has already about $80 billion invested abroad, has concentrated on reaching beyond its territory in search of oil and diversifying its world-wide facilities to help market its crude oil and petrochemicals. Given its rather small population of 1.5 million, Kuwait's own industrialisation potential in terms of large manufacturing complexes, such as steel mills, has been quite limited.

On the other hand, DFI from the DCs, especially from the United States, in the Middle Eastern OPEC countries was until the mid-1970s heavily concentrated in the petroleum industry (Ajami 1979, Chapter 2). Since then, however, manufacturing and services have become increasingly attractive to foreign investors. More recently agricultural and food processing projects have also acquired greater importance.

The spectacular oil-fueled boom of the 1970s in the Middle Eastern OPEC countries, despite its recent slow-down, has enabled them to begin acquiring the modern socio-economic infrastructures essential to rapid and sustained development. The big-ticket items, such as airports, communication networks, power stations and technical universities, are either on line or nearing completion. As these countries become more developed and acquire greater technological competence, they leave behind the old days of the large, ready-made turnkey projects bought from the United States and other DCs. They move toward the acquisition of duplicative and innovative technological capabilities besides the merely operational ones, through greater depackaging (unbundling) and selectivity of their technology imports.

Furthermore, the non-crude oil sectors of their economies are becoming relatively more important. For example, the non-crude oil part of the Saudi-Arabia's economy, which virtually did not exist a decade ago, is now larger by itself than the entire national Danish economy, having grown at an average rate of 14 per cent per annum (Lippmann 1983: 1). This should not be surprising in light of the fact that Saudi Arabia, with reserves of about $ 150 billion, has invested tens of billions of dollars in the acquisition of foreign technology, mostly in petrochemicals. It has also entered into several joint ventures with giant MNEs from the United States, Western Europe and Japan, as well as the fledgling third-world MNEs from South Korea and Taiwan. Saudi Arabia intends to become an important producer of fertilizers by combining foreign technological know-how with its huge reserves of natural gas.

Despite the recent complete takeover of its producing assets by the Saudi government, Aramco (the Arabian American Oil Company) has maintained its presence in Saudi Arabia on the basis of long-term supply contracts, service and management agreements. Saudi Arabia still needed US technical aid in oil exploration and production. Of all the old four US part-owners of Aramco, Mobil has continued to play a major role in Saudi Arabia (Business Week, 17 October 1983: 76–91). Presently it relies on Saudi Arabia for half of its crude supply. It is also participating in several industrial projects as the largest single foreign investor in Saudi Arabia.

In 1980, Mobil reached an agreement with the Saudi Arabian government worth several billion dollars. Mobil agreed to build an oil refinery and a petrochemical complex with access to cheap feedstocks, both export-oriented, in Yanbu. It also committed itself to training Saudi personnel to operate and manage these facilities. In return, Mobil acquired the right to buy an extra 1.4 billion bbl. of Saudi crude oil over two decades.

Recently, the newly-founded Saudi Arabian Basic Industries Corporation (SABIC), the holding company for Saudi Arabia's state-owned industries, has begun its global marketing of petrochemicals (The Economist, 10 December 1983: 71). It has decided to testmarket its plastics directly, rather than through Western chemicals companies.

SABIC expects also to begin producing, by 1985, ethylene and derivatives and methanol in its Saudi plants. Two-thirds of these plants' outputs will be targeted for export. Initially, SABIC is expected to channel about one quarter of Saudi Arabia's exports of petrochemical products. This share may double by the late 1980s. SABIC's Western joint-venture production partners are expected to account for the remaining half.

Now let us look at a unique case of a potential ITT with novel implications. In January 1984, Saudi Arabia concluded a major arms agreement with France (The Economist, 21 January 1984: 31–32). According to this accord, the Saudis agreed to buy from France an antiaircraft missile system for $ 4 billion. The Saudi defence minister, Prince bin Abdul Aziz, was quoted as saying that his kingdom 'contributed huge amounts of money' to the development by the French of the Shaheen (Arabic for 'falcon') anticraft missile system's technology.

The Saudi-French arms accord was said to have stipulated 'that no country, including France, can use the new technology in the missile system without Saudi approval' (The Wall Street Journal, 27 January 1984: 27). This was reported to have been the first case ever of a country financing the development, in another country, of a completely new military technology.

We do not know whether any Saudi military/technical experts were directly involved in the development of this new missile system technology. We can speculate, however, that the Saudis may benefit significantly from the installation and experimental operation of this system in the Gulf region. This may be a prelude to possible joint-ventures with Western arms producers in Saudi Arabia and elsewhere. Furthermore, there may be important spillovers into civilian applications from these military technological ventures. The case of another Middle Eastern country, Israel, in its successful joint ventures with US arms producers comes to mind here.

The Middle Eastern countries now offer significant potential to foreign investors and technology suppliers in developing their indigenous technology and training local manpower toward the further advancement of food production, food processing and handling, minerals exploration, water and its environment, and permanent energy sources. Fields such as building materials, processing of data in local languages, health care, security systems and irrigation equipment are especially in need of the technological and managerial expertise that can be provided by primarily the United States and other DCs.

These countries continue, however, to benefit substantially from technologies transferred from the newly industrialised countries (NICs) such as Brazil, South Korea, Taiwan and Turkey.[2] For example, Libya still relies heavily on Turkish know-how for developing its socio-economic infrastructure. It as well as some other OPEC countries such as Iraq and Iran have presently very close commercial, industrial and educational ties with Turkey. Turkish contractors and suppliers are now well established in the construction industries of Algeria, Iraq, Kuwait, Libya and Saudi Arabia.

Often Turkish construction technologies and their application are more appropriate for the local conditions of the Middle East than those available from the United States and other DCs. Turkey's industrial and technological ties with the Middle East are further strengthed by the growing DFIs in Turkish financial and industrial sectors from the oil-producing countries of the region. In fact, Turkey, given its strategic location as a regional power, nascent NIC status, recently closer cultural and religious ties with these regions, is bound to play a more pivotal role in their further development. It will serve as a wider and busier technological bridge between the DCs and its LDC neighbors, as itself climbs up the international technology ladder.

In 1981, Saudi Arabia, Kuwait, the United Arab Emirates, Qatar, Oman and Bahrain, all countries of the Arab (Persian) Gulf region, established the Gulf Cooperation Council (GCC). The objectives of the GCC are to:

(a) share manpower and financial resources regionally,
(b) allocate industrial projects regionally,
(c) eliminate intraregional tariffs, and
(d) form a common market in the Gulf region.

The GCC is clearly a very encouraging development for future inward DFI and ITT in the Gulf region. As the phenomenal growth of US DFI in Western Europe that followed the formation of the European Economic

2 For an analysis of the recent trends in DFI and ITT among LDCs, see Agarwal (1984).

Community (EEC) in 1958 demonstrated, common markets can be a strong, attractive force for DFI and ITT. Furthermore, the GCC, if successful in developing itself into a common market, may well show the way toward the establishment of a larger one, including if not all then most members of the OAPEC (Organisation of Arab Petroleum Exporting Countries).[3] It should be remembered that the formation of the EEC was motivated and encouraged by the earlier formation and successful performance of the customs union among Belgium, Netherlands, and Luxembourg (Benelux).

3 See Askari and Cummings (1976, Chapters 12 and 15) for an in-depth analysis of the problems and prospects of regional integration in the Middle East.

Part Two
Management Practices

Chapter 7
International Business and the Middle East:
Recent Developments and Prospects

Riad A. Ajami

In recent years students and practitioners of international business have devoted a considerable degree of attention and analysis to the environment of international business and the resultant interaction between the multinational enterprise and developing host societies. That their effort and attention is justified need not be dewelled upon at great length. It is crucial to note, however, that the intrusion of multinational enterprises into traditional developing countries sets in motion social and economic forces likely to bring about massive changes within developing countries. This observation is especially true when western multinational corporate actors, coming from advanced industrial countries, interact with traditional societies and economies such as the Arab states of the Middle East and North Africa.

7.1 Industrialization, Modernity and Social Change: A Major Issue of Concern

Western industrialization took place over a long period of time, concomitantly the structure of western society was being altered. New institutions and socio-economic values unfolded to accommodate the process of industrial transformation. The process was sequential in that each unfolding stage rested upon the development of requisite skills, technology, material and intellectual values and social organizations (Lewis 1969). Levy wrote of this process:

> There were thousands of steps of this sort in the process – all of them quite gradual by contrast with the vast majority of those facing members of any relatively non-modernized society. The first steam engines could be constructed, and were constructed out of the metals

available and by the blacksmiths available. This kind of direct conversion of the materials and skills by hand is often out of the question in many cases for late-comers (Levy 1966: 768).

Arab society, like all late-comers, has had to condense the industrialization process and shorten the time span required, thus superimposing modern values and institutions upon an existing traditional social and cultural structure. The result is a patchwork quilt consisting of modern and traditional social and economic institutions (Higgins 1977: 99–122).

The Arab societies and the multinationals provide a picture of paradox. The Arab countries are traditional while the multinationals, coming from western industrial countries, represent modernity. The operations of multinational firms inevitably induce social and cultural change. Though cultural change can hardly be attributed to just one factor, the multinationals were, nevertheless, agents of change and modernization. Contrasting modernity with a traditional social order, Reinhard Bendix (1978) suggests that one of the consequences of modernity is a breakdown and disruption of the traditional order where accepted authority loses sanctity. Another consequence of modernity is the disolution of some traditional pattern and a drift towards a functional separation of the sacred and secular.

Traditional Moslems exposed to modernity through interactions with multinational firms confront such a challenge. Rapid economic growth and social change often destabilize value systems and established ways of life, thus causing individual conflict and dissonance. Overwhelmed individuals respond by retrenching into their culture and into familiar established ways of life, often rejecting the source of change.

Saudi Arabia, a paragon of Islam piety is an example of a society which is facing internal instability as it moves toward industrialization. On November 21, 1979, the first day of the fifteenth Islamic century, a group of Moslem traditionalists took over the Grand Mosque in Mecca, Saudi Arabia, demanding less development, not more. By labeling the government modernization program as irreligious, the Saudi dissendents were condemning an economic transformation process which was brought about with the collaboration of the multinationals. The dissendents perceived the unfolding change as a threat to the traditional social order. Jonathan Raban speaks of the impact of rapid social and economic change upon a traditional Arab society like Qatar. Of the Qatari, he writes:

In the city of Doha, Qatar 'the whole delicate structure' of the Arab culture 'appeared to have fallen disastrously apart. Objects, people, clothes, traditions and technologies were swirling about in an unholy stew. Nothing matched. Everything grated against everything else. There was a kind of fever in the air as if some violent chemical reaction were going on, creating a new and particularly nasty variety of toxic gas (Fuller, 1980: 18).

Confronted with this, technocrats and Islamic reformers desiring industrialization and modernity, have sought to mediate and ease the impact of this economic transformation process upon their society. At a conference hosted by Duke University in North Carolina, phrases like "An Islamic framework for development and modernization," and "modernization without westernization" were echoed by a number of Saudi officials, educators and technocrats (Malone 1979: 40). These men, though ardent believers, seek to modernize but not necessarily westernize their society. They are rethinking and interpreting Islam in terms which makes Islam relevant to today's world. Equally they are arguing that the rejection of technology and economic transformation do not fit Islam. As members of that society, the reformers believe that the respect for traditional values can coexist with their vision of an industrial Arab society. Samy Mosley, Yanbu Engineering Director – General for the Saudi Royal Planning Commission, speaks of this:

"Old Yanbu was built on traditional and religious values, where the new Yanbu will be built on traditional, religious and modern values by modern methods." (McConahay 1979: 5).

In the same vein, an Islamic scholar suggests:

"The problem isn't modernization," he says. "The problem is certain aspects of modernization. Improving the standard of living in keeping with Islamic principles. We need hotels, but do we need casinos? Moslem conservatives don't object to foreign investment; growth is fine, but what kind of people do you create at the top? People who live in affluence and forget Islamic duties?" (Wall Street Journal 1979: 19).

In the same vein, Salem Azzam, Secretary-General of the Islamic Council of Europe, suggests:

Islam favors modernization when this means new schools, hospitals, roads, houses, industrialization, and fair play for the people. Then he said: "modernization doesn't mean pornography, extramarital sex, alcoholism drug addiction, gambling, juvenile delinquency and big crimes. We reject these evils in any society and say they are totally unrelated to progress and modernization." (Wall Street Journal 1979).

To the reformers, international business and Islam can coexist. Through the former, Arab society can fruitfully link itself with world commerce so as to satisfy its basic economic needs; through the latter it can maintain its moral purpose by following the principles of the "Shariaa." Egypt is an example of such a society where the two coexist:

In terms of westernization, modernization in Egypt – in education, culture, the economy, even industry – started early in the 19th century, long before its appearance in any other Islamic country. Spread over such a long period, it has not produced the stress evidenced elsewhere, where its sudden introduction has disrupted the social fabric. On the contrary, modernization and westernization have come to be associated, in the Egyptian mind, with the power and influence which the country commanded under Mohammad Ali in the first half of the 19th century. They are also associated with the leading cultural and intelectual place which Egypt has occupied among Arab countries (Wahby 1979: 4).

In conclusion, if the Moslem reformers carry the day, as I believe they will, the multinationals will find individuals within Arab countries who will welcome their economic contributions. The potential problems of industrialization and social change pose a threat to multinational firms – host Arab society interactions, however, a viable and accommodating mode can be reached. The inflow of foreign workers and managers is an equally vexing problem.

7.2 Inflow of Foreign Workers and Technicians

The Arab states, in their drive to industrialize, are confronted with the knowledge that the task requires vast numbers of technocrats and skilled workers. The fact that this cannot be created overnight, means a great dependency on expatriates. According to Reuber, one of the consequences of industrialization "alien personnel and practices and introduced into the local scene: that local arrangements and habits are challenged and local beliefs are threatened" (Reuber 1973: 16). A preservation of the traditional social order without "contamination" thus becomes difficult. Because Islam represents a total culture, the inflow of foreign personnel makes it difficult to preserve a traditional Islamic way of life.

Libya, as well as the gulf oil states of Kuwait and Saudi Arabia are becoming concerned about the number of foreign personnel. In Saudi Arabia the foreign labor force, which the government wanted to keep below 850 000 workers by mid – 1980s, is estimated to number over one million today. The impact of 1.2 million expatriates within a population of four million is considerable. Yet Saudi Arabia, the other Gulf states and Libya need skilled manpower if they are to successfully carry their five year economic developmental plans. Libya's expenditures for its five year plan, which ended in 1985, represent only 70 percent of the allocated budget. The government's desire to speed up investments, so as to achieve the desired economic growth targets, is handicapped primarily by a shortage of skilled manpower. The future of the vast industrial Saudi complex at Yanbu is in doubt due to the lack of Saudi manpower. The number of non-Saudi personnel in Yanbu sets that industrial community apart from the rest of Saudi society. It is foreign looking, and will be so for some time to come due to the lack of a sufficient number of indigenous Saudi's to run it. This represents a source of concern to the Saudi government. A Saudi official comments on this state of affairs: "If outsiders run it, we have defeated our purpose." (McConahay 1979: 5).

The shortage of indigenous skilled human resources is a source of continuing anxiety for the Arab states. The governments are acutely aware that further development means more foreign labor. When facilities are completed they must have the skilled workers to staff them, and the prospect of more expatriates is troubling. Multinational firms, which can contribute to increasing and upgrading the indigenous human resources of the region, are likely to be more welcome.

7.3 Subcontracting: A Mode for the Development of Local Enterprise

The development of a viable indigenous private sector is another source of concern for host Arab society. Arab decision makers are interested in the growth of an Arab private sector within the domestic economy. In Saudi Arabia, the Saudi Organization for Consulting Services, a government agency, was created recently to facilitate the growth of an indigenous Saudi capacity in engineering and technical services. The purpose of the agency is to ensure that Saudi businesses will be given a preference over foreign enterprises when bidding on governmental projects. Ahmad al-Tueirji, Vice-President of the agency, points out that over 90 percent of engineering and technical services in Saudi Arabia, are provided by non-Saudi enterprises, which over the last twenty years "have not attempted to train Saudis to carry out such services which form the cornerstone of development." (Middle East Economic Digest 1979: 45). Thus in the interest of promoting an indigenous private sector, the Saudi government initiated the practice of granting projects to national enterprises or joint-venture enterprises, even when the bid prices are higher than those offered by wholly-owned multinational firms. Speaking of this, Yousif al-Mamadi, the Saudi Deputy Commerce Minister, stated, "we are willing to sacrifice 1 to 2 per cent additional cost, provided it results in a transfer of technology" (Middle East Economic Digest 1979: 8).

The growth of small and medium size Saudi enterprise is an equally troubling issue. Statements about "corporate barons" who could act to stifle the growth of small and medium size Saudi enterprises are echoed in a number of Arabic newspapers. Because of the large size of projects initiated by the second Saudi Five-Year Plan, small and medium size firms are unable to bid and compete against large joint-venture firms (Saudi-foreign enterprise) with substantial assets and capital. In recognition of this problem, the trend today, in Saudi Arabia and elsewhere in the Gulf is to divide up projects, thus making it feasible and manageable for local businesses to participate in the bidding process. Similar trends are also evident in Qatar. According to a recent government declaration, foreign firms will be excluded from bidding for projects costing less than $ 100,000. Multinational firms can still bid to manage large scale projects, however, through dividing up projects and subcontracting they can continue to do business in the Arab world. Subcontracting helps indigenous enterprise development and improves local managerial skills. The advantage of this arrangement to the multinationals is the freedom from the burden of managing small local operations at which they could be at a comparative disadvantage. Multinational firms should find this development acceptable for conducting international business.

Another issue of Arab concern is the hostility to their investments and oil money within Europe and the U.S.A. Concerns that the Arabs will control major European and U.S. corporations are commonplace in western economic circles. Statements about Arabs purchasing vast amounts of agricultural land within the U.S.A., thus pushing up prices of land are echoed in the American Congress and at farmers' gatherings everywhere. Laws and regulations to screen foreign investment in the U.S.A. were primarily motivated by the fears that the Arabs, with their newly found wealth, will take over control of major industries in the U.S.A. In Europe:

> Fears that OPEC's new wealth would lead to a wholesale Middle East takeover of Europe's industrial corporations prompted many German industrial chieftans to advocate protectionist measures aimed at keeping out what the popular press called 'bosses in burnouses' (the traditional Arab garment) (Myall 1979: 21).

Arab investors are arguing that their U.S. investments in industries, land, and agriculture is miniscule. Though hard data is not available, it is estimated that total OPEC countries' share of direct foreign investment within the U.S. is less than 1% (Foreign Investor 1978). Published figures by the U.S. Department of Agriculture indicate that Arab concerns own less than 615 acres out of a total of 1,046,000 hectares of cultivated land owned by foreigners within the U.S.A. (Middle East Economic Digest 1979: 20). Thus America as well as the rest of the industrial world will have to advance avenues of mutuality so as to make that exchange beneficial to both if they are to have excess to Arab oil. Otherwise the Arabs will have no incentive except to keep their oil in the ground.

7.4 Third World Linkages

Another example of third world linkages is the transfer of skilled and semiskilled labor. The U.S. Fluor Corporation has recently announced its intention to transfer approximately 4000 skilled Indonesian and Philippine workers to Algeria. The firm has been awarded a $ 330 million contract by the Algerian state-owned oil concern, Sonatrach, to build a gas recycling complex. According to a Fluor official, this is a desirable form of conducting international business because, "There is a lack of skilled manpower here. We think that we can use the people we have already trained on one of our projects in Indonesia to help in the construction of the plant here. Sonatrach has agreed to this" (Blum 1979: 25).

A parallel example of third world labor involvement in the course of Arab economic development is the possibility of using Chinese workers. China is trying to make inroads into Arab business by offering to supply skilled and semiskilled labor. Advertisements by the Chinese Guandong Manpower Service Corporation, offering teams of workers to contractors in the Arab world, proliferate Arabic newspapers. The chinese agency offers several hundreds to several tens of thousands of skilled workers for monthly salaries, not exceeding $ 450 (Breeze 1979: 6). The promise of this linkage is yet to materialize. In light of the Grand Mosque takeover, traditional Arab Gulf states, such as Saudi Arabia, are, however, weary about allowing substantial number of socialist-communist expatriates to work among the Saudis.

7.5 Conclusion

Arab policies toward the multinationals can be placed along a continuim, as shown in Exhibit 7/1.

At one end of the continuum the climate for multinational corporate linkages can be labeled as regulative-restrictive, and the other open-door. Egypt, Tunisia, Lebanon, Jordan and Morocco policies range from promotional to opendoor. The policies of Saudi Arabia, Kuwait, the United Arab Emirates and the other Gulf mini-states, with the exception of South Yemen, can be characterized as promotional. The climate in Algeria, Iraq, Libya and Syria ranges from regulative-restrictive to promotional. What-

Exhibit 7/1: Arab Country Policies Toward The Multinationals

Arab Country Typologies			
	Algeria Iraq Libya Syria	Kuwait United Arab Emirates Saudi Arabia Qatar	Jordan Lebanon Tunisia Morocco Egypt
Policy Alternatives	Regulative- Restrictive	Promotional	Open-Door

ever the policies are, even in the most restrictive group of countries, the multinationals are nevertheless playing an essential role in the process of economic development, a process which is to propel the Arabs into an industrial age. The Arab oil states are conscious of the limitations of an oil-based economy, and are weary of the fact that their oil will be depleted within two to three decades, long before developing an alternative economic base.

Inspite of the wave of nationalization of oil investments, the oil-producing states remain connected to the oil companies through joint-venture, service contracts, and as of recently "processing agreements." Petromin, the Saudi national oil concern, is about to conclude a processing agreement with two major multinationals. Under the terms of the arrangement, the foreign firms will refine and market Saudi crude oil on behalf of Petromin. Abu Dhabi and Kuwait are also seeking processing agreements and joint-ownership of refineries located outside the Middle East. Kuwait has just concluded an agreement for a joint-venture with Gulf Oil to acquire a South Korean refinery. Kuwait will supply crude oil, and Gulf the management and marketing of the output. One can thus speak of a symbiotic relationship between the Arab oil-producers and the multinationals. Arabs own crude oil and the multinationals have managerial services and marketing outlets. Aware of the vital link which the multinationals can play, Arab decision-makers are prudent enough to pursue policies of connectedness to the firms. The destabilization impact of industrialization is an issue that host Arab countries must deal with by creating social and economic structures to minimize the impact of this economic transformation process. The multinationals must accommodate this process by following social and economic guidelines of host Arab countries.

Chapter 8
Managerial Practices in the Middle East

Ugur Yücelt

8.1 Introduction

In the management literature, there are numerous discussions of the ways in which managers are typically affected by their cultural and social backgrounds, as well as by behavioral and economic factors. The family structure and the relationship between family members, the degree of acceptance of authority in the society, economic conditions and the overall standard of living, and personal and behavioral characteristics of managers contribute to differences in their management styles in different nations (Glaser 1971; Kavcic, Rus, and Tannebaum 1971; Melikian 1956, 1959). Despite this proposition about the factors which affect management styles in general, studies dealing with practices in developing countries demonstrate very little managerial orientation.

The purpose of this chapter is to point out management styles prevailing among managers in both the private and public sectors of Middle Eastern countries. Although the empirical analysis focuses on Turkey, the findings and conclusions are relevant to the managerial cultures of other Middle Eastern nations. Therefore, this chapter also discusses the applicability of different management systems and considers the impact of management behavior on orderly decision making.

The countries of the Middle East have distinguishing economic, cultural, social, and behavioral characteristics. They own rich oil reserves and rank among the wealthiest nations of the world. For example, in terms of physical wealth, one study ranked Saudi Arabia as 26th, Iran 34th, Egypt 39th, and Turkey 51st out of the sixty richest nations of Europe, North and South America, Asia, and Africa (Haner 1980). GNP, per capita income, and consumption figures of Middle Eastern countries reflect higher averages than those of the developing countries of Asia and Latin America (The Europe Year Book 1982).

With regard to social values, cultural norms, and behaviors, the people of the Middle East and Westerners are clearly dissimilar. One study stated that Saudis do things at a leisurely pace and are unmindful of interruptions; Westerners, however, set time standards and objectives for completion of tasks (Daniels and Ogram 1982). In addition, Middle Easterners are highly sensitive to face-to-face criticism, and they place great value on hard work and personal friendship (Lee 1979).

These differences in behavior and motivation in the various cultures of the Middle East help to explain differences in management styles. In terms of humanistic values, among the sixty nations of the world, Haner (1980) ranked Egyptians as 30th, Saudis 32nd, Iranians 44th, and Turks 45th. When the human and physical values are combined, Saudi Arabia was 31st, Egypt 38th, Iran 40th, and Turkey 51st. This study stated that Turkey might move to a higher rank, if an authoritarian government takes power.

As in every nation, managers of the Middle East work to satisfy their basic needs for goods, clothing and shelter. Because satisfaction of higher level needs (social, esteem, autonomy, and self-actualization) depends upon what motivates individual managers, differences in motivation help to explain individual management styles (Harrell 1971). Middle Eastern managers rank self-actualization as the most important higher need, followed by social need, esteem, security need, and autonomy (Badawy 1980). However, the greatest managerial dissatisfaction is in the areas of autonomy and self-actualization (Haire, Ghiselli and Porter 1966; Howell, Strauss and Soreson 1975).

8.2 Theoretical Explanation of Management Styles

Likert (1976) examined management styles and related them to a wide range of factors, including: leadership, motivation, communication, interaction, decision making, goal setting, and control. He developed the famous four-systems model, in which he stated that there are basically four management styles: a) System 1 – Exploitative-Authoritative; b) System 2 – Benevolent-Authoritative; c) System 3 – Consultative; and d) System 4 – Participative-Group. The System 1 style manager does not have any confidence or trust in subordinates. He holds all of the authority, and subordinates do not participate in decision making. There is very little upward communication, and subordinates experience fear, punishment, distrust, and occasional rewards. System 2 managers, on the other hand, have some confidence and trust in subordinates. However, subordinates still are not free to discuss job-related problems with their managers, and there is only minimal upward communication and interaction with superiors. Orders are issued to instruct and to comment on job-related matters. System 3 style managers have complete confidence and trust in subordinates. In this style of management, subordinates feel free to discuss job-related matters with their superiors, and experience both rewards and occasional punishment. Communication is in both directions (downward and upward), and subordinates interact with superiors without fear in decision-making. System 4 style managers, in the last and best system, allow subordinates to discuss and interact in job-related matters with complete confidence and trust in their superiors. In this system, group problem-solving and other group functions are permitted to achieve maximum efficiency and high productivity. Subordinates are highly motivated to achieve organizational goals, and fully participate in decision making. There is always a free, uninterrupted flow of communication from one part of the organization to another.

Likert (1976) stated that any organization may be characterized by one of these systems. However, the greatest attention should be directed to the System 4 style of management, which is the ideal for profit-oriented organizations concerned about employee well-being. Indeed, each style of management evolves over a certain period of time, and the System 4 style should be the goal of those organizations seeking to be the most creative, successful, and effective (Kavcic, Rus and Tannebaum 1971).

The application of the Likert System theory demonstrates that highly industrialized nations tend more toward System 4 and less toward System 1, while, in less industrialized nations, management systems tend more toward System 1 and less toward System 4. Also, an organization applying System 4 tends to produce higher morale and higher productivity, because morale and productivity tend to increase as an organization moves from System 1 to System 4 (Likert and Likert 1976). In Yugoslavia, for example, a study demonstrated that the less successful organizations apply System 2 style of management, and the more successful ones, the System 3 style. In Sweden, another study showed evidence that district sales managers of the System 4 type had considerably higher sales volume than did the district sales managers who exercise the System 1 style of management. In Japan, one study placed the average mean management score of high productivity firms between System 1 and System 2. Another Japanese study showed that the high productivity managers in Japan are much more like System 4 style managers than those of System 1. A study in the Arabian gulf region demonstrated that Middle Eastern managers perceive their organizations to be operating in the System 3 mode, and in interpersonal relations, there is a tendency toward participative management (Tannebaum, Mozina, Jerovsek and Libert 1970; Kavcic, Rus and Tannebaum 1971; Likert and Likert 1976; Abdulrahman and Hollingsworth 1983) Exhibit 8/1 shows differences between authoritarian (System 1 or System 2) and participatory (System 3 or System 4) styles, with managerial implications.

Managers of the Middle Eastern nations are considered authoritarian rather than democratic, and tend to discourage participatory decision making in

Exhibit 8/1: Implications of Different Management Styles

Implications	Management Styles	
	System 1/System 2 (Authoritarian)	System 3/System 4 (Participatory)
Motivation	None	Higher
Commitment	None	Higher
Appraisal	None	Contingent Upon Employee Performance
Knowledge about Subordinates	Little	Greater
Direction of Information	Downward	Upward
Interaction	Little	Greater
Decision Making	At Top	Throughout Organization
Goal Setting	Orders Issues	Group Decision
Rewards	Non-Existent	Contingent Upon Employee Performance
Development	Poor	Greater
Responsibility	None	Greater
Planning	No Involvement of Employee	Closer Involvement of Employee
Supervision	Greater	Less
Self-Discipline	None	Greater
Authority	High	Low
Freedom	None	Greater, Related to Achievement Objectives
Satisfaction	Low	High
Respect from Subordinates	Low	High
Feedback and Control	Poor	Greater

their workplace. They believe that authority will produce both higher morale and productivity in the workplace, while low morale and low productivity will be the result of applying participatory management systems. Research suggests that authoritarianism in the Middle East nations is caused partly by their educational systems and family structure, and partly by their culture and social values (Barret and Bass 1976; Mihcioglu 1970; Meade 1967; Meade and Whittacker 1967; Kenis 1977; Harrell 1971; Terril 1965; Lauter 1969; Ross and Ross 1971; Haire, Ghiselli and Porter 1966).

There are two different types of business organizations in the Middle East: a) privately-owned organizations; and b) state-owned enterprises. The state-owned enterprises have larger work forces, and contribute a great deal to the economic development of the Middle Eastern nations. However, despite size and importance of state-owned enterprises, they are unproductive, inefficient, and the largest money losers. The inefficiency is created by incompetent and unqualified managers who have little incentive to minimize production costs (Gillis and Peprah 1982; Charlton 1983).

Findings of several studies demonstrate that Middle Eastern managers tend to attempt to get results through authoritarian methods, rather than through persuasion and delegation of authority. They believe that subordinates are incompetent, and cannot be trusted to perform their jobs independently in a satisfactory manner; therefore, they strongly defend centralization of authority and insist that subordinates should be closely supervised and directed at the workplace. It follows then, that the managers do not have sufficient time for planning, coordination, and control because much of their time is devoted to the minor matters which could be handled by subordinates (Wright 1981; Zahra 1980; Anastos, Bedos, and Seamon 1980; Fazel and Jan-OleRay 1977; Pezeshkpur 1978; Skinner 1964; Himmetoglu 1983, Savage 1978; Stephens 1981).

In developed nations of the West, on the other hand, workers generally show low morale, low productivity, and a high degree of dissatisfaction with authoritative managers. When authority increases at the workplace, workers tend to quit within the first year of employment (Rey 1966). The European and American examples demonstrate that participatory management develops high morale, high productivity, and high satisfaction at the workplace. Therefore, in West Germany, plant workers have one-third representation on the supervisory board of directors. In Yugoslavia, self-management is widely practiced in almost every plant. In the U.S.A.,

Exhibit 8/2: Middle Eastern vs. Western Style Management

Implications	Middle Eastern Management	Western Management
Decentralization	Limited	Widespread
Authority	Executive Only	Dispersed
Delegation of Authority	Rare	Frequent
Superior/Subordinate Relationship	Formal	Highly Personal
Leadership	Based Upon Domination	Based Upon Experience, Intelligence and, Judgement
Trust in Subordinates	Non-Existent or Minimal	Great
Team Work and Cooperation	Non-Existent or Minimal	Great
Accountability	Demanded from All Subordinates	Determined According to Job Description
Control	Oral and Through Use of Accounting Information	Written and Through Performance Appraisal
Planning	Short-Term	Long-Term
Written Reports	Brief and Uninformative	Long and Informative
Staffing	Contingent Upon Affiliation, Friendship, and Right of Birth	Contingent Upon Qualifications, Training, and Experience
Learning	Memorization	Analytical methods and Problem Solving
Profit Objectives	Short-Term	Long-Term
New Ideas	Discouraged	Encouraged
Resistance to Change	Strong	Minimal
Group Membership	Based Upon Social Status	Based Upon Economic Sociopolitical, and Psychological Factors
Loyalty	To Individual Manager	To Organization

General Foods Corporation designed a system to run the manufacturing plant with minimum supervision (Kelly and Khozan 1980; Charlton 1983). Exhibit 8/2 shows the differences between Middle Eastern and Western styles, with managerial implications.

8.3 Empirical Analysis

In order to examine the management styles in the Middle East, a survey was conducted among 59 Turkish executives presently employed in five companies in Istanbul, Turkey. Four of the companies were private; the fifth was a state-owned enterprise. The industrial affiliation and sample size of each company is presented in Exhibit 8/3.

Exhibit 8/3: Characteristics of Companies (N = 59)

Name	Industry	Sample Size	%
Company I	Tire and Rubber	16	.27
Company II	Oil refinery	15	.25
Company III	Glass Fiber	10	.17
Company IV	Tools and Machinery	7	.12
Company V	Glass and Glass Products	*11*	.19

Of the 59 Turkish executives surveyed, 78 percent were male and 22 percent female. Data indicated that eight were presidents (14%); five, vice presidents (8%); 29, middle level managers (49%); 15, first level managers (26%); and two gave no response to occupation (3%). Forty-three of the respondents (73%) were 35 years old and younger, and 16 were over 36 years old (27%). However, 90 percent of those surveyed were between 26 and 45 years old; therefore, they were relatively young. Most (95%) had either business or engineering degrees and 5 to 10 years' business experience.

8.4 Research Method

A Likert-type questionnaire was adapted and translated into Turkish for this study. The questionnaires were hand-distributed to 100 randomly selected Turkish managers representing five different industries through their employment offices. A total of 59 usable questionnaires were returned.

The obvious reason for focusing on Turkey in the empirical study was that Turkey became industrialized in the 1930's and has an established industrial setting similar to other Middle Eastern nations (Eren 1963); therefore, Turkey's past and current experiences may provide the basis for some conclusions about the managerial styles in the Middle East.

A plotting technique was used to analyze the data. By use of mean scores, the plotting technique visually presents the data, and determines the Turkish executive's position in Likert's System 4 model. Because this method, although simple, is particularly useful in evaluating attitudes of respondents toward different management styles, it has been used successfully in studies similar to this one (Kavcic, Rus and Tannebaum 1971; Tannebaum, Mazina, Jerovsek and Likert 1970; Likert and Likert 1976).

Exhibit 8/4: Management Styles in Five Turkish Organizations

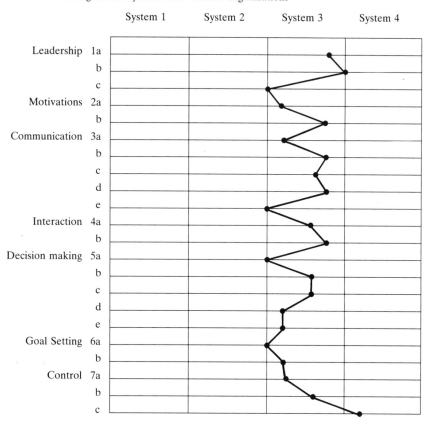

8.5 Findings

As shown in Exhibit 8/4, the plotted results indicated that the managerial style of executives in the sample was more inclined toward System 3, Consultative, and less toward System 4, Participative-Group.

When the data was plotted separately, System 3 appeared to be the most acceptable style in the majority of these five Turkish industrial organizations. For example, in Company I (manufacturer of tire and rubber products), System 3 was applied for leadership motivation, decision making, and goal setting; and in company II (oil Refinery) the executives

Exhibit 8/5: Management Style in Tire and Rubber Products Manufacture

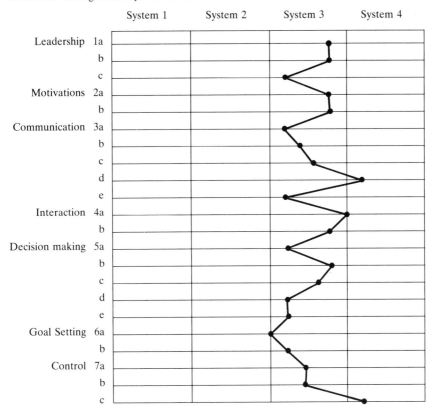

leaned toward System 4 in leadership and interaction, but were more inclined toward System 3 for all other variables Exhibits 8/5 & 6).

Exhibit 8/7 shows that in Company III (glass fiber manufacturer), the executives leaned toward System 2 for communication and decision making, and toward System 4 for control; they leaned more toward System 3 in motivation, leadership, interaction, and goal setting.

According to findings of Exhibit 8/8 in Company IV (tools and machinery manufacturer), managerial style leaned toward System 4 in communication, toward System 2 in goal setting, and toward System 3 in leadership, motivation, interaction, decision making, and control.

Exhibit 8/6: Management Style in Oil Refinery Company

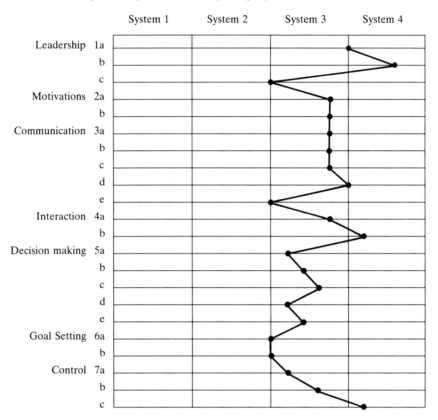

Company V (glass and bottle products manufacturer) was a state-owned enterprise and the oldest company in the sample. It was interesting to see that the executives of this company leaned more toward System 2 than did the executives in companies I, II, III and IV. Management style of executives in Company V was authoritarian in communication, decision making, and goal setting; participatory in motivation and control; and consultative in leadership and interaction (Exhibit 8/9). According to this evidence, it appears that traditional state-owned enterprises have more authoritarian structures than privately owned corporations in Turkey.

Exhibit 8/7: Management Style in Glass Fiber Manufacturer

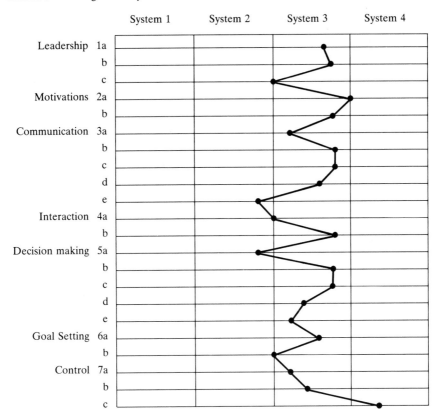

8.6 Conclusions and Policy Implications

Responses from 59 Turkish executives to the Likert-type questionnaire indicated that the Turkish managers lean less toward System 1, Exploitative-Authoritarian, and more toward System 4, Participative, management style in private organizations, and more toward System 2, Benevolent-Authoritarian, and less toward System 4 management style in traditional state-owned organizations. With these findings in mind, it appears that the decision making of young and well-educated Turkish managers tends to have a participatory character rather than an authoritarian one.

Exhibit 8/8: Management Style in Tools and Machinery Manufacturer

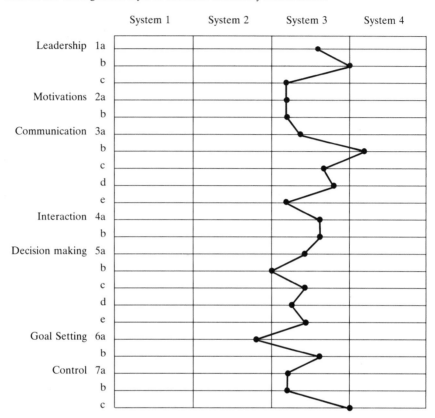

Effective participatory management requires well-trained and well-educated employees. It is not surprising then, that the better the education and training in an organization, the higher the participation and managerial efficiency. That is one reason why the Turkish State Planning Organization has recommended an alternative education system for Turkish pupils since 1961, and has encouraged individual development, free interchange of ideas, and a thoughtful, purposive approach to learning rather than dictation and imitation, both in the classroom and on-the-job training:[1]

1 Turkish industry started in the 1930's and has already completed the early stages of industrial development. Since the 1960's, the aim of the State Planning Organization has been to alter traditional management and production systems in Turkey.

Exhibit 8/9: Management Style in Glass and Bottle Products Manufacturer

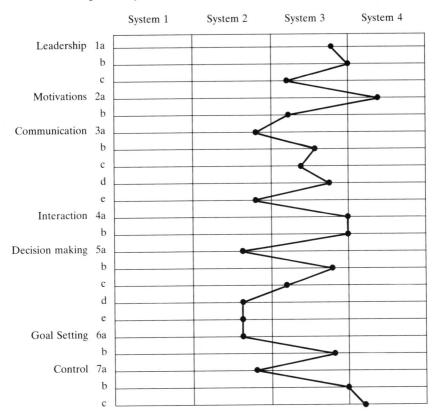

Accordingly, in the newly established private Turkish organizations, authority has become a less popular concept because newly trained managers understand the value of participative management, and are willing to apply it to achieve high morale, efficiency, productivity, and low absenteeism.

In the Middle East, therefore, it is necessary to introduce participative managerial systems in classrooms and train prospective managers before they assume on-the-job managerial responsibility. This does not suggest that they change their social values, culture, family structure, and individual pride; rather it proposes to narrow the gap between the management styles of Western culture and the Middle East nations. Then the Western businessmen working for multinationals in the Middle East may find a more productive and effective work environment.

The authoritarian structure of the Turkish State-owned enterprises is not different from that of state-owned enterprises in other nations (Gillis and Peprah 1982). Inefficiency, low productivity, backwardness, and high deficits are the result of this management system. The alternative is to adapt participative management through innovative managerial training on-the-job. Managerial culture in the Middle East can be improved if progressive and functional manners are introduced into the business environment.

Chapter 9
The Arabian American Oil Company (ARAMCO) and Saudi Society: A Study in Interaction

Riad A. Ajami

9.1 Introduction

As a major multinational enterprise, ARAMCO (the Arabian American Oil Company) plays a vital role in linking Saudi Arabia oil resources with energy dependent Western economies. Its crude oil output in 1979 supplied 17% of United States' oil imports, and as much as 20% of "Free-World" demand. In 1981, ARAMCO's oil represented about 45% of total OPEC output. ARAMCO was jointly owned by the government of Saudi Arabia (60%) and four major American multinational firms: Mobil, Exxon, Standard Oil Company of California and Texaco (40%).

Arab nationalization of Western oil investments began in 1973. Naturally ARAMCO became a target for complete takeover by Saudi nationalists. After years of negotiation, however, the Saudi government remained reluctant to completely take over ARAMCO. Today, ARAMCO continues to be run by the four multinationals. Furthermore, its domain within the Saudi economy is likely to grow because the Saudis have come to trust the companies and to look at ARAMCO as an efficient enterprise useful for the development of the Saudi economy. Through its service company, ARAMCO is supervising electrification projects in the Eastern province, in addition to its exploration and development of oil and gas fields offshore and onshore. Other activities indicative of further expansion of ARAMCO's role in Saudi economic life include a master gas gathering system and a transpeninsula pipeline. Moreover, it is developing billions of dollars worth of facilities to support the doubling of its labor force, thus suggesting that its role in the Saudi economy is unlikely to undergo major contraction when the government finally confirms ARAMCO's nationalization, as a result of its decree in March 1980 to increase its share of ownership to 100%.

9.2 Purpose of the Study

The purpose of the study is to assess the process of interaction between Saudi Arabia and the four American multinational firms, as well as to understand the effect of this process on both the firm and its environment.

This study proceeds from three basic propositions. One is that ARAMCO, in order to survive and grow, has had to change the environment in which it operates; the second is that ARAMCO has had to pay tribute to several traditional elements in the society in which it operates and has to de-Americanize its personnel in order to function properly in such an environment. The third, and crucial proposition to the success of ARAMCO, is the development and growth of indigenous Saudi technocrats. ARAMCO attempted and succeeded in developing a cadre of indigenous technocrats.

9.3 Research Focus and Methods

The major purpose of the study is to query the technocrats about the impact as well as the contributions of ARAMCO to Saudi society. Specifically, the study will be an attempt to see how important the following variables are to the Saudi technocrats in assessing the value of such a continued linkage to the American oil firms. These variables are:

(a) Influence on the way of life of Saudi Arabia, due to the presence of organizationally alien institutions,
(b) Contribution to economic growth and development,
(c) Rate of natural resource depletion,
(d) Opportunities for managers (skills transfer),
(e) Opportunities for industrialization.

A sample of 134 Saudi middle and upper level technocrats was selected. This sample came from Dhahran, Saudi Arabia. A structured questionnaire was utilized; however, the respondents were asked to add on any additional comments and concerns.

No human activity occurs in a vacuum. Thus the environment in which an actor acts is a crucial element in understanding both the actor and the environment. The process of interaction between the two is one that deserves attention and study. This observation is especially true when the actor and the environment seem to provide a picture of paradox and fundamental incompatibility. The Arabian American Oil Company viewed against a background of traditional Islamic society is a challenge to the student of organizations. This is by no means a modest attempt. Social change could hardly be attributed to one factor. But, nonetheless, ARAMCO seems to be an influential and important agent of change within Saudi Arabia.

As indicated earlier, ARAMCO has had to change the foundations of Saudi society in order to make the environment conducive to its enterprise. Saudi Arabia simply did not possess characteristics which would provide for organizational survival growth. Amitai Etzioni writes:

> The main sociological characteristic of modernization is differentiation. Differentiation is best viewed against the background of a primitive or traditional society. (Etzioni 1964: 106).

He also adds:

> Differentiation is essential for the organizational revolution for two related reasons. First, it allows the establishment of new social units devoted to specific functions, especially those of production and allocation, leaving social and normative integration in the hands of older, more traditional units, above all the family. Second, it makes possible the formation of artificial social units deliberately designed for the effecient service of these functions; such units have a set of norms and a structure (including an authority hierarchy) which have been tooled to fit the specific goal or goals of the organization (Etzioni 1964: 106–107)

To have this kind of a structure, ARAMCO set in motion forces which literally helped transform Saudi society. When the kingdom of Saudi Arabia was created in 1932, one year prior to the concession given to ARAMCO, there had been no background of foreign domination or external pressures, and the great majority of the population were tribal nomads. By definition, a tribal society is incompatible with modern organizations.

As a result of ARAMCO's operation, a new social factor has been introduced into the Saudi equation: the urban worker and manager. ARAMCO's native working force provides an interesting phenomenon. They belong to their society and yet they do not. Superimposed upon their old system is a new one more appropriate to the corporate culture. Corporations seem to and in fact have to create their own norm-structure. ARAMCO is no exception. It too has had to foster its values, norm-structure and its way of life.

With the majority of the Saudi working force owning homes around company installations and the majority of the rest of them living in company housing, a subculture has been created; a group of people with their own norms and way of life, a way of life that is destined to be different from that of the rest of Saudi society.

When taking the number of years as a criterion to measure the degree of adaptation of working force to the corporate entity, one fact emerges: the importance of the length of service of the Saudi employee as a socialization agent. In the early 1970's, over 70% of ARAMCO employees had a service of 15 years or more. These figures indicate a steady working force; one that has grown up with the corporation and, that is better suited for the purposes of the organization. The number of Saudi employees stands now at 56% of total employment.

Without skills and know-how, the Saudis could not get far in ARAMCO. But ARAMCO's training system must be given full credit. It started on the lowest possible level; elementary education for adults. Elementary schools were opened by ARAMCO and turned over to the Saudi government. Even education for females, until recently an alien thing to the Saudi environment, was pioneered by ARAMCO.

Modern medicine was introduced, and several agricultural products were supported by ARAMCO. In short, ARAMCO is considered by some to be the most important agent of change that has invaded Saudi culture. Be that as it may, ARAMCO has often found it advantageous to perpetuate the way things are; the emphasis upon the past and tradition.

Looking at ARAMCO's employee magazine, published in Arabic, *The Oil Caravan* (Kafilat az-Zait), one finds that it has articles on religious subjects, ancient Arab poetry and the glory of the past. Romantic stories, art works related to females, and contemporary issues are never to be found in ARAMCO's magazine. ARAMCO's magazine has done quite well. Its circulation is considerable, and it is read by its employees as well as the public. Thus ARAMCO has not only sought to restrict its contacts to the host government, but extend that to the public at large as well.

Another variable in ARAMCO's successful adaptation within Saudi Arabia rested upon the development and strengthening of the indigenous Saudi technocrats. The technocrat in general tends to be moderate, realistic and understanding of the company's policies. The position of the technocrat is very well expalined by J.E. Hartshorn:

> These youngish men differ rather significantly to the casual observer, at least from the similarly aspiring intelligentsia of other developing societies. Their education is sometimes technological rather than legal. Their ladder of advancement, has not been primarily political (Hartshorn 1962: 301).

Because of their technical competence and apolitical nature, the technocrats are easier to deal with. They are isolated from the feudal social structure of their society, and even more isolated from the radical nationalists. They are equally aware of the shortages of indigenous skills and are concerned with efficiency. A look at ARAMCO's technocrat is now in order.

9.4 Results and Discussion

The purpose of this section is to present an analysis of a set of variables measuring the attitudes and perception of Saudi technocrats toward ARAMCO and the related phenomenon of direct foreign investment by multinational corporations.

1. In your opinion is the overall effect of ARAMCO's activities in Saudi Arabia good or bad?

Very Good	Good	Neutral	Bad	Very Bad
1	2	3	4	5

In response to the Likert type question related to the overall effect of ARAMCO's activities in Saudi Arabia, 121 out of 134 respondents, 90%, are of the opinion that overall effects are good, 9% reported that it is a bag of mixed results, and 1% that it is bad.

As to the question of ARAMCO's contribution to economic growth and industrialization, the results indicate that 124, or 92%, of the respondents agreed with the following statement, while the remaining 8% took a neutral position with no respondent disagreeing.

2. Do you agree that ARAMCO's activities contribute to Saudi economic growth, development, and industrialization?

Strongly Agree	Agree	Neutral	Disagree	Strongly Disagree
1	2	3	4	5

3. Do you agree that ARAMCO's activities contribute to Saudi technical skill formation and skills transferred to Saudi managers?

Strongly Agree	Agree	Neutral	Disagree	Strongly Disagree
1	2	3	4	5

On the issue of ARAMCO's contribution to Saudi skills and managerial development, again there is a high degree of consensus with 93% of the respondents agreeing that ARAMCO has contributed to an increase in the level of managerial and technical development, while 7% took a neutral position. The spill over of ARAMCO's operation into the Saudi economy it must be said is considerable: the flow of managers and professionals out of ARAMCO and into other facets of Saudi economic life is one measure; so is the effect on increasing the number and formation of Saudi-owned business through local sub-contracting and purchasing. ARAMCO's purchases from local Saudi vendors and manufacturers are substantial. The following figures illustrate the point: 62.4% of $1.04 billion of world wide purchases by ARAMCO in 1980 went to Saudi vendors and manufacturers (Middle East Economic Digest 1981: 7).

As to the issue of payments for the perceived economic contribution of ARAMCO to the Saudi economy, there was a lack of consensus whether their payments are fair or excessive. Fifty-nine, or 44%, of the respondents indicated that the payments are fair, 16% had mixed feelings and 40% felt that they are excessive.

4. In relation to the economic contributions of ARAMCO to Saudi Arabia, do you believe that the payments which ARAMCO receives are less than the benefits ARAMCO gives to the country?

Fair	Somewhat Fair	Neutral	Somewhat Excessive	Excessive
1	2	3	4	5

To assess the concerns of Saudi technocrats over the issue of continued economic dependence upon foreign enterprises, and joint ventures, the following questions were asked:

5. Do you believe that ARAMCO's activities increase the dependence of Saudi Arabia on foreign firms?

Strongly Agree	Agree	Neutral	Disagree	Strongly Disagree
1	2	3	4	5

6. Do you believe that joint ventures with foreign firms are beneficial to Saudi Arabia?

Strongly Agree	Agree	Neutral	Disagree	Strongly Disagree
1	2	3	4	5

The first question asked whether ARAMCO's mode of operation and foreign linkages increase the dependence of Saudi Arabia upon foreign firms. Eightyfour per cent of the respondents disagreed, while 10% agreed that it does, and 6% held a neutral view. As to whether joint-ventures are beneficial to the course of Saudi economic development, 91% of the respondent, agreed that it is, and 9% had mixed feelings. This view is in accord with official Saudi thinking. Speaking of future foreign involvement in Saudi development through joint-ventures. Saudi Arabia's deputy commerce minister, Abdel-Rahaman al-Zamil, states:

> There is no particular rule that you must give work to Saudis, but in practice, if you look, you will find a lot of jobs are now open by limited invitation only to Saudis or joint ventures. If the worse comes to worst, you will find three quarters of them are Saudis and joint ventures, and one quarter foreign firms (Middle East Economic Digest 1981: 28).

On the sensitive issue of oil output levels, two questions were intended to shed some light on this hotly debated issue.

7. Do you agree that ARAMCO's oil production should be responsive to the needs of the oil consumers and the international economy?

Strongly Agree	Agree	Neutral	Disagree	Strongly Disagree
1	2	3	4	5

8. Do you agree that ARAMCO's production should be high enough to finance Saudi economic development only?

Less than 5 mbd	5–6 mbd	7–8 mbd	9–10 mbd	10 or more mbd

As to whether Saudi oil production levels should be in accordance with the needs of an energy hungry international economy or Saudi Arabia economic development needs, 70% of the sample disagree with the notion of linking Saudi oil output to the needs of the global community, 20% agreed, and 10% had mixed feelings. In response to the second question of what is a desirable level of Saudi oil output, 76% of the respondents indicated that it should be 5–6 mbd, while 10% suggested 7–8 mbd, and only 14% desiring 9–10 mbd. It must be stated, however, that the level of Saudi oil output is at best problematic. A number of Saudi elites would rather see the government stretch out the life of the oil reserves by producing at about 6 mbd, enough to finance Saudi Arabia development plans. This group points out, further, that oil in the ground is safer than surplus reserves which stand at about $ 100 billion. The lack of receptiveness of industrial economies to Arab oil funds and investments, they argue, confirms the wisdom behind this view.

The policy behind the higher level of oil production, however, can be explained by the following statement. Speaking of Saudi Arabia's position towards the oil consumers, King Fahd, Chairman of the Kingdom's Supreme Petroleum Council, stated, when asked about the continuation of ARAMCO's production of 9–10 mbd, "We feel responsible towards Saudi Arabia's friends in the world ... As a result, Saudi Arabia will extend the period of increased production by three more months to help stabilize the petroleum situation and allow the consumers to stock up." (Tanner and Close 1979: 3).

9. To what degree do you believe that the influence of Western ways of life, brought in as a result of MNF(s) activities, changed ways of life?

Small Change		Neutral		Large Change
1	2	3	4	5

10. Are these changes (Question 9) good or bad?

Good		Neutral		Bad
1	2	3	4	5

In answer to the question whether the intrusion of Western ways of life resulted in changing Saudi society, 66% of the sample believe that the influence has been large, 18% that it has been small, and 16% that it has been neutral. As to the perception that these changes are good or bad, 40% of the sample responded that the influence has been good, 18% had mixed feelings, while 42% indicated that the change has been bad.

Because the cultural impact has been viewed as good both and bad, the following two questions ought to shed some light upon this.

11. In your personal activities, to what degree do you feel it is desirable to adopt ways of life of MNF(s)?

Large Degree		Neutral		Not At All
1	2	3	4	5

12. In your personal activities, to what degree do you feel it is desirable to emulate work methods of MNF(s)?

Large Degree		Neutral		Not At All
1	2	3	4	5

In answer to whether it is desirable in one's personal activities to adopt Western way of life, 95% of the respondents indicated that they would not adopt Western ways, while 5% had mixed feeling, about such happenings in answer to the same question. With reference to the adoption of work habits, 79% of the respondents believe that it is desirable to emulate work methods and habits of Western enterprises, 13% had mixed feelings, while 8% indicated that they would not. Upon first glance, this may seem contradictory; however, it is not. The technocrats who are generally opposed to the intrusion of the Western ways of life into a traditional social order, nevertheless, understand the need for an efficient working industrial order.

13. Do you want a larger or a reduced role for ARAMCO in the course of Saudi economic development?

Larger		Neutral		Smaller
1	2	3	4	5

Finally, as to the feeling of Saudi technocrats towards a larger or a reduced role for ARAMCO in the course of Saudi development and economic transformation, 69% of the sample desire a larger role, 8% want a smaller role, and 23% believe that is should continue as is.

By way of final summation, the results of the study point that the technocrats view favorably the linkages between ARAMCO and the Saudi economy. These individuals are committed to the economic transformation and industrialization of their society, and because of this, they tend to see no substitute for multinational corporate linkages (Ajami 1979). The issue of a complete take over of ARAMCO by Saudi governmental agencies such as Petromin, or the Ministry of Petroleum and Minerals, is far from settled. Informed Saudi technocrats value ARAMCO's efficiency as a private commercial entity. Morever, they fear that its take over by a bureaucratic apparatus under the auspices of the government could result in stifling the operation and reducing the efficiency of ARAMCO. The technocrats concede that there are economic and cultural costs visited upon Saudi society as a result of the operation and activities of all multinationals. They also realize, however, that the alternatives to multinational linkage are costly: foregone opportunities for economic transformation and economic diversifications, exhausted oil resources without an alternative viable economic base. As to the cultural costs, they see these dislocations as manageable and inevitable. As all traditional societies thrust into modern industrial orders they are bound to face socio-cultural challenges to the established order. But that too, they recognize is the lot of all societies undergoing socio-economic change. The belief in Islam, and the cohesiveness of the family and tribal units, should in the short run allow the Saudi social system to withstand the challenges imposed by industrialization and modernity.

Chapter 10
The Relationship Between Managerial Decision Styles and Work Satisfaction in Saudi Arabia

Abbas Ali and Paul M. Swiercz

10.1 Introduction

In the management literature, there are numerious studies examining the relationship between work satisfaction and various individual and organizational outcomes. For instance, studies have shown employee satisfaction to be correlated with leadership style (Graen, Novak and Sommerkamp 1982; Keller and Szilagyi 1978), motivation (Lawler 1973; Kipnis 1964 and Jones 1980; Hackman and Oldman 1975), job characteristics (James and Porter and Lawler 1964), absenteeism and turnover (Hulin 1975; Porter and Steers 1973), role ambiguity (Beehr and Newman 1978 and Gupter and Beehr 1972), autonomy (Beer and Drexter 1983; Davis and Valfer 1966; Mann and Williams 1962), life satisfaction (Keand and McDonald 1978; Rousseau 1978), and goal-setting (Arvey, Dewhirsty and Brown 1978; Tosi, Hunter, Chesser and Caroll 1976). As indicated by these factors, satisfaction is generally held to be closely related to the well-being of organizations. That is satisfaction is used as an indicator of whether or not an individual's needs are being met through association with a particular organization. To the extent that the organization fails to meet the needs of its members, that organization performs at less than optimum levels. Thus it is considered to be a major variable in organizational life and a popular factor in both applied and theoretical research (Gruneberg 1974; Pulakos and Schmitt 1983).

Despite the abundance of research examining the work satisfaction variable, an extensive review of the literature reveals an insufficient amount of research on the relationship between managerial decision styles and work satisfaction, especially with respect to non-American managers. The purpose of this chapter is to report the findings of an empirical research study conducted to explore the relationship between managerial decision styles and work satisfaction in a developing country – Saudi Arabia.

Saudi Arabia was selected as the research site because of its unique characteristic of being both committed to rapid industrialization and to the maintenance of its traditional Arabic culture. As the richest and most sophisticated of the newly prosperous oil-producing countries, Saudi Arabia has become a testing ground for strategies aimed at integrating economic development with social tradition. Because of the social commitment to the preservation of traditional values, Saudi managers offer a unique population for investigating the relationship between non-Western decision-making styles and work satisfaction.

As indicated, the relationship between decision style and work satisfaction is an unexplored area. But there has been enough research to suggest that Arabian managers have culturally influenced decision-making styles. For example, El-Baruni (1980) discovered that Libyan managers have values indicating high concern for social welfare and low concern for profit maximization and industrial leadership. Askar (1979) in his research found that Egyptian managers tend to be moralistic and place high value on dignity, prestige, influence, and power. Murrell (1979) also found in the Egyptian management culture a bias against planning, tendency to disregard the necessity of continuous education, and the absence of a pioneering or innovative spirit. The findings of Zabra (1980) supports these observations and explains them by arguing that Egyptians, like many other nationalities in the Middle East, are fatalists – meaning that they share little appreciation for the values of time, planning, organization, and discipline. Moreover, this is reflected in the common cross-national problem of orienting native workers to an industrial environment.

Islamic cultures, of which Saudi Arabia is representative, also have in common a tradition of respect for the family. Thus, decision-making is centralized in those influential managers who have earned the trust and respect of the extended family. When changes are to be made, the process is initiated by key managers, but prior consultation with important family members is a necessary aspect of decision-making. This necessity of developing a consensus before making a final decision creates an atmosphere of open communication, but significantly slows down the speed of decision-making (Anastos, Bedos and Seaman 1980).

This family oriented decision-making style also has implications extending beyond the speed of decision-making. To the extent that organizational structure is developed by the Saudi businessman, it will be horizontal in nature rather than vertical. This reflects the notion of egalitarianism and facilitates decision-making by consultation and consensus. Therefore, the typical Saudi company structure will not be patterned after the organizational pyramid used in the West. Instead, it will be relatively flat with broad spans of control (Anastos, Bedos and Seaman 1980: 84).

Research reported in the literature thus far clearly suggests that culture influences management. As trends toward the internationalization of business continue to mature, understanding the nature of these cultural influences takes on added importance, especially in those circumstances where the traditions of the partner nations are widely divergent. This research is an attempt to shed light on the relationship between decision-styles and job satisfaction in Saudi Arabia – an Arabic country experiencing high levels of Western influence.

10.2 Research Propositions

Decision-making is probably one of the most important functions performed by business leaders. Most recent writers in the field maintain that managers can adopt different decision-styles, depending on the pattern of organization and individual characteristics (Steers 1977; Stogdill 1974; Vroom 1976). Likewise, job satisfaction is said to be a function of individuals and organizational variables (Strauss 1974: 307). With the discovery that both decision-style and level of satisfaction are situation dependent, recent research has had the objective of examining the situation for insights into the decision-styles likely to result in the highest levels of satisfaction for both managers and subordinates. In other words, work satisfaction is held to be dependent in part upon decision-making styles. No single decision-making style is appropriate in every situation; therefore, the highest levels of satisfaction are likely to occur in those circumstances where there is a high degree of congruence between the decision-styles and the situation. With these conditions in mind, some hypotheses are developed in order to examine Saudi decision-styles and their implications.

In their studies, Ritchie and Miles (1970) and Roberts, Miles, and Blankenship (1968) suggest that basic attitudes of trust and confidence in subordinates are associated with participative leadership behavior. And that to the extent that managers encourage participation on decision-making, there will be positive increases in both managerial and employee satisfaction and performance. Thus the following hypotheses were formulated.

Hypothesis 1: Participative managers are expected to be highly satisfied with persons in their work group.

Hypothesis 2: Autocratic managers are expected to have low satisfaction with persons in their work group.

Previous research shows that the attitudes and behavior of Arabic managers are determined to some extent by the cultural values and norms which prevail in that part of the world (Ali 1982; Almaney 1981; Nimir and Palmer 1982; Badawy 1974). Muna (1980) found in his studies that the consultative style is predominantly preferred by Arab executives. Wright (1981) has suggested that managers in Islamic organizations seldom delegate authority to their subordinates, and these managers are loyal to their immediate supervisors, rather than to their organizations. Accordingly, the following hypotheses were formulated.

Hypotheses 3: The consultative style is the predominant decision style of Saudi managers.

Hypothesis 4: Consultative managers tend to be highly satisfied with their immediate supervisors but less satisfied with their organization.

However, Ali (1982: 60) and Hudson (1977) have characterized the Arab's culture as authoritarian. In such cultures, there is a phenomenon of "non-decision-making" whereby superordinately situated managers control the behavior of subordinates through the manipulation and control of the environment in which the latter must operate (Bell and Leiden 1974). Managerial behavior, which remains strictly within the framework of the authoritarian and hierarchical structure of the organization, seeks to prepare subordinates to accept decisions already made by managers and to improve the individual manager's image in a society where tribalistic values still have some important influence. The intention of managers in this case is not to create a situation of real consultation, but rather to create a feeling of consultation by means of the leader assuming a particular style (Pateman 1970). This style is not similar to the consultative concept which prevails in the West. It is appropriate then to call such style *pseudo-consultative* so as to distinguish it from the consultative one. Based on the above discussion, the following hypothesis was formulated.

Hypothesis 5: A high proportion of Saudi Arabian managers exhibit a pseudo-consultative style.

Thus, these five hypotheses might be classified into three subcategories. Hypotheses one and two are traditional, in that they address the classical issue of participative versus autocratic decision styles and their relationship to satisfaction. Hypotheses three and four are more culturally specific. They concern themselves with the Saudi specific issues of consultative management, questioning the widely held assumption that Saudi managers are in fact consultative and the consequences of this decision style. Hypothesis five falls into a separate category because it most directly confronts the issue of cultural bias. It raises a question as to whether there is a distinction between the appearance of consultation and the reality of consultation. The implicit assumption underlying hypothesis five is that Western researchers have thus far failed to appreciate the subtlety of decision-making in alien cultures. Americans in particular live in a society distinguished by its openness and relatively straight forward patterns of communication. In contrast, the ancient societies of the Middle East are well known for their intrigue.

10.3 Research Methodology

Procedure

A convenience sample of eighty-three managers from three major cities in Saudi Arabia – Riyadh, Al-Huse, and Damman – was the source of data for the study. In order to encourage participation, the survey was administered in the Arabic language. Prior to its actual administration, it was rendered from English to Arabic and back to English again by an experienced translator in order to identify potential cultural biases. Few problem areas were identified and the final version was reviewed by an experienced Middle Eastern executive as a final quality check.

Personal distribution was adopted to overcome problems associated with the postal service in Saudi Arabia, to maximize the response rates, and to provide an opportunity to clarify questions concerning the purpose and method of response to the questionnaire. In most cases, questionnaires were left with managers and collected by research assistants.

Participating managers were assured that the questionnaire was for research purposes only and that they would remain anonymous. A total of 140 surveys were distributed, yielding a final response rate of fifty-nine percent.

Subjects Employed

Managers participating in the survey were employed in a variety of organizations including companies such as ARAMCO, Electric Company in the Eastern Region, The Public Electric Company, and a number of small private organizations. Exhibit 10/1 presents a brief profile of the sample. It shows that sixty-nine percent of the subjects worked in firms employing less than 250 employees. About sixty-nine percent worked in public enterprises, and over seventy-one percent were between the ages of thirty and forty-nine years. Over sixty-nine percent had a college or graduate degree, sixty-five percent had been working with the present company for two to ten years, and twenty-six percent were either general or assistant general managers.

Instruments

The primary instruments on the survey were the *Work Satisfaction Index* and the *Leadership Decision Style Index*. Work satisfaction was measured by items extracted from the Survey of Organizations, a popular questionnaire used by the Survey Research Center at the University of Michigan. It consists of seven subscales which measure satisfaction with persons in work group, supervisors, pay, job, organization, promotion, and future chances for getting ahead in the organization. Whereas the *Leadership Decision Style* scale is a modified version of the instrument used by Muna (1980: 136) and Vroom and Yetton (1973). Two modifications were made. First, it was our understanding that all managers display a variety of decision styles depending on the situation and the type of decision involved. Thus, we added the term, *Most Often*, to reflect this fact. Second, in the Arabic language, it is preferable to use direct pronouns. For example, "Ina" (I), rather than the indirect pronoun "Inta" (You); we replaced "You" with "I." The scale included a description of five alternative decision styles. Managers were asked to indicate the one style that best described their behavior. The five systems were:

    I. Most often I solve the problem or make my decision using information available to me without consultation with my subordinate(s).

Exhibit 10/1: Type of Organization and Personal Characteristics of Participants (N=83)

Variable	Frequency	% Frequency
1. *Managerial Level*		
General Manager/President	10	12
Assistant General Manager	12	14
Department/Office Manager	38	46
Section Manager	23	28
	83	100.0
2. *Size*		
50 Employees or Less	36	42
51 to 250 Employees	22	27
251 to 750 Employees	9	11
751 to 2,000 Employees	9	11
2,001 to 10,000 Employees	3	4
10,001 Employees and More	4	5
	83	100.0
3. *Ownership*		
Public	57	69
Foreign	9	11
Private	17	20
	83	100.0
4. *Age Group*		
Less Than 30 Years	23	28
30 to 39 Years	39	47
40 to 49 Years	20	24
50 to 59 Years	1	1
	83	100.0
5. *Educational Level*		
Completed Elementary School	2	2
Completed Intermediate School	9	11
Completed Secondary School	10	11
Associate Degree	5	6
College Degree	39	48
Masters Degree	7	8
Doctorate Degree	11	13
	83	100.0
6. *Number of Years Working With Company*		
Less Than 2 Years	6	7
2 to 4 Years	25	30
5 to 7 Years	18	22
8 to 10 Years	11	13
11 to 15 Years	14	17
16 or More Years	9	11
	83	100.0

   II. Most often I consult with my subordinate(s), but that doesn't mean that I give any consideration to their ideas and suggestions. (The intent is not to create a situation of real consultation, but rather to create a feeling of consultation.)

  III. Most often I have prior consultation with my subordinate(s). Then I make decisions which may or may not reflect my subordinate's influence.

  IV. Most often I share and analyze the problem with my subordinate(s) as a group, evaluate alternatives, and come to a majority decision.

  V. Most often I ask my subordinate(s) to make decisions on his/their own.

10.4 Research Results

In hypothesis 1, it was predicted that participative managers would exhibit a high satisfaction with persons in their work group. The results of the analysis of variance (ANOVA) presented in Exhibit 10/2 support this prediction. Managers indicating a participative style ($\bar{x} = 4.00$) are highly satisfied with persons in their work group.

The second hypothesis predicted that autocratic managers would be less satisfied with persons in their work group. This hypothesis was also supported. The autocratic managers scored significantly lower ($\bar{x} = 3.17$) on satisfaction with persons in their work group.

Exhibit 10/2: Mean Satisfaction Scores by Managerial Decision Styles and Anova Test

Variables	Persons in Work Group	Supervisor	Job	Organization	Pay	Promotion	Future in the Organization
Autocratic	3.17	2.33	3.88	3.56	3.78	3.89	3.73
Pseudo-Consultative	3.74	3.83	3.74	3.39	3.09	2.91	2.52
Consultative	3.63	3.19	3.50	3.26	3.06	2.91	2.66
Participative	4.00	3.88	4.68	4.56	3.25	3.41	3.41
Delegative	5.00	4.00	4.00	3.50	3.00	3.00	4.00
$F_{(4,78)}$	3.41*	4.74**	3.87**	4.10**	2.38	4.69**	3.40*

  * $p<.05$
 ** $p<.01$

Exhibit 10/3: Estimated Percentage of Saudi Managers by Decision Style

Style	N	Percentage
Autocratic	9	11
Pseudo-Consultative	23	28
Consultative	32	39
Participative	17	20
Delegative	2	2
	83	100

Interestingly, the results also indicated that while delegative managers are shown to be highly satisfied ($\bar{x} = 5.00$) with persons in their work groups, the consultative managers, on the other hand, tend to be less satisfied ($\bar{x} = 3.63$). No hypothesis was formulated in this regard.

The third hypothesis predicted that a high proportion of Saudi managers would prefer consultative styles. This hypothesis is supported by the results in Exhibit 10/3 which show that the predominant decision style (thirty-nine percent) of Saudi managers was consultative.

In hypothesis 4, it was predicted that the consultative managers would be satisfied with their supervisors and less satisfied with their organizations compared to other managers. The first part of the hypothesis was not supported ($\bar{x} = 3.19$). However, the results did indicate that the consultative manager was less satisfied with his organization ($\bar{x} = 3.26$) than the participative manager ($\bar{x} = 4.56$). The results also indicated that the pseudo-consultative, participative, and delegative managers tend to be highly satisfied with their supervisors. No hypotheses were formulated relative to these relationships.

In hypothesis 5, it was predicted that Saudi managers would exhibit a pseudo-consultative style in their conduct of business operations. The results in Exhibit 10/3 support this prediction. Twenty-eight percent of managers surveyed indicated they preferred the pseudo-consultative style.

The results in Exhibit 10/3 also indicated that the least preferred decision style was the delegative style (two percent).

The analysis of the intercorrelations between the various components of overall work satisfaction is presented in Exhibit 10/4. The results indicated that there was a high correlation between job satisfaction and satisfaction with persons in work group, organization, promotion, and chance for

Exhibit 10/4: Correlation Coefficients between the Items of Work Satisfaction Scale

	Persons in Work Group	Super-visor	Job	Organi-zation	Pay	Promo-tion	Future in the Organi-zation
Persons in Work Group	1.00						
Supervisor	.58**	1.00					
Job	.66**	.47**	1.00				
Organization	.51**	.48	.66**	1.00			
Pay	.06	.11	.18	.21	1.00		
Promotion	.24*	.13	.44**	.44**	.49**	1.00	
Future in the Organization	.25*	.13	.34**	.38**	.34**	.60**	1.00

* p<.02
** p<.01

getting ahead in the future, and between promotion and one's chance for getting ahead in the future.

10.5 Managerial Implications

The findings presented in this study provide support for previous research that a participative manager tends to have confidence and trust in his subordinates. Likewise, the autocratic manager tends to lack positive attitudes toward his subordinates.

Contrary to Badawy (1979: 294), this study indicates that participative management is not necessarily alien to Middle Eastern cultures. This result might be explained by (a) the Western influence on Saudi managers through educational and business contacts (b) the influx of multinational companies and (c) the effect of mass media.

With respect to the findings that Arab executives are not oriented toward delegative styles, this might reflect the general attitude of the Arab executive to be aware of the affairs of his business and the tendency to make decisions and conduct business in a more personalized manner.

The strong preference of Saudi Arabian managers toward consultative styles is consistent with previous findings. This preference demonstrates the influence of Islamic and tribalistic values and beliefs, as both Islamic and tribal law reinforce consultation in conducting all aspects of life. As mentioned earlier, it is the practice of tribal societies that members of the entire kinship network should be consulted on matters important to their welfare. In addition, Islam presents consultation as religiously positive – "This reward will be for those ... who conduct their affairs with consultation among themselves ..." (Sarwar 1981).

However, twenty-eight percent of the sample managers were oriented toward the pseudo-consultative style rather than the "pure" consultative method. This variance can be traced to the authoritarian element in the Middle Eastern culture, an element springing from several factors which have shaped the norms, values, and beliefs of contemporary Arabic society. These factors include the primacy of coercive force and instability in the succession process of the Islamic Polity (1977: 92), the centralized political systems which have evolved since the end of colonialism (Roy 1977), and the quality of leadership (Watt 1961). Two other factors involved are the fragmented kinship society and the generally poor communications in the region. Finally, the majority of the Middle Eastern states are dominated by Sunni, as opposed to Shi'ite, Islamic thought.* A cornerstone of Sunni doctrine is the legitimacy of authoritarian actions of the leaders of society. The conflict between authoritative and consultative trends and traditions in Arabic society, indeed, with Islam itself, is crucial to the understanding of the current tensions in the region, particularly as that tension is expressed in the business sector. Arabian managers display a pseudo-consultative style in order to reduce that tension, to create a supportive and cohesive environment around themselves.

The fact that the delegative and participative managers are highly satisfied with their superiors could reflect their attitudes of trust and confidence in people around them (superiors or subordinates). At the same time, the finding that the delegative managers are less satisfied with their pay and promotion than the autocratic managers, seems reasonable once we know that in Saudi Arabia, and in the rest of the Arab world, pay is determined without regard to merit and performance, and the promotion and salary increases are largely determined by personal connections and maneuver, nepotism, sectarianism, and ideological affiliations.

* The Umma of the Sunni sect in Islam has always played the role of legitimizing the authoritarian action of the leaders since the early days of the Islamic state.

Exhibit 10/5: Similarities and Differencies between Saudi Arabian and North American Managers

Predominant Characteristics	Saudi Arabian	North American
Decision Style	Consultative	Participative
Value Systems	Outer-Directed (tribalistic, conformist, sociocentric)	Inner-Directed (egocentric, manipulative, existentialist)
Authority Delegation	Low	High
Organizational Design	Flat, vague authoritative relationships, centralized authority	Tall, relatively decentralized with clear relationships
Staffing	Highly subjective selection depends on personal contacts, nepotism, regionalism, and family name	Relatively objective, standards developed and qualifications and experience considered
Performance Evaluation and Control	Informal, absence of systematic controls and established criteria	Formal criteria, e.g., cost reduction, quality control
Planning	Undeveloped, not highly regarded	Well developed, highly regarded

The above discussion and findings clearly indicate that, in spite of the fact that the Saudi manager's decision style and work satisfaction are in large part determined by cultural values and norms, they also share some similarity in their approach and psychological aspects to that of managers of other cultures. Exhibit 10/5 presents a summary of some of the differences between Saudi Arabian and North American managers.

10.6 Conclusions

The results of the study lent strong support of Bhagat and McQuaids' (1982) call for more cross-cultural research, especially research designed to help identify and explain the influences of culture on managerial performance. More specifically, this research demonstrated the necessity to develop new conceptual frameworks from which to launch these research efforts. The best example of this contribution was identification of the frequency of the pseudo-consultative style of decision-making. While perhaps a poor choice of words since they imply some degree of Western bias, this construct has significant potential for helping understand decision-making by Saudi Arabian managers. Since we now have a truer picture of the pseudo-consultative style it may be appropriate to re-examine Western decision theory as applied to Third World cultures.

While identification of the pseudo-consultative style was perhaps the most significant finding of the study, this research also supported the notion that there are culturally independent attributes of successful management. For example, the finding that Saudi managers utilizing a participative style tend to be highly satisfied with members of the work group parallel findings in Western studies. This suggests that participation, regardless of the cultural circumstances under which it is practiced, results in more potentially productive work situations.

10.7 Suggestions for Future Research

Suggestions for future research can be divided into two categories; those dealing with improved methodology and those dealing with new research avenues. With respect to methodology, the following are offered: (a) Survey methodologies in developing nations are not yet the preferred method. Simple problems like inadequate postal service and respondent distrust severely complicate the process and potentially bias the results. Personal interviews should be used when possible since Arabs are generally open to one-on-one communication, providing that the subject has trust and confidence in the researcher. (b) Special attention should be devoted to planning the research effort in order to minimize the risk of missing or misinterpreting results of the effort. The results of this and other research efforts clearly establish the influence of culture and inadequate planning will result in a failure to recognize subtle but important factors.

There are a number of research opportunities available to those interested in cross-cultural research and the following are intended to be examples. Possibilities include: (a) an expansion of the scope of the effort to identify the similarities and differences between Saudi Arabian managers and those from other Middle Eastern states; and (b) more effort needs to be extended to the task of defining the nature of the Arabian culture from a managerial perspective. Lacking are high quality observational studies which can serve as the source for the generation of hypotheses amenable to rigorous empirical research.

Chapter 11
Cultural Marginality in the Arab World: Implications for Western Marketers

Nabil Y. Razzouk and Lance A. Masters

11.1 Introduction

Western observers who have witnessed the rapid industrialization and recent socio-economic growth of several Arab states are often quick to discount the viability of the region as a market for their goods and services. Political instability, fatalism, growing nationalism and dealing with differences attributed to the Moslem religion are among the most frequently cited reasons by Western businessmen for not pursuing trade opportunities with the Arab world.

In the light of recent well-publicized events in the Middle East such as the Iran-Iraq War, the Lebanese Crisis, the Libyan invasion of Chad, the assassination of Egyptian President Anwar Sadat and the on-going Arab-Israeli conflict, it is difficult to write off political instability as an influencing factor when considering the prospects of foreign trade with Arab states of the region. However one must keep in mind that wars and hostilities have been the rule rather than the exception to everyday life in that region for centuries, and may well continue to mark the region's history for centuries to come. The point is that firms and individuals desirous of international trade in the Arab states should anticipate such conditions, and plan to deal with such exigencies as they would any other element in their external environment, that is, to work around them or adopt their marketing strategies accordingly.

Other beliefs among Western business people concerning fatalism, nationalism and backwardness among the Arabs are for the most part, gross misconceptions. Yet these factors no doubt remain strong barriers against increased foreign trade in Arab states. Several authors (Luqmani, Quraeshi and Delene 1980; Owen 1976; Muna 1980 and Rodinson 1974) all attribute the rise of these widely held "myths" to earlier accounts in which Western scholars attempted to explain the decline and prolonged stagnation of the Arab states and Islamic civilizations. In most of these studies, direct comparison was made between Christian or European civilization and the Arabs and their religion – Islam – without taking into account the differentiating historical, political, cultural, socio-economic or even geographical factors (Patai 1973).

Another confounding element in these early investigations was their attention focused on the rural areas of Islamic countries and looked at the behavior of village populations. Generalizations were made from these observations to all the Muslims in the region (Rodinson 1974), which would have been analogous to reporting conditions in rural Appalachia as being typical of the United States of America.

Equally misconceived are the claims that Islam is an anti-Capitalist and anti-progressive religion. A careful study of Islamic beliefs reveals its consonance with the rest of the world, and especially with capitalism (Luqmani et al 1980: 17–19). One can hardly call the modernization programs of the Gulf states anti-capitalist or anti-progressive, nor do most Arabs consider them anti-Islamic. The late King Faisal of Saudi Arabia who set the tone for economic prosperity in the Gulf states once declared that he wished for his country "... to achieve rapid economic growth and modernization without sacrificing the traditions of Islam and Arab culture." (Meirc 1977: 4).

Last in this series of trade barriers is the journalistic account in Western media of Arab nationalism. As an ideological movement, Arab nationalism has experienced a change of focus over the years. At first the movement was concerned with independence from the Ottoman Empire and the later European rule. Following independence, the emphasis shifted to the strengthening Arab unity. The prospects of a united Arab empire or some type of uniform Arab socialism while long awaited by militant Arab nationalists and equally feared by many Westerners, remain basically unrealized and perhaps an unattainable pipe dream. The continuous feud among neighboring Arab states, fueled by apparent and arguably growing ideological differences is likely to diminish the prospects of a strong Arab nationalism.

Replacing the dreams of Arab unity and brotherhood are the growing phenomena of cultural marginality and ambivalence. This situation may present both a threat and an opportunity for foreign trade with the Arabs.

The purpose of this chapter is to investigate the nature of cultural marginality and its resulting ambivalence in the Arab world, and to assess their impact on international marketing activities of North American and West European firms in that region.

11.2 The Nature and Origin of Arab Marginality

Cultural marginality has been defined as the "State of belonging to two or more cultures without being able to identify oneself completely with either" (Stonequist 1973). According to Patai (1973) individuals born and acculturated into one culture become culturally marginal when they are exposed to another culture, become attracted to it, acquire a measure of familiarity with it and strive to become full-fledged carriers of the new culture. Some exceptional individuals may succeed in this endeavor and become immune to ethno-centrism. The majority of cases however never completely succeed. Consequently these cultural marginals suffer from the inability to feel completely at ease or at home in either culture.

Cultural marginality has been most prevalent in the North African Arab countries of Morocco, Algeria and Tunisia, and in the Middle Eastern countries of Lebanon, Syria and Egypt. All of these countries have at one time or another come under Western control, predominantly British or French. More recently, cultural marginality has intensified in these states, and moreover has spread to several others in the region, especially the Gulf states.

As viewed by local governments and Arab nationalists, cultural marginality is a threat to tradition and Islamic civilization, but for Westerners interested in trading with the Arabs, this marginality provides a vast opportunity for marketing Western goods and services. Self image theory would suggest that people in this area would make purchases of goods that would facilitate their movement from their own self image to their ideal self image (Gaulden 1978), as shaped by their impressions of what belonging to Western culture implies. They acquire and use trappings of Western civilization such as language, food, clothing, and even social reform without ever feeling that they are indeed integrated into Western culture. It is this subconscious followership that presents the Western marketer with a mixed bag of market opportunities and environmental threats.

The origin of cultural marginality in the Arab world dates back to the military occupation of Egypt by Napoleon in 1798. Since that invasion, Arabs in Morocco, Tunisia, Algeria, Egypt, Syria and Lebanon have learned Western languages and culture and have increasingly become unable to identify with either of the two cultures. A Lebanese writer (Naccache 1961) expressed this phenomena when he noted "We orientals with Western culture live in a perpetual state of internal division."

During the colonial years and for some time after their independence, culturally marginal Arabs were enchanted with the French language and the continental, French way of life. While living in an Arab country, their heart was in France and in all their behavior they attempted to demonstrate their affinity with France and the French. In the post colonial decades, Arab marginality has intensified in magnitude and broadened in scope to encompass the rest of western culture, especially that of the United States. This change may be attributed to several conditions.

The first change is the growth of Mideast-West trade opportunities. The discovery of oil in the Middle East brought about an increased consumer and governmental demand for food products, manufactured goods and services which were available in the West. In this context of trade, Arab executives found themselves working closely with Western expatriates and businessmen, and the Arabs gradually acquired more Western norms and values.

The second condition is the drastic expansion of both business and holiday travel of Arabs to industrialized Western nations. Once more the petro-dollars in the Arab states created a new influence which made it feasible for thousands of Arabs to travel in Europe and the United States in search of cultural excitement and Western consumer goods.

The third element is the return to home of Arab students who have been trained and educated in the West. Literacy and mass education are two of the "Mass benefits" which Arab students who were sent away by their governments are now returning home not only with advanced degrees, but with distinctly Western ideologies.

Migration from the Middle East is the fourth consideration. The ongoing wars and turmoils in the Arab states have driven many families away from their home countries. Most have migrated to countries where they have other relatives or people with whom they have some familiarity. England,

France, the United States, Greece and Australia are among the most popular destinations of Arab emigrants.

The fifth factor is the communication revolution, as manifested in satellite transmission and emerging video technologies, is a powerful cause of Arab marginality. Western norms and lifestyles as epitomized in television programming are now carried into most Arab households.

The relative disenchantment of the Arabs with their "literary heritage" is another source of marginality. Some Arabs go so far as to blame their relative backwardness on their preoccupation with their literary and spiritual heritage at the expense of science and technological progress (Ayyad 1956).

A seventh condition contributing to growing Arab marginality is the shattered dream of Arab unity. The unrealized dream of a united Arab front and Arab brotherhood, and the continued military humiliation of the Arabs by Israel have driven many Arabs into a state of despair with feelings of cultural inferiority. The result is a strong desire to identify with the West and to acquire as many Western strengths as they might.

These are some of the more apparent or recognizable factors responsible for the growing marginality among Arabs. In spite of legislated traditionalism in some Arab states, the whole region abounds with viable marketing opportunities for Western goods and services.

11.3 Arab Ambivalence: A Love/Hate Relationship

Understanding the extent and direction of cultural marginality is important for prospective trade partners, but it is ambivalence, the result of marginality, that actually influences international marketing decisions. Ambivalence has been referred to as "The coexistence in one person of opposing attitudes towards the same object, or the simultaneous operation in the mind of irreconcilable wishes" (Merton 1976). These attitudes are often expressed in terms of love and hate relationships, and are aimed at two or more sources of marginality.

In the case of Arab marginalists, a set of ambivalences are directed toward the traditional culture and its carriers from which and from whom they have come away. The other set of ambivalences are aimed at the newly exposed

Exhibit 11/1: Sources of Ambivalence Among Arab Marginalists

Attitudes of the Arab Marginalists Toward their own Culture	
What They Love	*What They Hate*
• Familism	• Inter-Arab Strife
• Sexual Modesty	• Low Value of Time
• Traditional Arts & Crafts	• Extremes in Informality
• Verbal Arts (i.e. Poetry)	• Nepotism
• Personal Relations	• Lack of Industrial Mentality
• Hospitality	• Inefficiency in Government

Attitudes of the Arab Marginalists Toward the West	
What They Love	*What They Hate*
• Democracy	• Extreme Formality
• The Work Ethic	• Emphasis on Technology rather than People
• Value & Respect for Time	
• Mass Social Benefits (Education, nutrition, social security, etc.)	• The Sexual Revolution
	• Women's Liberation
• Systematic Approach to Work	• Extreme Individualism

to Western culture and its carriers with whom they seek to identify (Patai 1973). The solution for many of these ambivalent Arabs is to adopt as many good points of the West as possible which do not conflict with their cultural foci. Whatever cannot be adopted is often *adapted* to fit with desirable traditional norms. At the same time these individuals will attempt to discourage or do away with local habits or traditional modes of behavior which they consider to constitute a hindrance to progress and modernization. In a sense, the ambivalent marginalist is attempting to shape the "right mix" of Westernalization and Arab tradition (Muna 1980).

Exhibit 11/1 summarizes the source and direction of Arab ambivalence toward their own culture and the West. Only attitudes related to the focal areas of the Arab culture are considered for this discussion. Attitudes toward less central areas, although not listed, can be important to the prospective Western marketer because they represent a neutral zone which is not likely to elicit social resistance or psychological reactance.

11.4 Implications for International Marketers of the West

According to Muna (1980), there are two general types of cultural change. The first refers to the minor and insignificant changes in cultural features outside the focal areas of society. Changes in the national dress, diet, housing, entertainment or medical practices which take place within the established social structure. These changes do not alter the norms and structure of society substantially, and thus would encounter little or no social resistance.

The second type of change involves fundamental and substantial shifts in a society's social structure, institutions and focal areas such as religion, families, and so forth. These changes would be in one or more of its social, political, military, religious or economic institutions. Society would normally reject or resist change in the focal areas of its culture because of sentimental attachment to them and they would therefore command loyal adherence which would tend to hamper innovation.

Western marketers doing business with Arabs must concentrate on products or product categories with features that possess readily apparent benefits to be accepted with little or no opposition. These features also should lie outside the focal concerns of traditional Arab culture. Technological features which are not threatening or which maintain or might even enhance traditional values will be the most readily acceptable ones.

The traditional lack of concern with technology among Arabs indicates that there is no traditional opposition to technological advances such as television, video recorders, telephones, automatic washing machines, microwave ranges and so forth. However resistance could develop to such products if they appear to threaten the basic traditional values of the culture. For example television could threaten family cohesiveness if it were perceived to keep women away from their traditional home duties. Similarly computers would not normally elicit traditional resistance, but if they were found to foster introspection and individualism, they could face strong resistance because they could become a threat to the cherished sociable nature of Arabs.

Arab traditionalism plays a significant role in slowing or preventing the introduction of Western innovations in the areas which are linked to the basic cultural values. Among these figure such factors as familism, personal relations, sexual modesty, and to a lesser extent, traditional arts and crafts and verbal arts. These dimensions are held in high esteem not merely because they represent old traditions in Arab life, but also because they are revered by Religion (Patai 1973). Recognition of these dimensions and their sanctity to Arabs need not be a threat to international trade. On the contrary, several Western products and innovations could be brought into the Arab world and successfully marketed as developers and enhancers of the basic and focal values. For example, washing machines could enhance the quality of family life by freeing the wife-mother to spend more time with the children and husband, or to attend to other household responsibilities. This type of appeal is in consonance with the traditional Arab values of familism and the restricted role of women, so it is not likely to elicit significant resistance. However, as message strategy with an appeal that emphasized life simplification or women's liberation from traditional roles would very likely fail. The same principle would apply to the marketing of a host of convenience oriented durable goods popular in Western cultures.

Pricing of Western products sold in Arab states is affected by the degree of manifested marginality and ambivalence just as are the product and promotion decisions. For example, Lebanese consumers are usually prepared to pay premium prices for American made soft goods such as running shoes, brand name sports and leisure attire, or even brand name infant attire such as Carter, Health-Tex or Curity. Manufacturers of less popular brand marks may also be able to command higher prices for their products because of the consumer's generalization of quality across a broad spectrum of American goods.

In the area of channels of distribution, growing marginality and ambivalence have broadened the scope of the market for Western goods beyond the boundaries of the large metropolitan cities to the small and remote Arab towns. Many of these village people have family or friends who work in a city and who bring home Western products. Accordingly, the villagers are just as anxious to identify themselves with the Modern. Most of these "New Marginalists" have to travel to the larger cities to acquire the Western goods they desire. Regional shopping facilities or distribution centers could enhance the prospect of volume sales in Arab states. As long as the present degree of ambivalence and marginality exist, an intensive distribution strategy may prove to be quite effective.

11.5 Conclusions

It is likely that the present demand for Western goods and services may persist in the Middle East for some time, but not with the same intensity as the present. Vast opportunities exist for marketing products of Western manufacture which enhance the focal areas of the Arab culture, or those products to which the Arab culture has traditionally been indifferent and noncommital. Sensitive consideration must be given to the selection of product categories and specific products and brands which are directly or indirectly consonant with the critical concerns of the Arab culture. Price skimming and charging what the market would bear would work well for Western products in popular demand. Distribution of Western products in the Arab world should be more intense because of the broadened scope of demand.

Yesterday's traditions and the dream of Arab nationalism have for the most part been replaced by marginalism and ambivalence. Successful marketers will capitalize on this opportunity while maintaining a sensitive concern for Arab culture. Marketers will also do well to remember the lesson of Iran, where too grand and rapid a Westernization was not acceptable to the clergy, with the resulting upset and reversals.

Part Three
Marketing Practices

Chapter 12
Consumer Market Environment in the Middle East

Lyn S. Amine and S. Tamer Cavusgil

12.1 Introduction

North Africa and the Middle East as a region is a vast geographic area embracing many disparate ethnic groups, languages, cultures, economic and political systems. Moving from Morocco at the Western end of the Mediterranean sea to Iran on the borders of South-East Asia and then north to Turkey, one becomes aware of an immense variety of marketing opportunities within this region. Typically, North Africa and the Middle East include the following countries: Morocco, Algeria, Tunisia, Libya, Egypt, Israel, Lebanon, Jordan, Syria, Iraq, Iran, Saudi Arabia, Kuwait, Bahrain, Qatar, United Arab Emirates, Oman, North and South Yemen, Sudan, and Turkey. Several "natural" or voluntary groupings of nations have evolved in this region. These groupings can be explored as distinct market segments or as sub-markets. These are as follows:

- "Maghreb": Morocco, Algeria, Tunisia;
- OAPEC (Organization of Arab Petroleum Exporting Countries): Algeria, Libya, Saudi Arabia, Kuwait, Qatar, United Arab Emirates, Iraq;
- Arab Common Market (ACM): Iraq, Kuwait, Jordan, Syria, Egypt;
- Regional Cooperation for Development (RCD): Turkey, Iran, Pakistan;
- European Economic Community Associates: Turkey, Morocco, Algeria, Tunisia;
- Casablanca Group: Morocco, Egypt, Ghana, Guinea.

In order to escape the pitfalls associated with the "self-reference criterion" (whereby foreign markets are compared and contrasted with the researcher's home market), we will focus our attention on three nations within this region, namely Morocco, Turkey and Saudi Arabia. Given the geographic distance between these three markets, one would naturally expect to find considerable differences in the respective marketing environments (Elbashier and Nicholls 1983). However, as it will be demonstrated in this chapter, a number of important commonalities exist, giving rise to the familiar "feel" of markets throughout the region. Two major themes will be developed: a) Environmental Factors – Converging and Diverging Characteristics and b) Market Commonalities. These themes are, of course, very important in developing effective marketing strategies to exploit the vast market opportunities of the region.

This approach is highly relevant to global corporations interested in the region as it allows them to identify macro segments both within and between nations, which in turn allows more efficient market penetration (Levitt 1983). The general premise is that, apart from some dissimilarities, these three markets share a unifying religion, a well-defined set of socio-cultural values and traditions, and the similar goal of economic development (Luqmani, Quraeshi and Delene 1980). As well, peoples of the three countries have similar attitudinal orientations toward life and work.

12.2 Environmental Factors

In considering the particular "feel" and character of a country's market environment, it is necessary to examine those specific environmental factors which play a determinant role in the way of life (Douglas and Wind 1973–1974). These environmental influences include topography, historical and political factors, socio-economic and cultural factors, and technology. They will be discussed in turn.

Topography

When speaking of North Africa and the Middle East, one tends to assume that the whole region is a barren wasteland of sand. Even in the desert states of the Gulf, this is no longer an accurate picture as showpiece parks and verdant private gardens are created with the aid of modern technology. In Saudi Arabia, agricultural production reached $1.5 billion in 1982. Irrigation is successfully producing tomatoes, squash, potatoes, lettuce, wheat and alfalfa in the desert. Hydroponic techniques and other experimental methods are also offering new possibilities (Mason 1983).

The stereotyped desert image is particularly unrealistic in Morocco where a conducive climate, a phosphate-rich subsoil, and unlimited irrigation water from rainfall, wells, ground water, and Atlas Mountain sources, all combine to support a thriving agro-industry and a growing export trade in citrus fruits, canned vegetables, juices, and condiments. Morocco is also one of the leading fish producers of Africa, a fact often overshadowed by its reputation as the world's leading phosphate exporter. In addition, the lush orange and olive groves of Marrakesh, the golden beaches of Agadir, and the ski resorts of Ifrane are new tourist playgrounds for Gulf State visitors wishing to vacation in an Arabic-speaking environment.

Turkey enjoys the benefits of a more northerly, temperate climate and Mediterranean topography. This country possesses a substantial amount of fertile farmland and a diversified base of natural resources and minerals. Significant achievements in the modernization of the agricultural sector over the years have produced an economy which is self-sufficient in agriculture. In fact, Turkey is an exporter of a variety of commodities including cotton, cotton yarn, hazel nuts, figs, raisins and many fruits and vegetables. Being surrounded by three different waters (Black Sea to the north, Aegean Sea to the west, and the Mediterranean to the south), the country is well endowed with seafood products. However, this industry remains underdeveloped due to the lack of sufficient infrastructure, processing capabilities, and marketing expertise.

Historical and Political Factors

Historical and political factors impinge upon the marketing environment of a country because in many cases, administrative structures are a legacy of former colonialism and are currently in a state of evolution. This is especially true in Morocco, a French Protectorate until 1956. French is the accepted language of business, and evidence of the French culture is found in every walk of life. The political regime is a religious monarchy with an elected parliament. King Hassan II whom one may term a "working King", is revered as the direct descendent of the prophet Mohammed and thus serves as the Defender of the Muslim faith.

Saudi Arabia, also a Kingdom, is led by King Fahad, a charismatic figure who also fulfills a political role as acknowledged leader of the Arab world. Saudi Arabia is paradoxical in many respects: it preserves the traditional values of Islam among its people and yet is host to vast numbers of immigrant workers and expatriate managers who are necessary for its rapid industrialization programs (Tuncalp and Yavas 1983: 5). In contrast, lifestyles in Morocco are becoming visibly more modern for many segments of the population. Each year, the number of foreign (mainly French) managers, teachers and professional experts is being steadily reduced through non-renewable contracts and the relentless program of "Moroccanization" in all sectors.

Turks are the descendants of the Ottomans who ruled the Middle East, North Africa, and parts of Europe for more than five centuries. The modern Turkish state was established in 1923 as a republic. Its first president, Atatürk, had a strong desire to make Turkey a modern "Western" state. Atatürk was also responsible for organizing the grassroots movement to seek the country's independence from the invading forces after World War I. Being established as a secular state, modernization of government, judiciary, education and other aspects of the culture was facilitated. Turkey has now had experience with a multi-party parliamentary system for over 60 years, but this is often interrupted with typically brief military takeovers. A proliferation of political parties and the resultant ineffectiveness of coalition governments has been a source of turmoil, often necessitating intervention by the military.

Socio-Economic and Cultural Factors

Major economic differences between Morocco, Saudi Arabia and Turkey arise principally from the availability or lack of natural resources; and yet at the same time, many common cultural characteristics prevail due to the unifying power of Islam (Almaney 1981). Turkey's population is 98 percent Muslim. In Muslim Morocco, one also finds the largest concentration of Jews in the region, outside Israel. In Saudi Arabia, Islam is a dominant feature of everyday life as seen in the ritual of daily prayer, conservative lifestyle, Koranic law, and the annual influx of pilgrims to the two holiest cities of Mecca and Medina.

In total contrast to Saudi Arabia with its 2 million foreign workers and experts (equal to double the number of employed Saudis), Turkey and Morocco provide "guest workers" for West Germany, France, and other European countries. Foreign remittances from workers abroad are a substantial part of the national budget in both countries. Workers returning home bring with them the visible symbols of success (an automobile, TV, video and stereo equipment, household appliances, etc.) along with changed value systems. Thus, whether it be in Saudi Arabia, Turkey or Morocco, Western value systems and lifestyles are grafted onto the traditional way of life either from within by local nationals, studying and working abroad, or from outside through the presence of foreign workers.

In all three countries age distribution of the population is heavily skewed due to high birth rates and improved health care. Indeed, it is estimated that Morocco has 50 percent of its population below the age of twenty. Actual size of population varies greatly between the three countries with approximately 11.1 million in Saudi Arabia, 20 million in Morocco, and 47.7 million in Turkey. Thus, although many environmental characteristics are similar, the dimensions of the problems or opportunities vary radically from one country to the next.

Typical of many developing countries, the population in both Turkey and Morocco is characterized by a striking dualism – rapid urban growth and slow rural development. Both economies are largely agricultural with more than one-half of the population living in rural areas. Progress toward a modern economy is well under way but under-utilization of national resources is a major problem. Standards of living in rural areas remain persistently low. In Morocco, the legal minimum salary for agricultural workers in 1980 was 9.80 dirhams (DH) per day ($ 1.96), compared with 1.96 DH per hour in industry and commerce, equal to 15.68 DH per day ($ 3.14). Despite the broad range of "traditional" and "modern" industries, these only account for 10 percent of total employment in Morocco. It is not unexpected then that unemployment, under-employment and rural migration to urban centers are serious social problems.

In Turkey, an ambitious industrialization drive started in the 1950's, coupled with a very rapid rate of population growth, have created serious strains on the economy. Until recently, an import-substitution strategy was employed which tended to create an inward-oriented and less efficient industry. Failure of the export sector to keep up with imports meant that the country would have to engage in substantial foreign borrowing. Today, the country is heavily in debt. However, a recent surge in exports to Middle Eastern countries such as Iraq and Iran, and a new policy of trade liberalization have together provided some relief from this pressure.

In many respects, Saudi Arabia appears markedly different from Turkey and Morocco due to its virtually unlimited opportunities derived from oil wealth and new-found precious mineral deposits. Five-year economic development plans promoting rapid industrialization, the creation of essential infrastructure, and compulsory education all combine to provide the basis for a modern way of life. The Kingdom is now self-sufficient in Saudi instructors for primary education, thus liberating this sector from "foreign" influence. The number of female students receiving secondary education was almost 39 percent in 1982. Although Saudi women are required to observe a strict code of dress in public, are not allowed to drive, and must attend segregated schools, some 3,380 women graduated from teaching institutions in 1982 and were all appointed immediately to teaching posts (Mason 1983). However, this success belies the dilemma of the educated woman in Saudi Arabia whose opportunities for work are severely restricted both by the family, social pressures, and the State. In 1981 only 130,000 women of working age were actually employed and most were in segregated professions such as education and medicine (Elliott House 1983).

Male graduates in the vocational trades such as welding, carpentry, electrical wiring, plumbing, and automobile repairs are each entitled to a $ 29,000 loan for starting their own business. One unexpected problem arising from the use of immigrant workers in Saudi Arabia is the disaffection of Saudis for applied skills which are regarded as lower status. Also, local employers find it difficult to recruit Saudi graduates into managerial positions since they expect higher salaries simply because they are Saudi (Kaikati 1976).

An important feature in this region is the link between ethnic origin, social class and occupation. For example, the Berbers in Morocco and Yemeni workers in Saudi Arabia dominate the retail food sector. The Berbers are a racial subgroup originating from the Atlas Mountain regions (Soussi). Their language differs from Moroccan Arabic and is used as an effective barrier to would-be newcomers to the trade. The people from the area around Fez enjoy a higher social status, largely due to their greater wealth from the wholesale textile industry. They are recognizable by their accent and generally fairer complexion than the principal Arab ethnic group. In further contrast, in Casablanca migrant Indians from South-East Asia have made important in-roads into the retail apparel business.

Technology

A common goal of each of the three nations is technological independence from developed countries. To achieve this, a sound industrial base is required, along with a solid education system. However, a third factor, lack of trained local manpower may represent a considerable hurdle, as in the case of Saudi Arabia. In contrast, Turkey and Morocco have a ready supply of labor but the industrial base is too narrow and the educational/training system insufficiently organized to match job opportunities with employment demands. Thus, progress in one field of development is often held back by deficiencies in other fields.

With regard to communications systems, television and telephone services are well established in all three nations. Indeed, in Saudi Arabia these services are among the most advanced in the world. Cable, microwave and satellite communication systems are being put in place to link 28 Arab and Mediterranean countries. Technology even serves to make the experience of pilgrims to Mecca more comfortable with air-conditioned, plastic-domed resting places.

In the business world, however, simple technologies such as telephone and telex are often replaced by the prefered face-to-face business meeting. Cultural traditions still place more value on the personal, rather than impersonal mode of business throughout the region. Time is not a critical factor when trying to reach a business agreement (Badawy 1980).

Looking to the future, it is hoped that new and evolving technologies will release even more of the potential for development shared by these countries. For example, solar energy techniques are being actively studied in Morocco, along with means of extracting oil from oil shale (reserves of which were recently discovered in the Western Sahara). Innovative agricultural methods and water-treatment techniques are being pursued in Saudi Arabia. In Turkey, significant achievements have been made in the modernization of agriculture. Indeed, Turkey is now a major supplier of foodstuffs to the Middle Eastern countries. An active program of petroleum exploration is also underway in Eastern Turkey.

From this discussion of environmental factors, numerous points of convergence and divergence have been identified. Potential for future development at the national level varies significantly between the three countries due principally to differences in natural resources, terrain, size of population, economic health, and the people's attitudes to life. In the following section we will identify those commonalities which cut across national boundaries to reveal a number of homogeneous market segments at the consumer level.

12.3 Market Commonalities

The dominant market commonalities can be categorized along the following dimensions:
a) Drive for modernization
b) Demand for products and services
c) Consumer behavior and retail practices

Drive for Modernization

It might be argued that in pursuing a modern standard of living, one is basically striving for a middle-class way of life with all the material benefits of a comfortable home, secure job, educational and health services, means of communication (automobile, TV, telephone), and recreational facilities. In both Turkey and Morocco, a small upper-class composed of successful entrepreneurs and professional experts, and an embryonic middle-class of salaried white-collar workers are currently enjoying most or all of these benefits. In Saudi Arabia, in contrast, there is no real middle class; the "middle-class way of life" is the preserve of a small social elite. While not necessarily poor, 85 percent of the adult population in Saudi Arabia is illiterate. In Morocco and Turkey, a substantial majority of the population is still illiterate and far from sharing the benefits of modern living.

In striving to achieve modernization, the challenge of Turkey is to make its developing industry and agricultural sector more competitive by international standards. Important steps have already been taken recently in terms of opening up the country's isolated economy to international competition. Full membership in the European Economic Community will be a welcome move in that direction. Thus far, the Turkish economy has not been able to make full use of foreign technology, capital and know-how. Negative and indifferent attitudes of successive governments have generally discouraged inflows of capital and technology. Recent governments, on the other hand, have indicated a strong desire to encourage foreign investment in Turkey – a positive development.

The challenge for Morocco is to widen its industrial base and achieve greater operating efficiencies in the agricultural sector in order to create jobs for the unemployed and better exploit both the capabilites of the under-employed and the capacity of capital equipment. Twenty-five industrial and artisanal zones have been designated to spread manufacturing activity outside the congested coastal strip from Casablanca to Rabat, respectively the commercial and administrative capitals. Joint ventures with foreign firms are encouraged within the limitations of compulsory 51 percent Moroccan ownership. Diversification of export markets is a further priority. Traditionally France has been Morocco's principal trading partner. Currently efforts are being made to develop other markets for simple, good quality, unbranded goods such as bicycle saddles, shoes, and apparel in the U.S., Canada, sub-Saharan Africa and Brazil. Individual industries have already achieved significant successes, as in the case of the pharmaceutical industry which is one of the leading suppliers for Africa.

While modernization problems are considerably less in Saudi Arabia, the challenge there is clearly to achieve independence from both foreign labor and the reliance on one source of income (Turner 1982). In manufacturing companies other problems include under-utilization of capacity, high managerial turnover, and lack of experience among newly-graduated Saudi managers. For all three countries, imbalance in all its forms is a major national preoccupation in pursuing modernization goals.

Demand for Products and Services

Exposure of individual consumers to advertising by global corporations creates similar needs to buy and enjoy across national boundaries and income groups (Arbose 1981 and Jory 1983). Moreover, when purchase of the product is assimilated in the consumer's mind with a modern way of life, then consumers, and particularly young consumers will readily accept the innovation. This explains the rapid penetration of such products as chewing gum and skateboards in Morocco, resort homes on the Mediterranean coast of Turkey, and Western fashions for wear at home in Saudi Arabia.

Even where lack of income and older age would appear to inhibit new product acceptance, one finds plentiful evidence of TV sets and radios in simple country villages and even in shanty towns on the perimeter of Casablanca and Ankara. Similarly, refrigerators are common in many of the poorest homes; the benefits offered by such products are clear to all. Three sources of market supply operate: imports, local manufacture, and blackmarkets. In Turkey and Morocco, import controls have been used to protect naissant local industry, while in Saudi Arabia import duty is 3 percent unless there is a local manufacturer, in which case the duty is 20 percent. Very often in this region a "made abroad" label is considered synonymous with a guarantee of quality and reliable performance, not always assured with locally-made items (Bilkey and Nes 1982). Where import controls exist, black-markets tend to develop either in areas close to source-countries (e. g. the port of Tangiers is close to Spain), or in poorly policed areas (e. g. the war zone in the Western Sahara).

Further examples of the consumer's willingness to abandon simple and traditional but inefficient products are the substitution of 3-cylinder Honda pick-up vans for the horse and wagon in Morocco; and heavy agricultural equipment for the horse (or camel or donkey) and plough (International Harvester, John Deere, Ford, Volvo, etc.). Global corporations which recognize this latent market for reliable technological goods produced at reasonable prices are in a strong position to penetrate these vast new segments which vary little from country to country (Levitt 1983).

At a higher level of sophistication, hi-tech consumer products find eager buyers in North Africa and the Middle East (Young 1977). For example, solar energy units, cordless telephones, video cameras, multi-system TV sets (Pal/Secam/etc.), microwave ovens and so on are all compatible with the way of life that the new elite aspire to in these countries. Buying power in this second segment of affluent consumers is a function of either inherited wealth, commercial success, or professional expertise. For example, in Saudi Arabia, a small group of dominant families holds controlling interests in many types of business and as "channel captains" for distribution systems represent not only important individual targets for consumer products but also important sellers of such products through their numerous business activities (Kaikati 1976).

In all three countries, government incentives and protection of local industry have encouraged many local businessmen to enter the manufacturing and commercial fields. In markets where demand typically exceeds supply for consumer products, entrepreneurial success is fairly easily achieved. The third group of affluent consumers, the professional experts, are able to achieve a high standard of living since skills and expertise are also at a premium. It is not uncommon in Morocco and Turkey to find an individual filling three full time positions owing, quite simply, to the narrowness of the professional market – for example university professor, private consultant and government advisor. In this up-market second segment, demand for consumer products and services is virtually identical to that in developed countries for automobiles, household appliances, electronic equipment, vacations, insurance, office equipment, and so on. The only obstacle to actual purchase may be such environmental factors as import controls or inconvertible currencies, or marketing factors such as lack of a sales representative or after-sales service in the country.

A third, middle-of-the-road market segment is composed of the embryonic middle-class where the head of the household typically has a modest but regular income (for example, office workers, bank employees, service workers, etc.). Here basic consumer products have found ready acceptance mostly due to convenience but also due to connotations of modernism – for example, household detergents and cleansers, personal care items (toothpaste, facial tissue, lotions, cosmetics, razor blades), food products (yogurt, desserts, soda, candy), toys, pens, magazines, cigarettes and so on. The brand-name products of Procter and Gamble, Unilever, Colgate-Palmolive, Nestle, Gillette, Coca-Cola and Pepsi-Cola are as familiar in these markets as they are in their domestic markets. Strong brand loyalty among consumers has in many cases been achieved by being first in the market; from there, the brand-name becomes assimilated over time with the generic product itself as in the case of Tide (detergent), Kleenex (tissues), Palmolive (dishwashing liquid) and Nescafe (instant coffee).

Thus we see that behind the mystique of these three markets in North Africa and the Middle East there exist a number of thriving consumer market segments. In many ways these are not only similar from one country to the next, but also are very little different from consumer segments in developed countries, as far as demand for products in concerned. It is in the area of consumer behavior and retail practices that some major differences from the Westernized model appear.

Consumer Behavior and Retail Practices

Consumers in this region are intrigued by novelty and new product launches of consumer goods such as foodstuffs or household products are almost always associated with wide-scale purchase and experiment. Word-of-mouth advertising is a specific phenomenon not to be under-estimated by any marketing company and rumor-mongering is a well-established social habit. A product which fails, which is associated with any scandal or which does not perform as advertised, is doomed to suffer the consequences for a long time. An example of a product which disappeared from the market in Morocco due to the destructive power of such word-of-mouth communication was a locally produced infant weaning food, Actamine 5, rumored to be made of fish. This came about from a misinterpretation of a TV commercial where fish and fresh meat were shown on one side of a weighing scale and the baby food on the other side to demonstrate its high protein equivalence (Amine, Vitale and Cavusgil 1983).

The fascination with novelty often takes the form of simple curiosity and a desire to imitate. Both the consuming public and the business community are rapidly attracted to any new form of advertising or retail practices. For example, during the year of the World Cup for soccer (1978), the multinational marketing company, Bayer, took the initiative of using animated insects playing soccer as a storyboard for a TV commercial promoting a household insecticide spray in Casablanca. Thereafter followed a veritable epidemic of animated commercials promoting local products and issues ranging from strawberry jam to banks to family planning. Thus innovation, whatever its form, is soon rendered standard practice and the search for new ideas begins again.

Consumer shopping behavior is very similar in all three countries (Amine, Vitale and Cavusgil 1983 and Yavas, Kaynak and Borak 1982). Taking the example of the retail food market, this is made up of countless very small neighborhood grocery stores which typically cannot physically accomodate more than ten customers at any one time. Food purchasing by consumers involves many visits per week and often, two or three visits per day. Items are bought in small quantities for consumption the same day. Credit is widely used and food prices are strictly controlled by governments (Kaynak 1980). The Moroccan state actively intervenes to impose regional quotas on deliveries in times of shortage. Butter and milk are often in short supply during the hot summer months when animal feedstuff levels are at their lowest. State intervention in distribution is institutionalized by means of "offices" which buy, distribute and commercialize staple foods and products such as tea, sugar, milk, flour, tobacco, etc. Regional quota systems are applied to regulate supply and demand. A Compensatory Fund operates to stabilize staple food prices, and "flying teams" attempt to exercize control by spot checks on retail prices. In contrast to the retail food market where prices for processed foods are strictly controlled, haggling over prices is standard practice in most other areas of consumer buying in Turkey, Saudi Arabia and Morocco such as apparel, household appliances, automobiles, and even rent for apartments.

Although innovation in the areas of products and communications finds easy acceptance at the consumer level, service innovations present more problems since they require changes in basic lifestyles. This explains to some extent why supermarkets and department stores have not been successful so far in North Africa and the Middle East (Yavas, Kaynak and Borak 1981 and Kaynak and Cavusgil 1982). Some change is coming about in Saudi Arabia where several U.S. supermarket chains are experiencing rapid growth. Initial acceptance is attributed to strong patronage by the huge expatriate community there, no doubt happy to rediscover one-stop shopping, so familiar in developed countries. Local consumers however are also adopting the concept and the whole operation functions within the constraints of a deeply conservative Muslim community (e. g. store closures during prayer times, no pork products on sale, meat processing according to religious procedures, and so on) (Tuncalp and Yavas 1983).

Elsewhere, supermarkets are not widely accepted. The three basic household purchases – produce, meat, and grocery items are spread over several types of outlet e. g. corner shops, specialty stores, public markets, and itinerant street peddlers (Goldman 1982). In many cases, the supermarket appears out of step with life in this region since it reduces employment possibilities in the retail sector, precludes haggling, limits produce choice and does not offer the same opportunity for social interaction. This was clearly demonstrated by the failure of the Migros-Turk venture in Turkey (Kaynak 1980). Furthermore, the basic advantage of supermarket shopping, buying in volume at cheaper prices, is linked to the need for some sort of transportation – either to carry purchases home or simply to reach the new stores which are often located on the periphery of major cities (due to lack of available space downtown).

Other concepts in the modernization of retailing, such as the department store and vertical marketing systems, have not made any significant progress either in these countries, probably because inefficiency results in higher, rather than lower prices to the consumer. However, where the consumer is motivated by prestige rather than economy as in Saudi Arabia, then not only department stores but also the whole concept of downtown mall shopping have been adopted (Mason 1983). In Casablanca, one new department store and a downtown pedestrian mall were recently inaugurated but do not pose a serious competitive threat to established "souks" due to generally higher prices targeted at the status-conscious consumer.

12.4 Conclusions

From this analysis of Morocco, Turkey, and Saudi Arabia emerges a picture of three very different nations – different in regard to the past, present and future evolution of multiple environmental characteristics. In some respects, one may even argue that the three countries have least in common with respect to the future – continued wealth and prosperity in Saudi Arabia, struggling efforts to maintain growth in Morocco, and the continuing burden of foreign debt in Turkey. Yet our analysis has revealed a number of market commonalities which permit global corporations to cut across geographic distances and economic disparities to identify relatively homogeneous growth segments which span national boundaries. These segments polarize into the new elite segment; the young and upwardly mobile segment; and the traditional mass market of the poor who, despite their low levels of income, still aspire to enjoy the benefits of modern marketing.

Elsewhere in the region (Iran, Libya, Egypt), Islamic resurgence erects barriers to consumer marketing by global companies. Products and services conceived and/or manufactured in the West are seen as symbols of a new "imperialism of values" (Eilts 1982). Not only the products but also marketing systems (advertising, sales promotion, etc.) are rejected in favor of a return to or maintenance of the supposedly "simple life". However, in Morocco, Turkey and Saudi Arabia, a more enlightened approach to modern marketing is evident: joint ventures, licensing and local manufacturing make foreign technology available locally while, at the same time, promoting employment, increasing foreign direct investment and expanding the industrial base.

Thus, in concluding our analysis, we believe that there is strong evidence that the three boundary nations of this region, Morocco, Turkey and Saudi Arabia share more common characteristics than differences with regard to market segments. Clearly, effective market segmentation should be the starting point in developing marketing plans. The presumption that each country is different and therefore requires tailored products and marketing strategies is likely to result in much wasted effort and many lost opportunities.

Chapter 13
An Analysis of the Current Status of Marketing in the Middle East

Awad B. El-Haddad

13.1 Introduction

Marketing neglect permeates developing countries causing social and economic development to flounder. Serveral reasons have been advanced for this neglect. This chapter attempts to asses the status of marketing in developing countries, with particular reference to Egypt. It also identifies some of the different factors hindering marketing development in these societies, based upon an analysis of the industrial sector of the Egyptian economy which has been chosen to provide an illustration and foundation for discussion.

Examination of the literature on economic development reveals that marketing in developing nations has not generally been appreciated, and attention has concentrated on production, finance, and other activities presumed to contribute more toward development. Despite the application of the theories of economic development planning, many of the developing countries, as Littlefield (1968) argues, continue to show serious growing pains. A high rate of capital formation and capacity expansion in the manufacturing sector have failed to generate the rate of growth hoped for by economic planners. A good number of these pains, in view of an increasing number of observers and students of economic development as well as marketing scholars, are caused by neglect of marketing (Drucker 1958; Kindleberger 1958; Rostow 1965; Moyer 1965; Bartels 1976; and Padolecchia 1979). Marketing difficulties have so far hindered the full utilisation of the installed production capacity and led, therefore, to low capital productivity and a low rate of growth in national income. Although this chapter primarily deals with the development of marketing, no implication is intended that this is the sole requisite of advance or that marketing progress constitutes a panacea. Therefore, it is important to establish that marketing should be considered along with continued development of infrastructure, capital formation, fiscal and agrarian reforms, efficient management, education improvement and other developmental activities that are all of great importance which have synergistic effect.

To date, however, marketers have done very little to convince public policy makers in developing societies that marketing principles and research methods can vastly improve the chances of attaining their economic development objectives (Richie and La Breque 1975). Few people in the marketing profession have given more than lip service to the possibility of applying or modifying marketing knowledge constructively in an environment which lacks in current affluence, but is full of opportunities for the future (Shuptrine and Osmanskie 1975). Furthermore, a survey of marketing literature suggests that the subject of marketing in economic development has little interested marketing scholars. It is not dealt with in basic marketing texts (Bertels 1976). This relative neglect of marketing in economic development can be broadly attributed to a number of reasons which are worthy of mention:

a) The intangibility of marketing. One reason for the neglect of marketing stems from the nature of marketing activity as being intangible and difficult to quantify compared with production, where accurate quantitative information is obtainable and important for planning purposes.

b) The association of marketing with high-level, not low-level economies. Marketing scholars have been concerned with marketing in developed rather than underdeveloped economies. This is understandable because the growing surplus of products early in this century created an emergency to find new routes to the consumer. Marketing was therefore conceived in industrial economies where individual, private enterprise responded to new market ideas.

c) Lack of attention to marketing problems in the Economist's model of competition. Western economists, preoccupied with a perfectly competitive model, assume the existence of a more or less adequate marketing system in their analysis. In other words, developmental plans ignore marketing, assuming that it is a passive activity which will somehow be performed once production is increased.

d) The view that marketing is a wasteful activity inappropriate to economies with an endemic supply deficiency. In these economies there is always the belief that it is production, not marketing, that is needed, since demand exceeds supply for most products and services.

e) Difficulty in transferring modern marketing concepts and know-how from developed to developing countries. Of all skills, marketing skills may be the most difficult to transfer from one country to another.

In summary most marketing scholars would probably agree that marketing has been generally ignored in developing nations. Consequently, it is not playing an important role in economic development. Beyond such bases for conclusions, there are some empirical data available to support the same viewpoint (El-Haddad 1980).

13.2 The Egyptian Economy – Historical Background

Egypt has been a socialist country, with a centrally planned economy, for the last twenty-two years. Egypt's transition to a socialist state was accelerated after 1961, when the 'Socialist Laws' were enacted, nationalising most of the economic activities in the country. Dissatisfied with the economic results of this move, however, the new Egyptian leadership[1] seems to be convinced of the necessity of having to go back, step-by-step, to the free market system which prevailed prior to 1956, when the Suez Canal was nationalised (O'Brien 1966). Implicitly, Egypt is using foreign investment as a vehicle to achieve this end, through what is now called the 'Open-Door' policy.

13.3 Wholesale Nationalisation of the 1960s

In July 1961, a series of laws were enacted to provide for the largest nationalisation movement in Egypt since the early part of the 19th century. These nationalisation laws radically changed the economy, with the public sector emerging as the main economic power to gain complete control over the majority of the economic activities. Thus, the idea of national planning was accelerated by the nature of the events that followed so rapidly after the

---

1 By the new leadership is meant President Sadat who took over after President Nasser's death in 1970.

Revolution, rather than as a result of preconceived socialistic or communistic economic doctrine. The first Five Year Plan, 1960–1965, reflected this shift from market capitalism to what was called Arab Socialism[2].

13.4 The New 'Open-Door' Policy

After President Nasser's death, it became clear to the new leadership of the country that the existing economic policy was not conducive to the attainment of the stated objectives. Egypt was plagued by unemployment, low wages, excess capacity, inflation and population explosion and overstretched balance of payment as a result of the excessive foreign loans (Abdelwahed 1978). Egyptian leaders decided to open the door to foreign investors, particularly those from Western countries, to take advantage of the high concentration of educated and cheap labour and raw materials. They were encouraged to bring with them their modern technology and know-how, which were needed for the country's economic development. A new Law was passed in July 1974 (Law 43 for 1974 Concerning the Investment of Arab and Foreign Funds and Free Zones) offering maximum guarantees against nationalisation as well as incentives through tax examption, and tax holidays for extended periods of time.

13.5 The Industrial Picture

To most observers in the developing world, economic development is virtually synonymous with industrialisation and has been regarded as being a key indication and measure of economic development.

Egypt is no exception. Most general comments as to the nature of the Egyptian economy, whether they related to the degree of public control, the patterns of wage development, or future growth rates, refer primarily – and sometimes exclusively – to the industrial sector (Mead 1967). Rightly or wrongly, and like so many other countries at a similar stage of development, Egypt is a country with 'industry on the brain'. Before 1952, the

---

2 Arab Socialism is a socialist philosophy which depends heavily on both Arabic and Islamic heritages. It is very little related to Marxism. Leninism. Among Arab countries which apply this philosophy are Iraq, Egypt, Syria and Algeria.

Egyptian economy was literally stagnant; it was still very poor by Western standards, but since the 1952 Revolution much industrialisation has been taken place. A great drive towards self-sufficiency after the 1956 war resulted in an intensive industrialisation programme which began tentatively in 1957, but was later incorporated in the five year economic and social plan, 1960–1965, which calles for an expenditure of £.E. 1.7 billion for economic development, of which £.E. 425 million was invested in the industrial sector[3]. Since then industrialization has received the major share of investment funds. The latest figures of the current 1982/83–1986/87 five year plan indicate that the industry proportion of gross fixed investments accounts for 26%, the largest single allocation to one sector. Share of industry in GDP accounted for 13.6% in 1982–83. It provides jobs for about 1.5 million, and wages in this sector arrived at £.E. 13.3 million in 1982–83. This amounted to 35% of all wages paid to various sectors of the economy[4]. The main conclusion to be derived from the statistics shown is that the industrial sector is of prime importance to the Egyptian economy.

13.6 Marketing in Egyptian Industry

Industrialisation in developing countries, including Egypt, has been given greater emphasis than marketing in relation to economic development. Although there are some arguments for giving special encouragement to industrialisation, this encouragement should be provided in such a way as to stimulate the development of a marketing system which promotes greater efficiency in the use of economic resources. The progress of developing countries depends not only on the development of an efficient marketing system (Higgins 1959; Moyer 1965).

The adoption of ambitious industrialisation programme in Egypt has imposed a burden on the inefficient marketing system of the economy, suited largely, as El-Sherbini (1964) pointed out, to the service of handicraft industries and import-export trade. This was far from being a healthy situation as structural disequilibria are likely to take place when effective means of mass distribution are not available to take care of mass production.

3 At the time of this study 1 £E. was equal to US 80 cents.
4 Ministry of Industry and Mineral Wealth, Annual Report on Industrial Sector achievements (1982–83: 30–35).

The neglect of marketing in most Egyptian industries has been documented in a number of empirical studies (Boyd et al. 1961; Saddik 1973 and Abu-Gomaa 1974). In the absence of a competitive market to regulate the economy, Boyd et al. (1961) argue, Egypt must somehow take some steps to incorporate the marketing concept into the thinking of management. Failure to do so will prove increasingly costly and will minimise Egypt's chances of sustaining its economic growth programme.

The need for a marketing orientation has been underlined by the new 'Open-Door' policy which has encouraged the formation of new companies to compete with the state-owned firms. It has also led to relaxation of import controls, and consequently created a more competitive situation.

The present study is an attempt to fill, partly, the gap concerning the neglect of marketing in Egypt's economic development. Its main purpose is to describe and evaluate the role of marketing in facilitating economic growth in the industrial sector of the Egyptian economy.

13.7 Methodology

The data[5] were gathered as part of a larger study based on a survey conducted during the period between November 1979 to March 1980 by direct personal interviews with senior executives in 30 public industrial companies operating in Egypt. The data were collected by means of questionnaires. Two kinds of questionnaires were developed and used in conducting the interviews: (a) structured questionnaire, which was directed to the Chief Marketing Executives in the firms visited. The aim was to obtain information relating to marketing policies and practices; also to generate data about their attitudes to marketing and the marketing concept. (b) semistructured interview schedules, which served as a flexible framework for investigation in order to determine other senior managers' attituedes to marketing and its role in economic growth.

5 The data from which this paper is developed were collected during a five months period of 1979–1980 which the author spent in Egypt.
6 Industries represented included both consumer and industrial products viz, textiles, food, chemicals and metallurgical industries. They also included both exporting and non-exporting industries.

A stratified random sample of 30 public firms, from the various sectors of the manufacturing industry[6], was selected. Eventually, 116 interviews were completed with Presidents, Marketing Managers, and other Senior Managers in the firms visited.

13.8 Management's Concept of Marketing in Egypt

The study findings indicated that there is a distinct lack of appreciation of the meaning of marketing. The majority do not fully understand its meaning. Those who do, tend to believe it is inapplicable in their companies. When asked to define the meaning of marketing, managers were inclined to view it in a narrow and/or traditional sense. To many, marketing is no more than 'selling'; to others, it is synonymous with promotion and publicity. But marketing as an integrated business activity designed to relate the firm to its market is far from being realised.

13.9 Attitudes Towards the Marketing Concept

An attempt was made to assess the overall attitudes of managers in the firms visited toward the marketing concept. In other words, the extent to which marketing and non-marketing managers accept the philosophy of the marketing concept was assessed. This was followed by the determination of the extent to which the marketing concept is put into practice, i. e. the actions taken by the firm to translate this philosophical foundation in terms of directing more effort to understanding potential user needs, and making use of such marketing tools as marketing research and marketing planning.

a) Adoption of the Marketing Concept

The study findings indicated that the majority of respondents agree with the textbook definition, and with the tenets of the marketing concept. A great number of managers in the firms visited have favorable attitudes toward the marketing concept.

However, the general feeling is that while they were quick to say that they understand and believe in the marketing concepts, their actions show otherwise. In other words, managers may merely be paying lip service to the concept without actually implementing it. Consequently, one has to distinguish between the acceptance of the marketing concept as an idea or a philosophy, and whether or not the management put it into practice in the day-to-day operation of the firm. Therefore, a company cannot be regarded as marketing orientated if it only accepts the ideas of the concept.

b) Degree of Implementation of the Marketing Concept

A number of yardstick were chosen to measure the implementation of the concept. Below is an analysis of the more easily quantifiable aspects of the marketing concept. These aspects are: (i) Customer orientation; (ii) Profitability of marketing operations; and (iii) organisational characteristics of the chief marketing executive.

(i) Customer Orientation

A number of measurements were chosen to asses whether a company actually regards customers' needs to be amongst the most influential factors in its decision making. These measurements are as follows:

– *Establishment of a Marketing Research Department with one or more full-time employees*

Only eleven out of thirty firms visited have marketing research departments reflecting something less than a complete customer orientation. Moreover, the issue of whether or not these departments are actually engaged in orderly marketing research activities is debatable. The view that marketing research departments exist only on paper, but do not work, was expressed several times by a number of forthright senior executives whom the author met.

– *Use of Marketing Research to Determine Appropriate Pricing, Promotion and Distribution Strategy*

With regard to using marketing research to determine an appropriate pricing strategy, althouth 14 out of 30 firms reported using this type of marketing research, in most cases the respondents considered economic studies relating to pricing, notably cost studies, to be marketing research studies. Six out of thirty firms are engaged in marketing research to determine an appropriate promotion strategy and twelve out of thirty firms reported using marketing research in determining their distribution strategy.

Overall, the firms in our survey exhibit only limited customer orientation in terms of their use of marketing research.

(ii) Profitability of Marketing Operations

Do the marketing programms of Egyptian manufacturing firms emphasise profitability of operations? Exhibit 1 reveals that they do not. Respondents were asked if they examine the profitability of their products, customers, salesmen and territories.

(iii) Organisational Structure of Marketing Department

Another test for determining if the marketing concept has been applied is to investigate the status of the Chief Marketing Executive. He should be at the same level of the firm's organisational chart as the top financial and manufacturing executives. Also, he should be accorded a title such as 'Vice-President – Marketing' and be directly responsible to the president of the company. Furthermore, one of the basic requirements for organisational application of the marketing concept is the integration of all marketing-related activities under the authority of the chief marketing executive.

– Organisational Status of the Chief Marketing Executive

Most companies accord the Chief Marketing Executive a status which reflects a general marketing orientation. In fact as many as 90% of the firms visited gave him an equal status to that of the Chief Production Executive.

– Title of the Chief Marketing Executive

The single most common title found among all firms visited is that of Commercial Manager or General Manager for commercial affairs (22 out of 30); Assistant General Manager for financial and commercial affairs (2 companies); Sales Manager (5 companies); and only one firm uses the term 'marketing' in the title of the Chief Marketing Executive.

Exhibit 13/1: Profitability Orientation of Marketing Programmes

Percentage of firms Examining the Profitability of Products, Customers, Salesmen and Territories			
Firms Examining Four Areas %	Firms Examining Three Areas %	Firms Examining Two Areas %	Firms Examining One Area %
7	17	33	43

Although it is argued that formal titles are of little or no significance and do not necessarily indicate differences in the nature and sophistication of the tasks performed (Saddik 1969 and Al-Mauthen 1978), it is our view, however, that titles have their implications and reflect, to some extent, what is meant by marketing in the view of the Chief Marketing Executives. The prevalent attitudes, as indicated from the field survey, consider the term 'marketing' as being synonymous to selling. Consequently, marketing, in their view, is the responsibility of Sales Managers who are – from an organisational point of view – responsible to the Commercial Managers. Thus, Sales Managers are performing relatively limited tasks compared with the Commercial Managers. Therefore, designating the 'Commercial Managers' as 'Marketing Managers' may lead to a broader understanding to the concept of marketing on the part of management.

– *Extent of Integration of Marketing functions under the Chief Marketing Executive*

Marketing in the majority of firms visited tended to be a fragmented assortment of separate functions which lacks co-ordination and synthesis. Frequently, certain important functions are not put under the control of the Chief Marketing Executive, such as price and product decisions.

The main conclusion to be drawn is that one can hardly find a firm which has implemented the concept in each of its details as recommended in the literature. The only facet where compatibility with the marketing concept was found is the organisational position of the Chief Marketing Executive where he was accorded, in most cases, a status equal to that of the Chief Production and Financial Executives.

13.10 Marketing Polices and Practices

Marketing Planning:
Generally, the majority of companies have poor planning systems in comparison with the requirement of the marketing concept, and some companies do not plan at all. This poor performance is demonstrated in both the scope of planning and formalisation of the plan process itself. Profit goals and competitive goals, like determining market share and introducing new products, are the most neglected areas in planning. This is to be expected since enterprise managerial decisions are not based on profit

motives, but on implementing plans and goals given by central planners. On the whole, marketing planning as a process involving the determination of marketing goals and the means of their achievement was alien to the vast majority of firms studied.

Product Development:
Marketing has little or no say in product development. Such an activity is thought to be the exclusive responsibility of the production unit. This is because most enterprises are followers and not leaders in the field of product development. Egyptian management looks abroad for new product ideas and products, and in most cases there is a tendency to divorce product design and development from the needs of the local market. Thus, most companies in Egyptian industry are imitative rather than innovative. As Saddik (1973) pointed out, many Egyptian companies have let their sense of purpose become dominated by the economies of scale and the achievement of efficiency in production to the extent of pushing innovation and customer satisfaction into the shade. It was found that the main strategy of growth is to rely heavily on existing products and old markets. Overall, most companies display a lack of marketing orientation in their product policy.

Pricing:
With regard to pricing, the study findings revealed that despite the fact that the background data and actual decisions which include recommended pricing policies as well as pricing proposals are generally made by the manufacturing firms, prices are fixed by government agencies outside the company. Consequently, the vast majority of firms disregard pricing as a major element in their marketing strategy, where price control and the need for government approval insulate them from the market and puts limits on price flexibility. Price administration is regarded by most companies as a permanent ill in business-government relations. Generally, the findings of the study revealed more cost orientation in price setting than market orientation. A cost-plus approach was mentioned by 26 out of 30 firms visited as the major factor considered in determining the price of their products.

Promotion:
Generally, advertising and promotion activities are accorded a secondary role in the total marketing strategy, where they are regarded as of minor importance in a shortage economy. In addition, there are some governmental laws which reduce substantially the money allocated for advertising.

Most companies use advertising on social, political and religious occasions. In general, advertising is informative in nature and not strictly linked with particular product emphasis. The majority of firms determine their advertising budgets by methods far removed from the application of the marketing concept, and evaluating advertising effectiveness is almost non-existent.

Personal selling is the least popular promotion technique used. This conclusion may be explained by the fact that since these companies are working in a sellers' market, the buyer almost always takes the initiative and contacts the seller. Consequently, most manufacturers find themselves free of pressure to please and attract customers and, therefore, they feel that there is little need to develop an aggressive sales-force. As a result, little emphasis was placed on the selection, training and control of salesmen. The situation, however, is changing – althouth slowly – towards more emphasis on the sales-force especially since the advent of the 'Open-Door' policy, and there is a need now for a professional sales-force to serve both domestic and foreign markets.

Distribution:
As fas as distribution is concerned, central control and the expansion of public activity in marketing has substantially increased. As a result, most of the products have to be marketed through government-owned middlemen, and government-owned co-operative retail stores are given the first choice of scarce consumer goods. It is to be noted that the government's control over the public sector companies' channels has caused these firms a lot of problems, that is they have little or no freedom regarding the services offered to middlemen, particularly in terms of credit and profit margins. Long credit periods and high profit margins offered to middlemen by importers and private firms lead to the result that the imported products are preferred and attentively marketed.

Marketing Research:
Egyptian industry has a long way to go to make effective use of marketing research. The quantity of research ostensibly performed is perhaps greater than one might expect, but respondents undoubtedly overstate the amount of research actually done. The quality, because of such factors as poor secondary data, lack of competition, and lack of commercial research facilities, is generally poor. Its scope is often limited to the solution of urgent current problems, especially when heavy inventories are accumu-

lated. Almost none of the firms visited conceive of marketing research as a process including the gathering of data for the purpose of planning, controlling and evaluation of marketing activities.

Egyptian industry is still obsessed with a production oriented philosophy. Most businessmen in Egypt are preoccupied with production and government relations problems rather than with consumers. Buyers were more or less expected to buy what was produced, and in many cases they did. The marketing concept with its total integration of business activities designed to provide customer satisfaction at a profit is a long way from being adopted and implemented in Egypt. If the Egyptian experience can be extended to other developing nations, modern marketing is not playing an important role in economic development.

13.11 Factors Deterring Marketing Development

The variables which this study has examined have been classified into five main factors as follows:

First, is the dominance of a sellers' market in most industries in which demand exceeds supply for most products. Egyptian industry, for a considerable number of years, has witnessed the rapid growth of a sellers' market because of limited productive capacity and lack of key raw materials, particularly from abroad. Management's prime concern has been with output and production problems. Satisfying a hungry market has been the paramount concern and marketing has been given little attention in an atmosphere where production generally lagged behind sales, and where shortages and waiting lists are familiar phenomena for many industrial and consumer products.

Although the study findings revealed that the majority of managers interviewed regarded marketing to be important in times of shortages, one can hardly argue that Egyptian firms are prepared for shortages situations with a predetermined marketing strategy. Most firms visited have not considered the appropriate adjustments in their marketing strategies. They are facing the shortages situation either by doing nothing (only putting customers on some form of allocation or rationing, and stretching out the promised delivery dates) or by aggressive de-marketing. A great number of companies have neglected the final consumer or user. In this way, these companies have reduced product quality, lessened the contents of packaged products, raised prices, and reduced customer services.

Second, lack of competition is also among the factors impeding marketing development in Egypt. The exercise of a high tariff policy to protect local industry and the excess demand over supply has led to less concern with consumer needs and a lower standard of marketing services. Until very recently, many businessmen, rather than meeting competition by emphasising customer satisfaction, have preferred to avoid it by seeking industry agreement or government protection.

However, the adoption of the new economic liberalisation policy as from 1974 has affected the structure of competition in two ways:

a) The number of new firms established under the new investment law (Law 43 for 1974) is increasing, causing an important influence on the stateowned firms' competitive behavior.

b) Even more important is the gradual relaxation of Tariff barriers, import restrictions and other protectionist measures which has opened the door to strong competitive forces.

The results of the study indicated that Egyptian companies, as a result of the 'Open-Door' policy, seemed more concerned with competition than ever before. Although there is little obvious change so far in their competitive behavior, there is already a marked awareness of increased competition in nearly all the firms visited. Therefore, one may conclude that the 'Open-Door' policy is releasing gradually the most influential forces for strengthening the role of marketing. First among these forces is increased competition.

Third, is the shortage of able professional marketing staff, with 83% reporting a shortage of marketing staff. This leads to poor performance in the marketing area, which leads, in turn, to lack of faith in marketing. Shortage of marketing staff can be attributed, as the results of the field study indicate, to several reasons:

a) In the early 1960s, selection, background, and training of management for directing the public sector implied a production oriented approach. The dominant idea was that industry and production, in general, are basically an engineering problem, and hence engineers should fill the managerial positions. This approach implied lack of managerial know-how in relation to marketing.

b) Modest standard of marketing training. Marketing training programmes attract only a few participants. This is partly because most of these programmes are of a theoretical nature, indicating that there is a gap between the academic and corporate life in Egypt. This is due, in part, to the non-involvement of many of the academicians in consultancy work which is not sufficiently encouraged.

c) The effect of the 'Open Door' policy, where the new firms have attracted the most experienced skills in marketing and other areas through higher wages and incentives. In addition, the emigration of Egyptians abroad has led to loss of qualified manpower in the area of marketing and has badly hit middle management and the skilled labor of the public sector.

d) Modest standard of marketing education at the university level. Education in marketing is largely theoretical and has little or no link with the reality of the market. An Anglo-American orientation is prevalent in teaching material, and this usually leads to the overshadowing of local materials and local orientation. Also the link between research effort and industrial application is weak. As a result, the impact of research in practice, is minimal.

Fourth, is the difficulty in transferring modern marketing concepts and technology to developing countries. The study findings revealed that a direct or rigid transfer of modern marketing concepts and practices to developing nations is inappropriate. This is because of the fact that these concepts and techniques are constrained by environmental factors which impede their transferability and applicability in developing countries. However, the vast majority of managers interviewed was in total agreement that developing nations should utilise the marketing knowledge and experience accumulated over the past three decades by developed countries, but with some modifications that have to be made in order to suit the new environment.

Fifth, the business-government relationship was examined in terms of its influence on marketing development. One conclusion which came from the field work was that current government policies do not provide enough incentive for businessmen to adopt and implement the marketing concept. It was found that the freedom of management of the firms in our sample to establish an optimum marketing strategy is limited. Management cannot consider the different elements of the marketing mix as factors under its own control, but factors determined by macromanagement decisions.

Another conclusion was that the obstacles to efficient and dynamic performance in the public sector companies are attributable to a wide set of economic policies and to the heavy burden of administrative controls. Public ownership, by itself, need not cause such problems. Egypt may not gain very much from a reform which restores the ownership of industry to the private sector, but does not change the other features of the policy framework (Mabro and Radwan 1976). The features and policies of the system restrict the freedom of management in more fundamental ways, such as:

a) The firm does not have the power to use its profits to expand or invest, as the investment decisions are centralised in the ministries. It can, of course, make suggestions and submit projects. But the right to dispose of some of the profits for the growth of the firm is an important incentive for improved performance and innovative activity which the system fails to provide.

b) Firms have little or no freedom on prices, which are fixed by other agencies. The price system insulates the firm, to a significant extent, from the market.

c) Lack of direct access to foreign markets entails economic losses because the export potential is not fully exploited and because import delays lead to the emergence of idle capactiy or the costly building-up of precautionary or stand-by inventories.

d) The labor laws prevent the companies from dismissing workers, save in very exceptional circumstances; and the employment policy forces them to overman the plant and the offices. Labor – despite profit-sharing and representation on the board – is not provided with sufficient merit incentives. Wages are determined according to rigid scales, with automatic annual increments. Promotion to senior jobs depends more on the length of service than on merit.

In the light of these deficiencies, reform should probably start with: a relaxation of unnecessary controls; a simplification of administrative procedures; a redeployment of redundant workers and employees in fields which paradoxically suffer from lack of manpower (education, rural services); changes in price and other economic policies.

13.12 Implications of the Study for Business Scholars

The findings of this study have implications for the scholars of marketing as follows:

a) The study adds support to the view that marketing should essentially be regarded as the tool of demand management, rather than demand stimulation. Stimulation is a function appropriate when a company has overcapacity, but marketing can face different marketing tasks and demand situations. Each task, as Kotler (1973) noted, calls for a specific type of problem solving behavior.

Thus, by recognising marketing's goal of managing customer demand, the concept of marketing will be broadened to deal more closely with the problem of scarcity that permeates developing nations. If so, it follows that in order to make use of this conclusion in practice; decision-makers will have to develop appropriate marketing strategies to suit the shortages' situations.

b) The study also focuses attention upon a number of environmental variables which have, heretofore, received little attention, but have made significant impact upon the development of marketing in developing nations. Studies concerned with marketing outside advanced free enterprise economies are in most cases a direct application of marketing approaches which have been developed in advanced economies. As such, environmental factors are typically given a brief introduction rather than detailed analysis.

c) With regard to the issue of transferring modern marketing concepts and technology from developed to developing countries, the study indicated that differences in local environment, views, traditions, and culture among both sellers and buyers, as well as in socio-economic and political systems, call for most careful adaptation in the transferring of marketing technology from developed to developing nations.

The above conclusion is in line with Baker's assertion (1979) that differences between developed and developing nations do not deny the relevance of marketing to the latter, merely a better understanding of its application. Thus, a challenging opportunity lies before the marketing profession. A large field of economic development calls for new interpretations and applications of marketing philosophy and technology. Thus, by applying

modern marketing concept and techniques to developing nations' problems, we broaden and deepend the marketing discipline. In fact, marketing
as a field of knowledge needs to give close attention to the very different
and varied situations which the developing countries can provide to broaden its own base. As Austen (1977) indicated, any applied science, but
particularly an applied social science, tends to hover uneasily between being
aridly theoretical and a collection of 'cook book' prescriptions applied and
applicable to a narrow range of ephemeral situations. It is only by interchange of theory and practice over wide and divergent range of living
situations that a discipline like marketing can broaden and deepen, while
enhancing rather than reducing its practical relevance. Nowhere could
marketing find a better range of empirical test beds than in the developing
world.

13.13 Implications of the Study for Western Businessmen

While Egypt is typical of many developing countries and is therefore
usefully employed as an example, the analysis indicates the idiosyncrasies in
its environment of particular interest to marketers. These implications are
discussed below:

a) Despite government actions to limit the freedom of marketing decision-
making is a potential problem area, it is, however, reassuring for the
multinational enterprises that Egypt is moving slowly towards a more
liberal trade policy. One of the most significant actions taken by the
Egyptian Government in this regard was the introduction of the policy of
more open and market-oriented economy. The development of the Egyptian market through foreign investment is welcome in the form of joint
ventures with the private and/or public sector. Priority is given to those
projects designed to generate exports, encourage tourism, or reduce the
need to import basic commodities, as well as the projects which require
advanced technical expertise or make use of patents or trade marks. These
economic liberalization measures constitute a big push toward the revitali-
zation of Egypt's economy through combining foreign capital and technology with Egyptian labour. Consequently, the role of the private sector in
the country has been enhanced.

However, it is to be emphasized that the problems of the foreign business-men with respect to Egypt's new 'Open-Door' policy, as Mahmoud and Rice (1984) indicated, lie in the risk of policy reversals. Unless carefully and gradually implemented liberalization often creates social and political ten-sions that can force a government to abandon or change drastically the policy. For example, early in 1982 the Egyptian government placed a high priority on intermediate and capital goods rather than luxury non-essential imports (Middle East and African Economist 1982c). Therefore, Western businessmen have to consider this new emphasis on the production sector rather than the consumer sector.

In many developing countires, and for a variety of reasons, their govern-ments have expanded the public sector activity in marketing. This should not preclude marketing development. International businessmen are ex-pected to function within the purview of the general plan, for government interference in economic activity, especially in developing nations, has become imperative. Therefore, Western businessmen should realize the fact that whether achieved through micro or macro-marketing manage-ment, through private or public initiative, economic development through marketing depends upon one's appreciation of marketing theory. As Bar-tels (1976) argued, it is not a question of who *owns* marketing institutions, or who *does* the planning – public administrators must be as knowledgeable of marketing as private entrepreneurs. Perhaps more efforts should be directed to the marketing orientation of officials in public administration. Perhaps more also to macro-marketing polices in developing countries.

In addition, the government involvement in economic planning has some implications for Western businessmen. They are advised to deal with an Egyptian partner. Dunn (1979) noted that because of market and legal factors, even multinational companies which usually sell direct in other overseas markets find local partners indispensable in the Middle East. Knowledge of local trading practices and customs is often essential in making a sale. Also, concluding a transaction or bidding on a project often takes a long time. The government is frequently the ultimate customer in Egypt. Knowledge of government buying procedures is therefore critical to sellers. This knowledge, however, is difficult to obtain without local part-ners. Finally, there may be continuing problems with quotations, financing, import regulations, and collections that are best solved by a local partner.

c) Egypt enjoyed overall economic growth during the years 1977–82 due largely to petroleum exports, remittances, tourism and Suez Canal reveneuss. The country maintained annual real gross national product growth rates ranging from 8 percent to 10 percent (Business America 1982a). Per capita income in Egypt is US $520 (Middle East and African Economist 1982b) which puts Egypt in the middle range of developing countries. These economic growth rates together with Egypt's large population (44 million in 1982)[7] lead to an increase in the size of the market for goods in Egypt.

However, interested Western businessmen would be unwise to ignore the effects of the dual economy problem upon the size of the market for certain goods in Egypt. As Mahmoud and Rice (1984) pointed out the real opportunities for international marketers frequently lie in regional and cultural segments rather than in thinking about a broad, national-market opportunity. For example, the market for most consumer and durable goods is concentrated in Cairo and Alexandria, where a large demand for foreign goods exists. Market opportunities also extend to Port Said and other cities around the Suez Canal.

Therefore, it may be necessary to conduct market research assessment for each sector. Most international marketing textbooks discuss the marketing implications of economic dualizm (Cateora 1983).

13.14 Directions of Research on Marketing in the Middle East

Many kinds of research are needed in the Middle East Countries as more modern marketing systems evolve. Marketing research is necessary for policy makers in government agencies and private enterprises to improve the utility of new marketing facilities and enhance the value of marketing services (Kaynak 1982). Among the areas that need further research and refinement are the following:

a) Marketing research on the actual process of attracting foreign investment as a means to stimulate economic growth. Namely, how to attract foreign investments to LDCs. This study can be predicated on seeking answers to two fundamental questions:

7 Egypt Investment and Business Directory 1983/1984, Fiani and Partners, 23.

(i) That the problem of attracting foreign capital is a problem in marketing and, therefore, is subject to marketing analysis; and

(ii) that the application of a well defined marketing plan will contribute to the attraction of foreign capital and technology.

b) Marketing research on the nature and patterns of marketing adaptation that should made by international business firms in their marketing efforts designed to serve the Middle East market.

c) Marketing research can be undertaken to determine if foreign companies operating in the Middle East are marketing innovators and as a result to assess the validity of the premise that foreign companies can act as change agents in the spread of marketing technology to the Middle East.

d) Marketing research on the management of marketing enterprises, how decisions at the firm level can be improved and how marketing functions can be coordinated to improve the efficiency of firms. Also marketing research on market structure and marketing systems of the Middle East Countries, how marketing functions are organized, and where the locus of power is in the system (Kriesberg 1971).

Chapter 14
An Export Marketing Model for Developing Middle Eastern Countries: What Lessons Countries of the Region Learn from Each Other

Erdener Kaynak and Metin N. Gürol

14.1 Introduction

Less-developed countries (LDCs) rely heavily on export marketing to obtain the foreign currencies necessary for their economic development. Marketing domestic products in foreign countries provides LDCs with a reliable source of income to purchase the capital goods they need for their development from the industrialized countries of the west.

Generally the exports of most LDCs consist of agricultural products and raw materials and semi-processed products, at best. But this over-dependence on primary products has proved to have many disadvantages, such as reliance on weather conditions, constant decline in prices due to competition between numerous sellers, and in recent years, the substitution of synthetic materials for natural materials. Therefore, if the aspirations of the LDCs of the world are to be fulfilled, high priority must be given to the marketing of manufactured products abroad.

Studying actual trade patterns of manufactured goods in the 1970's have led to an international "Product Life Cycle Model" (Abegglen and Rapp 1973:72). This model has many potential uses for LDCs in indicating the characteristics of successfully exportable products and the countries to which they should be marketed. For fast and efficient market growth, government planners and marketers could use these characteristics to select their export portfolios and target markets. Another research development in the 1970's, "Experience Curves", could be beneficial in ensuring the success of the export marketing strategy. The "Experience Curves" show that in a variety of industries, the total cost declines by a characteristic amount each time accumulated production experience doubles (The Boston Consulting Group 1970). If an LDC uses a model which combines "The

Product Life Cycle Model" and "Experience Curves", it could make better choices of exports and decrease costs and prices by large-scale production which would enable it to capture substantial shares of the world markets in certain industries.

Turkey is an LDC struggling with export marketing problems. Its major concern, as expressed in successive five-year development plans, is to shift the majority of its exports from raw materials and agricultural commodities to industrial goods. This has to be done in a relatively short period of time, 10 years, because in 1995, Turkey will be a full member of the European Economic Community (EEC). At the moment, the country is not ready for entry and cannot compete with the stronger, industrialized Western European countries who are partners in the Community. If industrialization is not accomplished within the allowed period, free competition with other member EEC countries will push Turkey back to an agrarian economy.

One of the main problems faced so far has been that no analytical studies of current Turkish export marketing have been conducted. This lays the foundation for such studies and proposes an "Export Marketing Model" for Turkey, which is based on the international product life cycle model and the experience curves. The Japanese have made very effective use of these two concepts in their export market development and can serve as an enlightening example in Turkey's struggle to become an industrialized economy by the end of this decade (State Planning Organization 1973:64).

14.2 An Overview of Turkish Export Marketing

For a long period, Turkish exports were mainly agricultural commodities and raw materials (Exhibit 14/1, Column 2). After 1968, manufactured product exports began a steady increase and the proportion of manufactured product exports in total exports increased from 13.5% in 1968 to 36% in 1980 (Exhibit 14/1, Column 8) (State Planning Organization 1980:65). Yet, lately, even this impressive increase has been below the goals set by the ambitious five-year-plans initiated in 1963 (Exhibit 14/1, Column 9). The main reason for this lag is the steadily rising oil prices that began in late 1973. Higher oil costs increased the export prices of most manufactured products, causing less demand for them in the importing countries (see Exhibit 14/2 for the effects of rising oil prices on percentage increase in exports).

Exhibit 14/1: Yearly Exports and Development Plan Goal Realizations

Year	Agricultural Products			Mining and Quarrying			Manufactured Products		
	Exports ($1000)	% of Total Exports	Plan Realization %	Exports ($1000)	% of Total Exports	Plan Realization %	Exports ($1000)	% of Total Exports	Plan Realization %
1961	282,482	81.5	–	18,256	5.2	–	46,002	13.3	–
1962	303,717	79.7	–	16,212	4.3	–	61,269	16.0	–
1963	292,239	79.4	103.5	10,479	2.8	59.9	65,369	17.8	136.5
1964	319,786	77.9	109.4	14,602	3.5	100.0	76,383	18.6	111.8
1965	360,796	77.8	110.8	19,674	4.2	145.7	83,268	18.0	117.3
1966	389,015	79.3	113.2	22,012	4.5	119.0	79,481	16.2	90.7
1967	426,039	81.6	111.4	18,606	3.5	79.2	77,689	14.9	74.7
1968	404,934	81.6	99.0	24,391	4.9	78.7	66,794	13.5	66.8
1969	402,010	74.9	91.1	31,759	5.9	94.8	103,065	19.2	102.9
1970	441,058	74.9	98.1	39,468	6.7	123.3	107,923	18.4	91.5
1971	489,700	72.4	105.1	37,159	5.5	88.5	149,734	22.1	113.4
1972	605,513	68.4	125.1	33,331	3.8	59.5	246,125	27.8	164.1
1973	831,291	63.1	141.6	39,565	3.0	98.9	446,227	33.9	163.5
1974	851,866	55.6	97.9	78,991	5.2	158.0	601,325	39.2	125.3
1975	792,630	56.6	69.2	105,566	7.5	111.1	502,879	35.9	66.2
1976	1,254,408	64.0	101.6	110,015	5.6	73.3	595,791	30.4	83.3
1977	1,041,401	59.4	71.3	125,851	7.2	90.0	585,774	33.4	65.1
1978	1,542,763	67.4	100.6	124,136	5.4	70.9	621,264	27.2	73.9
1979	1,343,632	59.4	81.2	132,480	5.9	98.1	785,083	34.7	81.8
1980	1,671,742	57.4	87.8	190,994	6.6	101.6	1,047,386	36.0	74.4

Source: Adapted from *Ihracat Istatistikleri* (Export Statistics) Study Center for Export Expansion, Ankara, Turkey (1981:2–4)

Exhibit 14/2: Percentage Increase in Exports

	1970–1973	1973–1976	1976–1979
World	22.2%	20.1%	21.1%
LDCs	23.7	34.1	28.9
– Petrol exporting countries	30.7	53.5	41.7
– Other LDCs	20.0	18.6	19.3
EEC	23.4	15.6	19.5
Turkey	30.8	14.2	22.2

Source: *Dördüncü Bes Yillik Kalkinma Plani, 1979–1983* (Fourth Five-Year Development Plan 1979–1983) State Planning Organization, Turkey (1979:55)

Turkey's decision to join the European Common Market (EEC) means that Turkey must change its present economic structure to resemble that of Western European countries. The five-year development plans emphasizing the increase of industrial products aim to achieve this change. The Ankara Agreement, signed on June 12, 1963, formally obligates Turkey to the following: establishing a customs union in the future; allowing the free flow of factors of production; abolishing different treatment of workers according to nationality; changing the Government's economic policies to resemble the EEC's economic policies. The procedures to be applied to Turkey during the transition period are specified in an amendment on November 23, 1970. The transition period will terminate in 1995, and at that time, Turkey will be ready to discuss the procedures to become a full member (State Planning Organization 1973).

The amendment became operational on September 1, 1971 and EEC countries abolished their quotas and import taxes on industrial products imported from Turkey. In response, Turkey must lower its trade barriers against imports from the EEC countries and abolish them by 1995 (State Planning Organization 1973). As a result in the future, the Turkish government will not be able to use some of the protective policies which contribute to the achievement of its goals for the development of the country.

The members of the EEC have the structure of developed economies. Their per capita income is much higher than that of Turkey. They are at a higher level of scientific and technological development (State Planning Organization 1973:124). In order for Turkey to participate in joint economic policy with these developed nations within 10 years, a model that will accelerate the growth of its manufactured exports is vital.

14.3 Current Status of Turkish Exports

Developing countries rely heavily on export marketing to obtain the foreign currencies necessary for their economic development. These countries, in most cases, need to work out the characteristics of successfully exportable products and the countries to which they should be marketed. For fast and efficient market growth, government planners and marketers could use these characteristics to select their export portfolios and target markets (Moustafa 1978).

In recent years, the present and future importance of certain foreign markets for Turkish exporters has revealed encouraging potentials. As a trading partner, West Germany still ranks first in all categories of products. However, in the last few years, the relative importance of West Germany and other OECD countries has diminished somewhat, with greater emphasis being placed on the Middle Eastern and North African Arab countries (see Exhibit 14/3). As a result of this trend, there has been considerable attention placed by successive Turkish governments as well as manufacturers on developing lucrative market opportunities in these markets.

Turkish exports, which diminished in 1979, have shown a remarkable increase especially after October 1980. Exports increased from $ 1,646

Exhibit 14/3: Export Destinations For Turkish Products

Export Destinations	Percentage Breakdown		
	1980	1981	Percentage Change
West Germany	20.1	13.4	−6.7
France	4.8	4.3	−0.5
Italy	7.4	5.4	−1.7
Switzerland	3.6	6.3	+2.7
U.S.A.	5.0	5.3	+0.3
Other OECD Countries	15.1	13.7	−1.4
Libya	2.1	8.2	+6.1
Iraq	5.3	12.3	+7.0
Iran	1.9	5.3	+3.7
U.S.S.R.	7.0	4.8	−2.2
Other Countries	27.7	20.7	−7.0
Total	100.0	100.0	

Source: Turkey: A Survey, *Euromoney* (February 1982:27)

Billion in 1980 to $ 2,609 Billion in 1981. In addition to this satisfactory volume increase, substantial structural changes have taken place in the Turkish foreign trade. For instance, the share of exports in foreign trade was 18.6 percent in 1979 and 17.4 percent in 1980, and increased to 38.6 in 1981. During the same period, the share of certain Arab countries (namely Iraq, Iran, Saudi Arabia, Syria, Jordan, Lebanon and Kuwait) went up by 28 percent as compared to 12.6 percent in 1979 and 14 percent in 1980. In 1980, Turkish exports to these countries alone reached $ 635,7 million, an increase of 170 percent. Of this figure, $ 287,8 million worth of goods went to Iraq and $ 119 million to Iran. Turkish exports to North African countries have also shown some increases in recent years. Their share in total Turkish exports of 5.5 percent in 1979 and 3.2 percent in 1980 attained 10.3 percent in 1981, with Libya holding the first place. In terms of export earnings from these countries, a $ 48.9 million figure jumped to $ 233 million with Libya's totalling $ 197 million (Export Trade 1981:8).

There is also a marked increase in industrial goods exported to Middle Eastern and North African Arab countries. Compared to 1980, a $ 236 million increase has been recorded, bringing the total industrial goods exports to the region to $ 368 million. The share of Middle Eastern and North African countries in Turkey's total industrial exports reached 58 percent. As well, a close to 200 percent increase in Turkish exports to Moslem countries shows the important development in the trade relationship of Turkey with these countries.

14.4 New Developments in the Theory of International Trade

The International "Product Life Cycle Model" Classical and neoclassical theories of international trade were very elegant; however, they failed to describe actual trade patterns. Therefore, business academics whose interests were practical problem solving developed the international "product life cycle model". Although this model was less elegant than traditional theory, it did turn out to be helpful in explaning trade flows of manufactured goods (Wells 1972:3 and 5).

The frist version of the model was described by Vernon (1966:199) as a three-stage process (Exhibit 14/4). Then Wells (1972) presented a five-phase model (Exhibit 14/5). In summary, the model suggests that "many

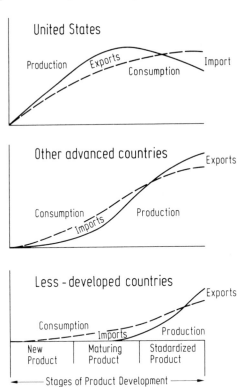

Exhibit 14/4: The Vernon Model

Exhibit 14/5: The Wells Model

Phase I	Phase II	Phase III	Phase IV	Phase V
All production in U.S.	Production started in Europe	Europe exports to LDCs	Europe exports to U.S.	LDCs export to advanced countries
U.S. exports to many countries	U.S. exports mostly to LDCs	U.S. exports to LDCs displaced		

Source: Raymond Vernon: International Investment and International Trade in the Product Cycle. *Quarterly Journal of Economics* (Vol. 80, May 1966:199 and L. T. Wells: International Trade: The Product Life Cycle Approach. In: L. T. Wells (ed.): *Product Life Cycle* and International Trade, Boston (1972:15)

Exhibit 14/6: Summary of Product Characteristics Throughout the Life Cycle

Characteristics	Stage of the Life Cycle		
	I. Introduction	II. Growth	III. Maturity
1. Technology	– rapidly changing and adapting to consumer preferences	– few product variations of importance with various degrees of refinement; process innovations critical	– both product and process stable; with no major design innovations of importance
	– closely held by innovating firm; no licensing or sale	– patent variations decrease monopoly of technology; some diffusion and licensing	– readily available and transferable
2. Production	– product centered – shortruns; prototype manufacturing	– shifting to process – larger runs; mass production introduced although techniques may differ	– process-centered – long runs; stable processes
3. Capital	– low use of capital; multipurpose equipment	– increased utilization	– high investment in specialized equipment
4. Industry structure	– innovating firm leads with others entering field to capitalize on success	– large number of firms; many casualties and mergers; growing integration	– number of firms declining with lower margins
	– know-how principal barrier to entry	– financial resources critical for growth	– established marketing position principal barrier to entry
5. Human inputs	– high scientific engineering and marketing skills	– financial and production management necessary to reduce costs	– unskilled and semi-skilled labor; marketing
6. Marketing and demand structure	– seller's market – low price elasticity; "snob appeal"	– balanced market – growing price elasticity	– buyer's market – high price elasticity for individual producers
	– high introductory marketing effort in communication and awareness	– beginning product differentiation; distribution critical	– high brand and product differentiation may appear through various means
	– high monopoly prices	– increased competition reducing prices	– lower prices and margins

Source: Jose de la Torre: Product Life Cycle as a Determinant of Global Marketing Strategies. *Atlantic Economic Review* (September–October 1975:10)

products go through a cycle during which high-income mass-consumption countries are initially exporters, then lose their export markets, and finally become importers of the product. At the same time other advanced countries shift from the position of importers to exporters later in time, and still later, LDCs shift from being importers to being exporters of a product" (Keegan 1980:266). At a later stage, De la Torre (1973:76–82) made an indepth study of the life-cycle concept to evaluate a product's performance in world markets, and to anticipate trends in international competitiveness necessitating strategic adjustments in marketing and logistics. He proposed a framework as an aid to the international marketing executive in evaluating his product's performance in world markets and, more importantly, in predicting changes in their performance over time. Having some concept of future trends in relative competitiveness, the firm can anticipate any changes in strategy necessary to reduce its vulnerability to changing trade patterns. This framework also assesses the suitability of a marketing strategy, designed for one market, for a different environment. In the past, discussion of life cycles typically has been limited to changing marketing characteristics. However, many other aspects of the product or its manufacture are also subject to significant variations throughout the life-cycle. Among them, changes in product and process technology, production processes, relative capital and labor intensity, and industrial structure are relevant to this analysis. Exhibit 14/6 summarizes these characteristics in terms of the first three stages of the life cycle (De La Torre 1973).

During the last stage LDCs get a chance to make a breakthrough into the big and rich markets of the developed countries if they realize the chance in time. The best example is standardized textiles. Other examples are standardized computer and electronic parts from other LDCs. The current growth rates for exports of manufactures from LDCs may indicate that they will soon become an important factor for European and American businessmen (Wells 1968:4). To this end, most LDCs have adopted policy reforms in favor of diversifying the composition of their exports which in 1970 consisted almost entirely of primary products and commodities (Hiemenz 1983; Havrylyshyn and Alikhani 1982).

14.5 Export Marketing Implications of Experience Curves

The experience curve concept dates back to the 1920's to airplane production, and subsequently has been improved and refined by the work of the staff of the Boston Consulting Group. The experience curve effect is distinctly different from the "learning curves" and "progress functions" in that it encompasses *all* costs (including capital, administrative, research and marketing – not only labor) and traces them through technological displacement and product evolution (Abegglen and Rapp 1973).

The Concept It has been shown that for a variety of industries, total cost in constant dollars will decline by a characteristic amount each time accumulated production experience doubles. This is true for entire industries as well as for individual companies and has been observed in many countries, including the U.S.A. and Japan. For more industries and products, the unit cost decline is about 20 to 30 percent for every doubling of accumulated experience. Though the precise reasons for this phenomenon are not well documented, it appears to be a combination of learning by doing, management experience, and economies of scale; it is an accepted part of cost-projection formulations in the aircraft and semi-conductor industries. The cost-experience relationship can be plotted on log-paper to give the industry (or company) experience curve (Exhibit 14/7).

Export Marketing Implications Export marketing policy significantly affects product costs because of the volume potential it affords. Freer trade can spell tremendous cost reduction to individual firms by allowing them to expand volume and thus, descend their cost/volume slope faster. If this analysis is carried to its logical conclusion, it also means substantial savings in resources for entire countries.

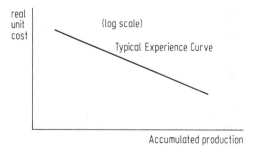

Exhibit 14/7: Industry Experience Curve

If two countries trade with each other, the costs of production can be lowered significantly for both. On the basis of experience curves, two economies of equal size can theoretically have potential cost savings approaching 30% by completely free trade between them, compared with full separation. Four economies of equal size can have cost levels approaching 50% of those which would be required if they were all separate, equal and self-contained.

The public policy issues in export marketing seem clear and straightforward. Very substantial benefits in terms of lower costs are potentially available merely by enlarging the scope of the free trading area. Thus technical investments will be more readily justified and progress will almost certainly take place faster in those economies which have the largest free trading area. The price of the cost savings is mutual dependence of the different parts of the trading area.

14.6 Japanese Export Marketing

The aggressiveness and effectiveness of Japanese export marketing are admired worldwide. Instead of every manufacturer trying to market his product abroad by himself, the Japanese use trading companies that are specialized intermediaries in worldwide exports and imports. The trading companies account for about half of Japan's total exports, and slightly more of its imports. The most basic function of the large trading company is to facilitate exchange between buyers and sellers in different countries. Among the large companies mainly responsible for the Japanese exports in the major product categories, the use of trading companies varies a great deal (Johansson 1981:16–18). There are three hundred major trading firms responsible for 80 percent of Japanese exports and imports, with a dozen large firms accounting for 60% of total trading company volume (Keegan 1980:126).

By design, Japan first exports to LDCs and then to developed countries. In the 1950's, approximately three-quarters of Japan's exports were shipped to LDCs. During Japan's rapid growth between 1950–1960, her export trade changed radically both in composition and destination. "By 1964 Japanese exports going to more advanced countries reached 50% of her total exports; and this percentage is still increasing" (Tsurumi 1972:162 and 178).

First, Japanese manufacturers satisfied internal demand for products that were produced overseas, and to do so, they had to purchase technology, usually from the U.S.A. Then they started exporting to LDCs in Asia where there was a growing demand for the product and no domestic competition. Frequently, Asian LDCs served as a testing ground for Japanese manufacturers in the world market. Japan's geographical proximity and the relative similarities of its socio-cultural background contributed to its success in these Asian LDCs. After a firm gained worldwide competitive strength, the Japanese manufacturers started exporting to industrial nations. Hence, the Japanese have consciously been taking advantage of the duality of their export markets (Tsurumi 1972:178).

14.7 A Turkish Export Marketing Model

Characteristics of the Middle Eastern and Western European Market

From the viewpoint of socio-economic development, Turkey is a country between the advanced and less-developed world, similar to the status of Japan some 25 years ago. Thus Turkey faces a dichotomy of her export markets: Middle Eastern countries as LDCs and Western European countries as developed nations.

Most of the Middle Eastern countries were part of the Ottoman Empire for more than five centuries. At the end of the First World War, the empire collapsed and Turkey, as well as most of the Middle Eastern countries, where invaded by forces from Europe. The Turkish War for Independence, the establishment of the Turkish Republic, and the reforms that created modern Turkey have been admired and taken as a model by many Middle Eastern countries. Many Arab nationalists idolize Atatürk, the creator of the Turkish Republic, and try to increase their contacts with Turkey, probably the most developed Moslem country in the world. Therefore, we can conclude that Turkey is closer to the Middle Eastern countries than to Western Europe both in geographical and cultural-political and psychological distances.

The Middle East has been going through a major change since the energy crisis of 1973. Dramatic rises in oil prices resulted in the accumulation of buying power which created more demand for consumer products and industrial goods required by ambitious five-year development plans. The

Middle East is an ideal market for Turkey in her efforts to export its
manufactured goods.

On the other hand, most of the sixteen countries in Western Europe have
highly developed economies and generate approximately 30 percent of
global income. Widespread industrialization, higher urbanization and literacy and the existence of customs unions or free trade agreements are some
of the characteristics of Western Europe. In a small area, 404 million people
live a prosperous life. Some of these countries have higher per capita
incomes and a higher standard of living than the United States (Keegan
1980:119). Western Europe is another ideal export market for Turkey
because, in addition to high purchasing power, the size of the market allows
largescale production facilities that will benefit from the experience curves.

14.8 Market Identification in the Middle East and
         North Africa

As the importance of these markets for Turkish manufacturers is increasing, the exporting as well as would-be exporting firms will have to engage in
more marketing research activity using numerous techniques to determine
the market potential. These manufacturers, in most cases, are forced to
make some quantitative estimates of sales opportunities for their products
in each target market. Such knowledge of market potential is the first step
in the preparation of an effective international marketing program (Fayerweather 1983).

Each Middle Eastern and North African country is characterized by specific
environmental conditions, such as cultural, socio-economic and technological development, which affect buying patterns and responses (Elbashier and
Nicholls 1983). These environmental factors can provide several indicators
of overall market response (Wind and Douglas 1972). Markets of the region
can be segmented in a two-step process. First the macro segment composed of individual or groups of countries can be identified, based on
national market characteristics. Then, within each macro segment, the
market can be further subdivided, based on customer characterization.

Through this approach, as seen in Exhibit 14/8, an initial screening of
countries and the selection of certain countries on the basis of national

Exhibit 14/8: A Construct for Assessing the Middle East and North Africa Markets

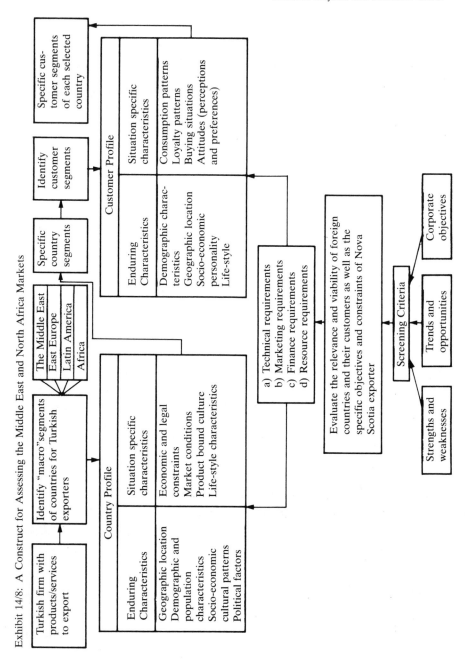

market characteristics are undertaken. Once markets have been segmented at the national level, they will then be further subdivided by customer characteristics. Two grounds for segmentation will be used: general characteristics and situation-specific characteristics. The classification of countries on the basis of national characteristics appears to provide only very weak indicators of marketing behavior in the Middle East and North Africa. Thus further investigation of both general and situation specific customer characteristics within each country market is required to identify relevant target segments.

14.9 Estimating Market Potentials

To become successful and establish a niche in the huge Middle Eastern and North African markets, Turkish manufacturers, like their counterparts in the more developed countries, need to have a comprehensive knowledge of the characteristics of the market place. Primary attention, therefore, needs to be directed to determining what the target markets need and want from Turkish manufacturers.

Once the Middle Eastern and North African countries to be investigated have been identified, the next step is to make an estimate of market size and market growth. Market potential analysis will be very useful in gathering pertinent data on the Middle East and North Africa markets which are to be used as the basis for managerial decisions (Douglas, Craig and Keegan 1982). After the initial screening process, the nature and intensity of both current and potential demand in each country of the area as well as the regional demand variations need to be empirically assessed for orderly export policy decisions.

Estimating market potentials in the Middle East and North Africa is typically quite difficult. Although there are numerous techniques which are used in determining market potentials, when the data are scarce one of these techniques becomes more readily useful than others. This technique is called the Multiple Factor Analysis. In an exploratory study using this method, an attempt can be made to establish market potentials for little known markets of the Middle East and North Africa. This technique allows the researcher to make inferences from known to unknown (Samli 1977 and 1979).

The Model The export marketing model we have developed for Turkey provides general guidelines which other LDCs could use. It is composed of five stages (Exhibit 14/9). They are as follows:

Stage I: *Product Selection*

The first stage of the model is to select the products at the threshold of being exportable from the LDCs. These should be products that are in or are moving into the mature phase and have the following characteristics:

a) high domestic raw material content,
b) a labor-intensive technology to benefit from low labor costs
c) standardization with long production runs that will allow functioning of the experience curves
d) highly price elastic demand
e) initially high domestic demand and later high international demand for the product.

Stage II: *Domestic Sales*

After selection of the products, investments are made to build the production facilities. Economies of scale are important considerations, but capacities are generally limited by the domestic consumption potentials. At this stage, technology is purchased from the developed countries, which sell it quite cheaply by contrast to the original research and development costs, since those expenses have already been covered during the growth phase of the product life cycle (PLC). Starting from a low base, experience is accumulated at a fast rate which in turn allows lowering of costs and prices.

Stage III: *Export to the Middle East*

After experience is gained and costs are lowered, bigger and relatively more capital-intensive production facilities are built, and exporting to Middle Eastern countries starts. International marketing experience is gained, and sliding further down the experience curve allows further lowering of costs and prices. This decrease stimulates additional domestic as well as international demand.

Stage IV: *Export to the EEC*

The EEC should be the main target of exports, since Turkey will be in this free trade area soon. In this stage, larger capital investments are made considering the substantial demand of the EEC countries. Since technology is the same and economies of scale are exploited, Turkey could use its lower labor costs to capture a substantial share of the EEC market in these highly price-sensitive products. Before exporting to EEC countries begins, the quality preferences and standards of EEC countries should be investigated, and necessary product improvements should be made to satisfy quality-conscious European customers.

Stave V: *Export to the U.S.A.*

The products that are successful in the EEC could be exported to the U.S.A., because mass production with lower labor rates, cheaper raw materials and perhaps newer plants may enable Turkey to produce at a lower cost than the U.S.A. Of course, ocean freight and U.S.A. duties should be considered as additional costs before deciding to export to the U.S.A. American producers pricing on full cost might be undercut if only marginal costs are used for export pricing in order to gain entrance to this competitive market.

An Example: A good example of a product that could be exported from Turkey to other LDCs and developed countries using this export marketing model would be textiles. Raw materials for textiles such as cotton, wool and silk are available in large quantities at low prices in Turkey. The textile is labor intensive industry, and the cost of labor is low in Turkey. Textiles are mature and relatively standardized products with, generally, price elastic demands. Since clothing is a basic necessity, textiles constantly have both a domestic and an international demand. The amount of textiles imported to the U.S.A. from LDCs like Taiwan and Korea indicates that the export marketing model developed above for LDCs is realistic. The model we have developed incorporates the use of the "international product life cycle model" and the "experience curves" to generate a model for an LDC with respect to its geographical location. Japan's successful experience in export marketing using a similar strategy offers a good example for the LDCs.

14.10 Conclusion

Among the EEC countries, Turkey has the least industrialized economy and the lowest labor costs. If it can plan its export marketing scientifically in the light of the latest developments in international trade theory and the Japanese experience, it could use cheap labor as a competitive advantage, slide quickly down the experience curve, and become the dominant producer of many of the mature products in the Community. Turkey is not doomed to regress to an agrarian society in the face of European competition, if it plans wisely and implements quickly.

Chapter 15
The Prospects for Export Marketing to Egypt

Gillian Rice and Essam Mahmoud

15.1 Introduction

Egypt, with a population of forty-seven million, is the most heavily populated Arab state. Egypt had the third largest gross consumption level in the
Middle East, after Saudi Arabia and Algeria, during the period 1975–80 (El
Naggar 1981). It is, therefore, an important market in the Middle East for
many American, European and Japanese firms. The estimated value of
exports in 1982 to Egypt from the U.S., the E.E.C. and Japan was $ 1,726
million, $ 3,611 million, and $ 383 million, respectively (United Nations
1982). Kaynak (1984), in a hypothetical grouping of Arab markets, classi-
fies Egypt as a growing stage country along with other nations such as Syria,
Jordan, Yemen and Sudan. He suggests that market prospects for these
countries are in food processing, tourism supplies and equipment, industrial
equipment, hospital equipment and health care products, textile machinery
and consumer goods. More specifically, an article in Business America
(August 20, 1983) notes that in the near to medium term, prospects are
good for the sale in Egypt of foodstuffs, construction machinery, and
telecommunications and electrical generating equipment.

Egypt enjoyed overall economic growth during the years 1977–82, the latest
period for which information is available. Due largely to petroleum exports,
remittances, tourism and Suez Canal revenues, the country maintained
annual gross national product growth rates ranging from eight to ten
percent (Business America August 9, 1982). According to the Business
America report, the outlook for these key activities remains good. These
major foreign exchange earners performed well in 1983–84 and allowed
Egyptian policymakers to proceed gradually on structural economic reforms (Business America August 20, 1983). Per capita income in Egypt is
U.S. $ 520 (Middle East and African Economist April 1982), which puts
Egypt in the middle range of all developing countries. This figure reflects

Egypt's large population, but living standards are admittedly poor for the majority of the country's inhabitants.

This chapter evaluates the prospects for export marketing to Egypt. The assessment of the marketing environment which follows focuses upon economic conditions, bureaucratic issues, the marketing infrastructure and socio-cultural factors. Many of the problems and opportunities the exporter faces in Egypt are typical of the Middle Eastern country-markets as a whole. Pezeshkpur (1978) and Elbashier and Nicholls (1983), however, emphasize the diversities among the individual Arab nations. They stress the idiosyncracies of each nation's social, economic and political environments, its market characteristics and its resources. In this chapter, the aspects of the Egyptian environment which are common to other Arab countries as well as those specific to Egypt are examined. The chapter concludes with a number of recommendations for international marketing managers.

15.2 Economic Problems and Market Opportunities in Egypt

The Dual Economy Problem

While per capita income and growth are important, it is the spread of wealth and the general level of discretionary income which influence major shifts in the demand for different groups of consumer products and services (Michell 1979). The presence of economic dualism (the coexistence of modern and traditional sectors within the economy) in Egypt means that it may be necessary to conduct market assessments and develop marketing plans for each sector. With respect to consumption behavior, Egypt does not differ greatly from most developing countries in having relatively low spending levels in the countryside. A Household Expenditure Survey of 1974–75 cited by Ikram (1980) reported an average annual expenditure of 375.42 Egyptian pounds for rural families and an average annual expenditure of 556.75 Egyptian pounds for urban families.[1] The lower spending by rural families is usually explained by incomplete monetization of the rural economy and lower markups on food. As in most poor countries (Kaynak 1980, 1981), the budget share devoted to food consumption is high: more

1 When this survey was conducted, 1 Egyptian pound was equal to $1.4.

than 50 percent of the budget for all consumer groups except the very richest (Ikram 1980). Among nonfood items, there is a sharp increase in expenditures on transportation and communications, most notably on automobiles, in the top income groups and on categories such as culture and entertainment. These increases simply reflect growing diversity in the consumption basket as income goes up. In addition, a considerable part of the expenditure of the richer class in Egypt appears to be spent on imported items.

The multinational marketing manager would be unwise to ignore the effects of the dual economy problem upon the size of the market for certain goods in Egypt. The real opportunities for marketers frequently lie in regional and cultural segments rather than in thinking about a broad national market opportunity. For example, the market for most consumer and durable goods is concentrated in Cairo and Alexandria where a large demand for foreign goods exists. Market opportunities also extend to Port Said and other cities around the Suez Canal.

In the last ten years, however, the government has been attempting to decentralize governmental authority in order to weaken this market concentration and develop the more rural areas of Egypt (Mahmoud 1973; Business International 1980). Little change has been achieved (Kurian 1982).

Government Economic Policies and Planning

Egypt suffers from a large chronic trade deficit, estimated to be approximately $1.5 billion in 1982 (Business America August 9, 1982). In early 1982, the Egyptian government placed a high priority on intermediate and capital goods rather than luxury non-essential imports (Middle East and African Economist, July/August 1982). This new emphasis on the productive sector rather than on the consumer sector resulted from both the decrease in available foreign exchange and President Hosni Mubarak's desire for a more equitable distribution of Egypt's financial resources. There are two basic components of market potential: the government's development plan and the consumer sector. In assessing and forecasting the economic environment, therefore, the international marketer must become familiar with the planning activities and the resulting plans of the Egyptian government.

Development planning is coordinated by the Ministry of Planning, the National Planning Committee and the Permanent Council for the Development of National Production. It is important to appraise the degree of commitment to planning and to the plans that actually exist. The problem for the firm exporting to Egypt is that the firm's own sales forecasts and strategic plans may depend to a certain degree on the government's economic plans. In many countries, for a variety of reasons, government actions may not follow published plans. For example, in Egypt, ministerial changes cause instability in planning and this affects the continuity of existing projects. The construction project to build the "Cairo International Market" (where the annual Cairo fair is held) took almost twelve years to complete due to the changing policies and priorities of the different Ministers in office (Mahmoud 1973). Problems of government planning associated with personnel changes are exacerbated because, contrary to Western organizations which tend to have comparatively stable goals, organizational goals in Moslem organizations (as in Egypt and other Middle Eastern countries) seem to shift with the change over of organization heads. According to Wright (1981a), this stems from a belief on the part of Islamic managers that corporate entities need strong leaders who are willing to force their wills on their organizations.

Bureaucratic Problems

For a variety of organizational and political reasons, the performance of the Egyptian bureaucracy is declining sharply in quality, when the desire to encourage foreign investment is actually calling for a more innovative, flexible and efficient bureaucracy (Ayubi 1982). This is perhaps the best known of the features of Egyptian management (Zahra 1980).

The principal criticism made by investors is the lack of coordination between various government agencies and their apparent inability to honor important undertakings (Business International 1980). For example, a customs exemption from the investment authority, GAIFZ,[2] does not automatically mean the customs service will abide by it.

Administrative difficulties are also faced by international marketers seeking to finalize their contracts and obtain payment for their goods. Normally a letter of credit is opened and cleared within a few days. With the public

2 GAIFZ stands for the General Authority for Investment and Free Zones.

sector,[3] however, this is a difficult and lengthy process taking anything between three and six months. The award must be approved initially by the central bank which acts as the agent for the Ministry of Finance. Every Tuesday, a special committee of the central bank meets in order to allocate funds on a priority basis. If the credit is not opened on one Tuesday, it has to wait until the next. There are also problems if the order is, for example, in Norwegian kroner or even sterling, as the vast majority of Egypt's trade is conducted in dollars. Other problems can arise because of the delay such as price rises and renegotiation of terms or finding a ship sailing for Alexandria when the letter of credit finally comes through.

In response to international marketers' complaints that they have been deterred by bureaucratic obstacles, Egypt is making efforts to clarify the investment situation and to speed up and centralize the investment approval process so as to attract new investors into priority sectors. For example, according to Business International (1980), GAIFZ is improving its promotion effort through trade missions abroad and through its own promotions department in Cairo where it has set up a special information centre. In addition, the Egyptians have promised to decide within 120 days of the submission of a feasibility study instead of taking longer periods (The Economist, July 2, 1983).

From a managerial point of view, little can be done to overcome the bureaucratic problems. Dealing with them requires patience, skill, sensitivity and flexibility. A fundamental goal should be to develop friendly alliances inside and outside the business organization (Wright 1981b). As is the case in most Middle Eastern countries, whatever precise formal arrangements have been worked out, the relationship between the parties determines the success or the failure of any undertaking. Particularly important to business undertakings is the establishment of ties with government officials, the business community (business leaders), and the company's bankers (Hall 1979).

---

3 The public sector accounts for 80 percent of industrial output and will continue to be a dominant force in the Egyptian economy. The demise of the public sector is not politically feasible, nor is it an objective of government policy.

15.3 The Market Infrastructure

In their discussion of marketing infrastructure, Douglas and Craig (1982) identify "integrative networks" which affect the feasibility or desirability of utilizing specific types of marketing programs and strategies. Integrative networks include a variety of factors such as the availability of television advertising and supermarkets, the development of the transportation network and the communication system (the physical infrastructure) and the existence of market research organizations. In this section a brief discussion of the typical problems arising from the nature of Egypt's integrative networks will be explored.

The Physical Infrastructure

The pervasive impression is that the physical infrastructure in Egypt is seriously underdeveloped. The telecommunications network is described to illustrate this. It has become totally inadequate to the needs of the economy. Egypt's density of 1.34 telephones per 100 population is significantly lower than that of other Middle Eastern countries (Iran, 2.00; Turkey, 2.52; Syria, 2.30; Iraq, 1.69). The telephone density in Cairo is about 5.0 and in Alexandria 3.4, compared with Algiers, 9.5 and Teheran, 8.2. As many as 1000 villages in Egypt do not have even primary access to telephone service, for example, a public call office (Ikram 1980). There are also problems with the existing telephone system. For instance, in an article in World Business Weekly (1981), it was estimated that in Cairo, 50 percent of the telephone lines can be out of service at the same time and 75 percent of all dialed calls fail to get through on the first attempt. Perhaps in no other sphere, however, has there been such a marked improvement in services as in telecommunications over the last six or seven years. Direct dialing to Egypt became possible in 1984 with the result that it has become much easier to call locations outside Cairo. The long term goal of Areto (the telephone organization) is to provide a fully comprehensive telephone system by the turn of the century. Many logistical problems still remain, however. The telephone directory is available in Arabic only, except in some embassies.

Marketing Research Problems

Egypt has a fairly well-developed statistical system that generates a considerable body of secondary data. The problems, however, are that these are not always conceptually useful for marketing purposes; they often are not available at the appropriate time (Ikram 1980); they are published in Arabic; and they may be unreliable indicators (Brasch 1978). As Keegan (1980) points out, these difficulties may not be of prime significance as it is the nature of marketing research everywhere that only a small amount of data in the typical study is obtained from public sources. Saddik (1973) comments that the number of independent agencies that offer professional research service in Egypt is very small. Companies capable of doing marketing research do exist (U.S. Department of Commerce 1981), but the familiar problems of undertaking marketing research in developing countries remain. These are problems of infrastructure, such as an absence of telephones; and of culture, for example, a greater reluctance on the part of people to talk to strangers and when people do respond, the existence of "courtesy bias" (Kaynak 1978; Yavas and Kaynak 1980). Almaney (1981) notes that in general, Arabs have a tendency to be highly secretive and do not like to give factual information about themselves to strangers and officials. Place of birth, age, occupation, parents, wives and children all are felt to be private matters. Although secretive about facts, the Arab is quick to express his feelings and therefore, psychographics and attitude-related research may proceed more easily.

Distribution and Control Issues

The organization of the retail trade in Egypt, as in other Middle Eastern nations, may cause marketing control problems for the international marketer. Egypt's retail trade is dominated by a large number of small, privately owned shops and vendors (Kaynak 1981).

Customer service at the retail level is poor (Saddik 1973) and pre- and after-sales service are provided at a level far below that given in developed countries. The wholesale and distribution operations tend to be carried out by vertically integrated merchants or public sector trading companies. The generally small size of firms and limited market opportunities (for example, because of low levels of consumer expenditure) often lead to local competition and long channels of distribution. The latter effect gives the distributor a predominant role (Hibbert 1979).

Regardless of the method of entry into the Egyptian market (for example, direct exporting, sales subsidiary, manufacturing subsidiary) and despite possible reduction of central marketing control, it is advisable to deal with an Egyptian partner. Dunn (1979) noted that, because of marketing-related and legal factors, even multinational companies which usually sell direct in other overseas markets find local partners indispensable in the Middle East. Knowledge of local trading practices and customers often is essential in making a sale. The government is frequently the ultimate customer in Egypt. Knowledge of government buying procedures is therefore critical to sellers. This knowledge, however, is difficult to obtain without local partners. Finally, there may be continuing problems with quotations, financing, import regulations, and collections that are best solved by a local representative.

Price Controls

Price controls are implemented by the Egyptian government on most goods, limiting the manager's freedom to control his marketing decision variables. For example, consumers purchasing more non-subsidized and especially imported goods face higher rates of inflation. Luxury commodities, in particular, tend to attract indirect taxes, sometimes referred to in Egypt as "price differences" (Ikram 1980). In 1983, however, government policymakers decontrolled the prices of some agricultural items (Business America August 20, 1983). The objective was to help alleviate the burden of subsidies on the budget and to encourage more efficient resource allocation.

Advertising Problems

The media are entirely state-controlled and function as organs of the state information department. Nevertheless, Cairo is the largest publishing centre in the Middle East and the media capital of the Arab world. Commercial advertising can be placed in newspapers and magazines and on radio, television, cinema and posters through the government-owned advertising agency. Even in the advanced sector of developing countries in the Middle East such as Egypt, however, modern advertising is relatively new. Consequently, the advertising techniques and the associated returns may appear highly uncertain to local business partners (Leff and Farley 1980). The problems that do exist therefore concern the appropriate amounts of advertising expenditure in addition to cultural adaptation of messages, brand names and packaging (Business America 1979) and media selection which is constrained by factors such as the reach of media vehicles and literacy rates (Kaikati 1979). Egypt has a relatively low literacy rate despite increased government emphasis on education which admittedly led to an improvement in the literacy rate from 26 percent in the sixties to 54.3 percent in 1980. Illiteracy remains high particularly among older people and this is of some significance for marketing because these people are responsible for most buying decisions (Leff and Farley 1980). The low literacy rate combined with low radio and television ownership[4] has clear implications for communications with customers. Marketers must use appropriate media such as billboards which are available and provide a useful medium of communication.

Another alternative is cinema advertising. Egypt is one of the leading film-producing and film-exporting countries in the Middle East. In 1974 there were 239 cinemas in the country and movie attendance was 70 million (Kurian 1982). Selected examples of the cultural implications for advertising are included in the following section.

15.4 Cultural Influences on the Marketing Effort

The marketing implications of cultural differences in Egypt may be seen in terms of a number of activities within the overall marketing function such as marketing research, the understanding of consumer behavior, organizational behavior and salesman activity, and marketing strategy formulation (Redding 1982). For example, the consumer base in a Middle Eastern nation cannot be understood by reference to Western models. The intensity of some cultural traits of the Arabs also varies from country to country and from one locality to another within the same country (Almaney 1981). In the tradition-bound societies of Saudi Arabia, Kuwait, and the other Gulf states, ancient Bedouin customs relating to hospitality, pride, honor, rivalry and revenge are still observed rather strictly. In the more Westernized countries of Egypt, Lebanon, Syria und Iraq, certain aspects of such traits as honor and vengeance are showing signs of weakness. In these more Westernized societies, nevertheless, Bedouin traits tend to be more visible and more deeply rooted as one moves from cities to rural areas.

---

4 Ownership of radio receivers in 1979 was 132 per 1,000 inhabitants; ownership of TV receivers was 32 per 1,000 inhabitants (United Nations Statistical Yearbook 1981).

Egypt is a predominantly Moslem country. An important feature of the socio-cultural environment, which may have implications for the success of Western-oriented products and advertising, is Islamic revivalism. Some observers believe that social conservatism has grown in Egypt as a social consequence of increasing contact with the oil-exporting states (Ikram 1980).

Reliance on purely economic or demographic indicators can foster misconceptions regarding the size of a market and consumer behavior if an in-depth understanding of Egyptian culture is missing. This can be illustrated by an examination of consumer decision-making. Because of prevailing natality and mortality conditions, the populations of developing countries are relatively young.[5] Consequently, much of the potential market, even for established products, consists of new buyers without firm preferences for specific brands of products (Leff and Farley 1980). The "teenage market" is very limited, however, despite the fact that demographically it comprises a sizeable portion of the population. Consumer decision-making depends partly on the fact that the father, in accordance with Islamic traditions, protects and provides for the entire family. The family members, in return, are to respect all the father's wishes and remain psychologically and physically under his domain. Obligations towards parents are sacred. From a marketing standpoint, questions may be raised as to the amount of a teenager's discretionary income. The tradition of deference to parental wishes is likely to affect buying patterns in clothing and leisure expenditure especially as it is normal to live at home until marriage. Products and promotional messages must be designed recognizing the authority of the father with respect to most family purchases. According to Luqmani et al. (1980), the image of functional products could be enhanced with advertisements that stress parental advice or approval; even with children's products, there should be less emphasis on children as decision makers. In addition, advertising appeals based on Western values of youthful looks and energy are likely to be less successful in Egypt where the older generation, in general, is much more respected. Signs of old age may be helpful; grey hair, for example, can represent wisdom through experience (Pezeshkpur 1978).

5 The population growth rate in Egypt for the period 1975–80 was 2.6% per annum; life expectancy at birth in 1979 was 75 years and the percentage of the population under 15 years of age in 1970 was 40% (Statistical Digest 1981; United Nations Statistical Yearbook 1981).

The position of women in Egypt can only be understood in the religious context of Egyptian society which has emphasized the seclusion of women and their domestic roles. Improved educational opportunities have increased their social and occupational mobility in recent years, but although women constitute about a third of total enrollment in universities, in the field of education as in other areas of Egyptian society, female emancipation is still in its early stages. The Islamic influence includes an obligation to conform to codes of sexual conduct and social interaction which may include modest dress for women in public. More colorful clothing and accessories are worn by women at home, however, so promotion of products for use in private homes could be more intimate – such audiences could be reached effectively through women's magazines (Luqmani et al. 1980). The use of magazines as a communications medium would necessarily be confined to educated women. In general, Western-style advertising using scantily-clothed models or sexual connotations may be offensive to the target market. Communications strategies, therefore, should avoid immodest exposure and sexual connotations in public settings.

Selling techniques must be adapted to the local culture if they are to succeed. The Egyptian culture is characterized by a much slower pace of life. What takes one day to accomplish in North America or Europe may take a week in Egypt. Attitudes towards doing business emphasize the importance of personal relationships (Fleming 1981). Arbose (1982) attributed the success of Japanese salesmen in Egypt to their appreciation of the local attitudes towards doing business. For example, the Japanese are more polite, patient, efficient, flexible, alert, neat and generous than their Western counterparts. The Japanese salesmen wait patiently and know the different attitudes Middle Easterners have towards time. It is advised by Business America (November 15, 1982) that such a patient style of market development usually leads to successful business dealings in Egypt. Furthermore, the fundamental Islamic concept of worship (five times a day while the timing of prayers varies) means that the foreign marketer has to take into account the variability and shift in prayer timings in planning sales calls, work schedules, business hours and customer traffic (Luqmani et al. 1980).

15.5 Conclusion

This paper has assessed the marketing problems and opportunities faced by international marketers in Egypt. The most common problems are caused by the following: the existence of a dual economy; government trade and economic policies and the risks of policy reversals; dealing with the Egyptian bureaucracy; an underdeveloped and unfamiliar marketing infrastructure; and a socio-cultural environment strongly influenced by Islamic tradition. Every aspect of the marketing function is affected; from market assessment, marketing research and market entry to the marketing mix variables, marketing organization and control. Specific marketing implications will, of course, depend on industry, product and firm characteristics. A number of general recommendations for international marketers are listed below:

a) The coexistence of modern and traditional sectors in Egypt's economy affects the market size for many goods. Market assessments must be conducted for each sector.

b) As it is difficult and costly to exploit market opportunities in rural areas, firms could concentrate on the markets in the urban centres, e.g., Cairo, Alexandria.

c) Because of the trade deficit, high inflation rates and a weak currency, there are import restrictions on many consumer goods. It is advisable to market products which satisfy governmental as well as consumer demands.

d) A good marketing information system should be maintained to minimize planning uncertainty arising from frequent ministerial changes.

e) The use of agents with influence in high places can help avoid bureaucratic delays.

f) A trustworthy and experienced Egyptian partner can help a firm to become familiar with local trading practices and gain control over the lengthy distribution channels.

g) Marketing research efforts should concentrate on obtaining primary data; available secondary data are out of date or not conceptually useful for marketing. It is also advisable to deal with an Egyptian marketing research agency, preferably on employing consultants who also have experience in the West, to facilitate language and cultural translation of research instruments.

h) Cultural adaptation of products is increasingly important as Islamic revivalism could limit market growth rates of Western consumer goods.

i) Limited managerial control over prices because of governmental control necessitates the use of non-price marketing mix variables to attract customers.

j) Relatively low literacy rates and low TV and radio ownership suggest the use of poster advertising with pictures or cinema advertising.

k) The international marketer must also appreciate the need to develop an understanding of the Egyptian business culture (slow pace, the importance of personal relationships, the influence of Islamic beliefs) and act accordingly.

The problems are typical of those encountered in all the countries of the Middle East. The importance of the different aspects of a company's external environment (social, economic, technological and so on) will vary according to different national markets, however. The implication for the international marketer is that he or she should develop an awareness or sensitivity to local conditions. The success of the multinational marketing manager will be measured by his or her abilities to appreciate environmental similarities and differences and to formulate his strategies accordingly.

Part Four
The Future of International Business in the Middle East

Chapter 16
Future Directions for Marketing and Management in the Middle East

Erdener Kaynak

16.1 Introduction

In 1980, among the top 27 importing Third World Countries of the World, ten of them were from the Middle East region. Saudi Arabia ranked first with $30 billion, Iraq was eighth ($13 billion), Algeria was thirteenth ($10.7 billion) and Libya was fifteenth with $9.9 billion worth of imports (Sinclair 1982). Table 16.1 depicts main Third World importers in 1980 and also clearly indicates the prominent place of some of the countries of Arab Middle East.

In the future, Middle Eastern business in order to grow and prosper will develop new policies and strategies regarding socio-economic and technological growth, horizontal and vertical integration, the common market, consumerism, competition and monopolies and foreign investments in the local market as well as in other Arab countries (El Naggar 1980:83). Above all, the spread of advanced management techniques in the Middle East will be a critical factor in determining the course of the regions development over the remainder of this century. As economies of the region grow, marketing will develop to fulfill the needs of different economies. One can easily postulate that the development of marketing institutions as well as management practices of Middle Eastern firms will parallel the stages of countries' economic development. The more developed a Middle Eastern economy, the greater the variety of marketing functions demanded, and the more sophisticated and specialized the institutions become to perform the needed marketing functions (Saddik 1973:80–81).

Having concentrated on basic infrastructure projects during late 1960s and 1970s, Arab Countries of the Middle East are now in a position to seek real business development opportunities during the 1980s and beyond. The most significant trend in the business sector development of Arab states of the

Exhibit 16/1: Main Third World Importers in 1980

Ranking	Country	$ Billion	% of Total	Cumulative %
1	Saudi Arabia	30,171	5.6	5.6
2	Brazil	25,002	4.7	10.3
3	Singapore	24,007	4.5	14.8
4	South Korea	22,297	4.2	19.0
5	Mexico	19,460	3.6	22.6
6	Nigeria	16,688	3.2	25.8
7	India	14,131	2.6	28.4
8	Iraq	13,048	2.4	30.8
9	Iran	12,246	2.3	33.1
10	Venezuela	11,155	2.1	35.2
11	Indonesia	10,834	2.0	37.2
12	Malaysia	10,820	2.0	39.2
13	Algeria	10,714	2.0	41.2
14	Libya	9,870	1.8	43.0
15	Thailand	9,214	1.7	44.7
16	United Arab Emirates	8,746	1.6	46.3
17	Philippines	8,241	1.5	47.8
18	Turkey	7,667	1.4	49.2
19	Argentina	6,600*	1.2	50.4
20	Chile	5,821	1.1	51.5
21	Pakistan	5,350	1.0	52.5
22	Egypt	4,860	0.9	53.4
23	Colombia	4,739	0.9	54.3
24	Kuwait	4,457	0.8	55.1
25	Morocco	4,261	0.8	55.9
26	Syria	4,124	0.7	56.6
27	Tunisia	3,540	0.7	57.3

* 1979

Source: Stuart Sinclair: The State of the Third World in 1982. In: Third World Economic Handbook Euromonitor Publications Limited, London (1982:12)

Middle East will be the rapid development of the non-oil sector of their economies. Although most countries of the region will use oil as a source of revenue, manufacturing and service industries will be the two sectors to develop at an accelerating rate during the coming decade. It is anticipated that the petro chemical and agricultural industries will be the two fastest growing manufacturing industries in the region by the end of this decade. Under the service sector, banking will have further growth so will other service industries like insurance, shipping and transportation.

As a result of this intense activity in the region, joint-venture projects have started to appear in the Middle East business arena. For instance, spectacular oil price increases over the years have given oil producing states the financial resources to start companies like First Arabian. As well, Kuwait Petroleum Corporation (KPC) the world's sixth largest oil company bought Santa Fe International-an oil drilling and engineering concern in 1981. This $ 2.5 billion acquisition of Santa Fe was a key element in the long standing plan of Kuwait to build KPC into a position of greater global dominance (Erdilek 1984:47). All these new Arab transnationals have developed unique ways of doing business, the trend has been for them to do business with companies in smaller countries rather than those of the major powers.

Most of the Middle Eastern countries have also enacted foreign investment laws and developed new management systems. Historical market skills are being adapted to new marketing and investment opportunities. Transferring modern and contemporary Western technologies has resulted in vocational and management training programs for indegenous managers and employees. For instance, a Foreign Capital Investment Code was decreed in Saudi Arabia in 1964. Accordingly, foreign investment was to be encouraged for non-oil economic development projects approved by the Foreign Investment Capital Committee.

16.2 Various Patterns of Development

The world will witness a tremendous change and transformation in the Middle East region in the near future. This change, unlike most previous occurrences, will take place in a more planned and orderly manner. In light of the constant structural changes taking place in the Middle East, there is need for a better coordination in socio-economic development policies among the various countries of the region. More emphasis will be given to manufacturing and processing sectors.

When one looks at the countries of the Arab Middle East, one discerns different types and degrees of development. For instance, countries like Kuwait and Saudi Arabia, which are very much dependent on oil revenue, are eager to speed up growth in economic sectors other than oil in order to diversify. Kuwait adopted the policy of encouraging foreign investment so as to attract the most highly developed technology and greatest expertise in non-oil sectors (Geyikdagi 1984:18). For instance, North American manufacturing companies are well placed to assist countries of the Middle East in utilizing computers, satellite monitoring, and breeding techniques to improve the region's food supply; in adopting microelectronic technology to decentralize production so that new manufacturing techniques can be integrated into rural societies; in dividing limited resources between telecommunications and transport which would enable villages and small industries to derive more benefits from new developments in communications technology (Roche 1980:9).

The various development funds that have been set up to spread Arab oil money among the various Arab countries should see to it that duplication is avoided as much as possible and that eventually an Arab common market is formed where each Arab country will specialize, under adequate protection in what it can produce best.

16.3 Business Policy Guidelines

In an effort to bring about the desired changes in the business system of Arab countries, the structure of their interdependence will have to be strengthened in the future through the potential transformations in the economies of Arab oil producing countries as well as by the overseas investment activities of these countries. It is stated that the course of events shaping the international environment of business during the next decade or two will be determined by a matrix of interdependent decisions: a) within Arab countries (Mainly OPEC countries), b) within Western countries (mainly oil importing countries), c) between the two groups (Sherbiny 1975:115–116).

16.4 Within Arab Countries

Understanding Arab consumers be it institutional or final is essential. As a result, consumer behavior studies and cross-cultural investigations of Arab consumers is highly desirable. To this end, there is a need for marketing executives to probe more deeply into why consumers behave in a certain way as well as how they behave. The existence of sub-cultures within the Arab world, and the speed and scope of change in the region is of paramount importance. Employing Arab nationals in more senior management positions will enhance the credibility of a Western firm. By doing so, Western companies not only will be more sensitive to consumer needs, this will also be an effective way of building up enduring business relationships with local companies. The business decision makers of the world have a role to play here and as such they should scrutinize most carefully the available opportunities for industrial investments in the Middle East region. Through this process, they will find out that many feasible projects can be identified and many profitable joint ventures can be established.

As well, there is need to plan and increase production so as to satisfy basic needs of the masses especially in poorer Middle Eastern countries. This could be achieved within a foreseeable future by using labor-intensive marketing and management techniques wherever appropriate (Meissner 1978:16).

16.5 Within Western Countries

Western companies need to approach cultural problems encountered in the Middle East in an organized, systematic way. As well, confrontation should be avoided as much as possible by establishing orderly accommodations among countervailing powers in negotiating prices and supply of raw materials. Although advanced management theories, concepts and techniques have been transferred from the West to the Arab Middle East with a reasonable record of success; but we cannot say the same for the transfer of management practices. In general it is rather difficult, at least in the foreseeable future to superimpose advanced management systems on societies who put more emphasis on human relationships and traditional values. For the time being, Western management and marketing techniques should not be transferred blindfolded for implementation in the Middle East setting (Badawy 1980:58). What is needed is an evolutionary type of adaptations rather than revolutionary changes.

16.6 Between the Two Groups

Certain countries like Britain, Sweden and Canada have a good cultural affinity and political links with Arab countries. These countries will have a competitive advantage which they could exploit more fully.

Most Middle Eastern countries, if not all, are in dire need to acquire advanced technology from the West. In most cases, foreign direct investment by multinational companies is the best way of transferring technology to the Middle East. As a result, countries of the region will provide Western firms with more and more incentives for manufacturing and processing investments.

As pointed out previously in this text that Arab managers favor a traditional managerial approach influenced by their culture, history and traditions. Western managers and multinationals doing business in the Middle East will have to be alert to the prevailing fundamental differences that exist between Arab managers and their Western counterparts. That is to say, understanding the cultural dimensions of communication – cultural empathy – is crucial in becoming successful in the region.

As succinctly put by Ajami (1979:139) in his thought provoking book – Arab Response to the Multinationals – the Arab countries see their relation with the Western industrial economies as one of a mutually advantageous bargain: raw materials for Western technology. The capital-surplus states in the Arab world are determined to move from supplying raw materials to manufacturing stages. This is the most important issue between these states and the multinationals. If this is successfully and smoothly managed, the already strong ties between the Arab countries and the multinationals will become even more durable and resilient.

In general every country needs rich oil-producing countries of the Middle East more than they need them and this trend will likely to continue for many years to come. Continued huge increases in the export rates of crude are unlikely to prolong, even though building capacity to export will proceed. For the rest of the decade crude exports are likely to be reduced. This trend, if materialized, will have an adverse effect on Western firms who are trying to market products and services to the region.

16.7 Future Market Scenarios in the Middle East

During the next decade, we will observe a tremendous change in consumer markets of the region. Successful marketing and business in the Middle East will be based on the ability to recognize new trends in consumer demand or help create new needs and take advantage of market conditions by developing the right product, at the right price and offer it at the right time.

The total population of Arab Middle East will increase 14.8 percent by 1990 and 28.2 percent by the year 2000. Not only will we see a tremendous growth in population of the region, we will also witness increases in adult literacy rate as well as increases in percentage of population of working age. Although incomes generated in the region will increase substantially and the real earnings of the population will double by 1990 creating higher standards of living.

In 1981 of the total $ 360 billion GNP created in the region, 11.5 percent is allocated to defense budget. It is expected that most countries of the region will still spend a substantial amounts of money on defense for armament purposes in the future. This situation, will, of course, adversely affect consumers' ability to buy certain other products. The standard of living as well as the living conditions of the population of the Middle East will improve rapidly. For instance, in the last two decades, most consumers of the region through mass media have been exposed to Western products/ services as well as to foreign habits. As well, the development of the organized travel industry will induce more travelling activity among middle and lower income earner Arabs. This activity, in turn, will equip these masses with newer tastes and purchasing patterns. In light of these changes, Western firms who do succeed will have spent sufficient time in trying to assess and understand conditions and develop products which meet the requirements of the new changing consumers of the Middle East.

In addition to changes in the socio-economic characteristics of consumers, we will also witness some substantial changes and developments in the marketing and business scene of the region. The major developments in the area of management and marketing can be summarized as follows (Vassiliou 1980:149–150).

a) The influx of increasing number of foreign suppliers who will be competing in more sophisticated markets of the Middle East. Because of increased importance of manufacturing and service industries in the region during the next decade, suppliers of capital goods and service companies will be in a better position.

b) It is estimated that not only will we see the increasing proliferation of retail stores, specialization of the retail trade will be the watchword of the

Middle Eastern distribution system. With increases in numbers and spread over the whole countries of the region, the larger stores will gain more prominence. With the emergence of vertical and horizontal integrations in the channel, for the majority of products, there will be fewer links in the distribution chain. It is also anticipated that most wholesalers will import on their own account and would perform direct distribution activities. In certain countries of the region laws require local agents or distributors to take part in importation of goods in the country. For instance ARAMCO routed 70 percent of its purchases through Saudi vendors in 1981.

c) With increased competition in the home market, the large indigeneous trading houses will change their structure and the organizational set-up as well as management methods and procedures utilized by these companies will look more and more like Western trading houses. For efficiency and growth, they will also have to diversify into different product/market areas. Limited market potential at home will force some of these companies to move overseas markets where market growth is not limited. Multinational Arab corporations will consolidate more power in Western societies by consolidating their power base as well as diversifying their product portfolios. It is anticipated that by the end of 1980s, the Middle East Market will be controlled by those companies which have reacted positively to recent developments and changes in the socio-economic, cultural, governmental and technological environments as well as the market conditions of the region and have adapted rapidly to the new conditions.

d) With proliferation of goods and services and creation of buyers' market conditions, increased demand for consumer protection will arise. In the first instance, we will see the active role of governments in the region in regulating the marketing of goods and services as well as educating consumers to be more knowledgeable and well-informed. Another area which will attract increased government and public interest will concern the protection of environment. Most governments of the Middle East will enact anti-pollution and environmental safety legislations to protect not only their natural resources, they will also ensure safety of their citizens. This move on the part of Middle East governments will have certain implications for Western firms which are marketing their products into the region.

e) The role of State trading in the Middle East markets is constantly increasing. Governments as well as the public agencies in the region get involved in foreign trade as entrepreneurs. Marketing products to governments or related agencies has, of course, its peculiarities throughout the Middle East, whether free market or public sector economies. In Lebanon, for instance, the government does almost all of its purchasing through bids, and generally only local suppliers. Lebanon-based representatives of foreign firms are allowed to bid directly. In Saudi Arabia, contracts are generally closed to foreign bidders (Business International 1975:180).

These enterprises particularly conduct foreign trade operations in goods which are destined for resale. The expansion of State trading in the Middle East will likely modify the role of multinational firms in the international trade of commodities in the region. However, in recent years, there are indications that many Arab State traders have recognized the multinationals' power and expertise in international marketing and now are seeking cooperation rather than counteracting. It is expected that this partnership will increase in the future for the mutual benefit of the parties. One positive fruit of this cooperation between Western multinationals and State enterprise of the Middle East is the formation of joint ventures and emergence of foreign direct investment by some Arab companies.

f) Western firms in doing business in the Middle East should thoroughly understand their own and the company's goals and foreign situations and establish appropriate objectives acceptable for both parties. Second, they must understand Arab business procedures in order to develop expectations regarding their time table for attaining objectives. Third, understand and adapt to the specific cultural differences existing in the Middle East in order to build and maintain effective interpersonal relationships. Fourth, choose a field representative who has the personal characteristics necessary for success in the specific Arab country and provide enough flexibility for the representative to adapt when necessary to accomplish long-term goals.

To this end, Western companies trying to market their products to the region should attempt to find out if their products have a current and potential demand in particular Arab markets. Should there be markets, what is the size and extent of that demand? What characteristics and specifications specific company products must have in order to be acceptable in Arab markets of the Middle East. As well, the nature of the pricing and commission structure existing for their products in the region need to be delineated.

In stimulating passive exporters as well as non-exporter North American and West European manufacturers to become involved with more trading with Arab countries of the Middle East, certain steps need to be taken by business firms as well as Governmental agencies. These steps are summarized below.

a) How can Western manufacturing/service firms at varying stages of international business involvement with the Middle East be identified? Detailed profiles of Western manufacturers at different stages of trade development with Arab countries need to be prepared.

b) What types of Western manufacturing/service firms should be targeted for export stimulation and promotion by governmental agencies? One would expect differences in terms of types of assistance required between small and large exporters, as well as between exporter and non-exporter manufacturers in Western world.

c) What types of marketing programs would be most appropriate in reaching and serving the particular needs of Arab Middle East? For instance, the purchase decision criteria are relatively alike in the region. Brand reputation comes first, with delivery number two, and after sales parts and service the third factor and price is the least important.

d) Trade information services of Western governmental agencies should be improved. Most specifically, specific information requirements of local companies must be borne in mind. Furthermore, in an effort to serve the information needs of companies, supply/demand studies should be carried out.

e) The determination of long-run export promotions and development objectives and policies is needed. All strategic planning should have a marketing orientation. This is to say that all company export objectives, policies and programmes should always be directed towards the immediate or ultimate satisfaction of customers in the Middle East export markets – customer-orientation.

f) Customer-oriented export policy requires important institutional changes. Western manufacturing/service firms must be exposed to the environment of the Arab market of the Middle East more directly and more readily. Marketing executives of the West should probe more deeply into why consumers behave in a certain way as well how they behave. The existence of subcultures within the Arab world must be reckoned with.

g) There ist also an important human element of customer-oriented export policy. Owners and/or managers of Western firms must be trained and educated and they should be convinced of the advantages of serving the needs of the Arab markets of the Middle East. This will necessitate a change in attitude and understanding on the part of manufacturers as well as willingness to understand the nature and demands of foreign markets. To bring about this needed change in manufacturers' outlook, universities, research organizations, media as well as individual governments could shoulder additional responsibilities.

h) Consumer behavior studies and cross cultural investigation of Arab consumers is highly recommended for those companies which have substantial Middle East involvement.

i) The present institutional set-up for exports and foreign trade in the West needs to be strengthened and upgraded. The specialized support system and the available infrastructural services related to the export need to improve.

j) To be able to compete successfully in the Middle Eastern markets, more product and market diversification among manufacturers of North America and West Europe must take place.

k) The importance of cultural factors in doing business in the Middle East is rather high. As well, economic factors and in many cases political factors were also regarded as even more important in the Arab world. Companies are recommended to approach environmental problems in an organized systematic manner.

l) Western companies are well adviced to consider employing Arab nationals in more senior managements positions. This will be perceived as a positive gesture by Arab companies.

References

Abdel-Meguid, A. (1978): Negotiations with Arab Countries. Wall Street Journal, (December 21): 14–15.

Abdelnasser, G. (1963): United Arab Republic. Information Department, Cairo, 27.

Abdelwahed, F. H. (1973): The Role of Public Policy Toward Inland Surface Transportation in Egypt. Unpublished PhD Dissertation, University of California, Los Angeles, 62.

Abdelwahed, F. H. (1978): Egypt's Road to a Mixed Economy. International Management Review 18,1: 24.

Abegglen, James C., and William V. Rapp (1973): Japanese Managerial Behavior and Excessive Competition. Multinational Business, Michigan State University, Division of Research, 72.

Abu-Gomaa, N. H. A. (1974): Marketing Policies in the Textile Industry. MSc Dissertation, Assuit University, Egypt.

Abuljobain, Nadim (1981): How to Sell Successfully in the Middle East. International Management 36,10: 61–63.

Adams, Charles (1974): How To Talk Business With Arabs. Forbes 114,6 (September 15): 106–110.

Advertising Age (1977): Elaborating on Issues. Problems for Marketers 48,28 (July 11): 76, 78–79.

Agarwal, J. P. (1984): Intra-LDCs Foreign Investment, A Comparative Analysis of Third World Multinationals. Kiel, Institute of World Economics Working Paper No. 198.

Ajami, Riad A. (1979): Arab Response to the Multinationals. Praeger, New York.

Ajami, Riad A. (1980): The Multinationals and Arab Economic Development. A New Paradigm. Journal of Contemporary Business 9,3: 3–20.

Ajami, Riad A. (1980): Multinationals and Host Arab Society, Management International Review 20: 1.

Albeik, Matt A. H. (1984): Marketing in Egypt and Libya – An Overview. In: Atlantic Canada Resources Management: Issues and Answers. Halifax, Nova Scotia, (October) 26–27: iii-10 to iii-17.

Algahanim, Kutabya (1976): How to Do Business in the Middle East. Management Review 65, 8: 19–28.

Al-Jafary, Abdulrahman, and A. T. Hollingsworth (1983): An Exploratory Study of Managerial Practices in the Arabian Gulf Region. Journal of International Business Studies 14: 143–152.

Ali, Abbas J. (1982): An Empirical Investigation of Managerial Value Systems for Working in Iraq. Unpublished Doctoral Dissertation, West Virginia University.

Almaney, A. J. (1981): Cultural Traits of the Arabs: Growing Interest for International Management. Management International Review 21, 3: 10–18.

Almaney, A. J. (1982): How Arabs See the West. Business Horizons 25, 5 (September–October): 11–17.

Al-Muathen, M. S. (1977): Marketing in Developing Countries – The Iraqi Situation. PhD Dissertation, Department of Marketing, University of Strathclyde, Glasgow.

Al Nimir, aud, and Monte Palmer (1982): Bureaucracy and Development in Saudi Arabia: A Behavioral Analysis. Public Administration and Development 2, 2 (April–June): 93–104.

Al Quraishi, and H. E. Abdulaziz (1980): Managing Saudi Arabia's Reserve Funds. Journal of Contemporary Business 9, 3: 31–39.

Amine, Lyn S., Edward Vitale and S. Tamer Cavusgil (1983): Launching a Weaning Food in a Developing Country: The Moroccan Experience. European Journal of Marketing 17, 5: 44–54.

Anastos, Dennis, A. Bedos, and B. Seaman (1980): The Development of Modern Management Practices in Saudi Arabia. The Columbia Journal of World Business 15, 2 (Summer): 81–93.

Arabs Own Little U.S. Land (1979): Middle East Economic Digest (October 19): 20.

Arbose, Jules (1977): Running Saudi Arabia's Biggest Trading Group. International Management 32, 5: 11–13.

Arbose, Jules (1979): The Middle East Mirage. International Management 34, 4: 20–24.

Arbose, Jules (1981): How to Sell Successfully in the Middle East. International Management 36, 10: 61–63.

Arbose, Jules (1982): Wise men from the East bearing gifts. International Management (May): 67–68.

Arvey, R. D., H. D. Dewhirsty, and E. Brown (1978): A Longitudinal Study of the Impact of Changes in Goal Setting on Employee Satisfaction. Personnel Psychology 31: 595–608.

Asfour, E. Y. (1972): Prospects and Problems of Economic Development of Saudi Arabia, Kuwait, and the Gulf Principalities. In: C. A. Cooper and S. S. Alexander (eds.): Economic Development and Population Growth in the Middle East, New York: Elsevier.

Askar, Samir A. (1979): Personal Value Systems of Egyptian Managers. Unpublished Doctoral Dissertation, Mississippi State University, vii.

Askari, H., and J. T. Cummings (1976): Middle East Economies in the 1970s: A Comparative Approach, Praeger, New York.

Austen, A. (1977): The Relevance of Marketing to Developing Countries, Paper presented to the Marketing Education Group of the United Kingdom and North Regional Workshop, (June). 1.

Ayubi, Mazih, N. M. (1982): Bureaucratic Inflation and Administrative Inefficiency: The Deadlock in Egyptian Administration. Middle Eastern Studies 18, 3: 186–229.

Badawy, M. K. (1956): The Future of Culture in Arab Society. In: La Queue (ed.): 462–477.

Badawy, M. K. (1979): Managerial Attitudes and Need Orientations of Mid-Eastern executives: An Empirical Cross-Cultural Analysis, Academy of Management Proceeding. Atlanta, GA (August): 243–247.

Badawy, M. K. (1980): Styles of Mideastern Managers. California Management Review 22, 2 (Spring): 51–58.

Baker, M. J. (1979): Marketing: An Introductory Text, 3rd ed; London: The Macmillan Press Ltd.: 389.

Baker, M. J., and A. B. El-Haddad (1981): Marketing and Economic Growth. Paper presented at the Annual Meeting of the European Academy for Advanced Research in Marketing, Copenhagen, Denmark, (March).

Bedore, James M. (1978): Saudi Arabia in a Changing World. National Westminster Bank Quarterly Review (February): 13–23.

Beehr, Terry A., and J. E. Newman (1978): Job Stress, Employee Health, and Organizational Effectiveness: A Fact Analysis, Model, and Literature Review, Personnel Psychology 31: 665–699.

Beehr, Terry A., and John A. Drexter (1983): The Relationships Between Role Stressors and Job Satisfaction: Social Support, Job Characteristics, and hierarchical Position as Moderators. Paper presented at the 26th annual meeting of the midwest Academy of management. Kalamazoo, MI (April).

Bell, James A., and Carl Leiden (1974): The Middle East: Politics and Power, Boston: Allyn and Bacon, Inc.

Bendix, Reinhard (1978): Kings or People: Power and the Mandate to Rule. Berkeley. University of California Press.

Berger, Monroe (1971): The Arabs' Attitude to the West. The Yale Review 61, 2 (December): 207–225.

Bhagst, Rabi S., and Sara J. McQuaid (1982): Role of Subjective Culture in Organizations: A Review and Directions for Future Research. Journal of Applied Psychology Monography 67 (October): 653–685.

Bilkey, Warren, and Eric Nes (1982): Country of Origin Effects on Product Evaluations. Journal of International Business Studies XIII, 1 (Spring/Summer): 89–99.

Boyd, Harper, W., Abdel Aziz El Sherbini, and A. F. Sherif (1961): Channels of Distribution for Consumer Goods in Egypt. Journal of Marketing 25 (October): 26–33.

Boyd, Harper, W. A. A. El Sherbini, and A. F. Sherif (1961): Egypt's Need for Marketing Management. Business Horizons 4, 2 (Summer): 77–84.

Bradley, David G. (1977): Managing Against Expropriation. Harvard Business Review (July–August): 75–83.

Brasch, John J. (1978): Sales Forecasting Difficulties in a Developing Country. Industrial Marketing Management 7: 354–360.

Brewer, Thomas L. (1983): The Instability of Governments and the Instability of Controls on Funds Transfers by Multinational Enterprises. Journal of International Business Studies (Winter): 147–157.

Brewer, Thomas L. (1983): Political Sources of Risk in the International Money Markets. Journal of International Business Studies (Spring/Summer): 161–164.

Brown, L. Dean, (1976): Perspectives on the Middle East. The Conference Board Record 13,2 (February): 38–40.

Business America (1979): Adapting Export Packaging. (December) 3: 1–7.

Business America (1982): Strong U.S. Interest Sustains Our Share of Import Market. (August 9): 31–2.

Business America (1982): EGYPT Adequate Market Research and Financial Support should Result in Successful Ventures for U.S. Firms. (November 15): 28–30.

Business America (1982): Strong U.S. Interest Sustains Our Share of Import Market. (August 9): 31–32.

Business America (1983): Egypt U.S. Traders and Investors Will Find a Strong Market. (August 20): 50.

Business International (1980): Egypt Opportunities for Suppliers and Investors. Business International (July).

Business Prospects in the Middle East (1975): Business International S.A., Geneva (April): 3–4, 165–183.

Business, Week (1979): Egypt: Teaching Bureaucrats That 'Time is Money' (December 31): 48 and 5.

Buss, M. D. J. (1982): Managing International Information Systems, Harvard Business Review (September–October): 153–162.

Button, K. R. (1978): Marketing in Egypt, Overseas Business Report, United States Department of Commerce, Industry and Trade Administration.

Campbell, D. I. (1982): Canada's Natural Advantage in Saudi Arabia. The Canadian Business Review (Autumn): 25–28.

Carter, Glen (1980): Modern Marketing Research in An Arab Environment. Paper Presented at the 33rd ESOMAR Congress Taking Stock: What Have We Learned and Where Are We Going? Monte-Carlo 14th–18th (September).

Cateora, Philip R. (1983): International Marketing (Homewood, Illinois: Richard D. Irwin, Fifth Edition).

Charlton, Jacqueline (1983): Employee Participation in the Public Sector: A Review. Journal of General Management 8: 62–78.

Comparative Study of Development Plans of Arab States (1976): United Nations, New York.

Consulting Aims to Train Saudis, (1979): Middle East Economic Digest (October 19): 45.

Cook, K. H. H. (1979): The Middle East. In: Felix Wentworth and Martin Christopher (eds.): Managing International Distribution, Gower Press, London: 161–171.

Copulsky, William (1959): Forecasting Sales in Underdeveloped Countries. Journal of Marketing 24, 1 (July): 36–40.

Corcoran, Kevin (1979): Britain's Mid-East Misses, Management Today (February): 90–94.

Cremeans, Charles D. (1963): The Arabs and the World. Praeger Publishers Inc., New York.

Cross-Fertilization with Algeria's Technocrats. Business Quarterly 45, 4 (Winter) 1980: 7–12.

D'Ambrosio, C. A. (1976): Principles of Modern Investments. Chicago: Science Research Associates.

Daniels, J. D., E. W. Ogram, Jr., and L. H. Radebaugh (1982): International Business: Environment and Operations, Reading, Mass.: Addison-Wesley Publishing Company.

Davis, L. E., and E. S. Valfer (1966): Studies in Supervisory Job Design. Human Relations 19: 339–352.

Dawson, Leslie M. (1982): Opportunities for Small Business in Third World Markets. American Journal of Small Business 7, 1 (July–September): 20.

De la Torre, Jose (1973): Product Life-Cycle as a Determinant of Global Marketing Strategies. In: Thomas V. Greer (ed.): Increasing Marketing Productivity and Conceptual and Methodological Foundations of Marketing. AMA Combined Proceedings Series 35: 76–82.

Devlet Planlama Teskilati Bulteni (1980): (State Planning Organization Bulletin) Ankara, Turkey: 65.

Dobson, Wendy (1979): Exports to Developing Countries: An Opportunity for Canada. C. D. Howe Research Institute, (July) 20: 2.

Douglas, Susan P., and B. Dubois (1977): Looking at the Cultural Environment for International Marketing Opportunities. Columbia Journal of World Business 12, 4 (Winter): 102–109.

Douglas, Susan P., and C. Samuel Craig (1982): Marketing Research in the International Environment. In: Ingo Walter, ed.: Handbook of International Business, New York: John Wiley and Sons, Inc.

Douglas, S. P., C. S. Craig and W. J. Keegan (1982): Approaches to Assessing International Marketing Opportunities For Small and Medium-Sized Companies. Columbia Journal of World Business 17, 3 (Fall): 26–31.

Douglas, Susan, P., and Yoram Wind (1973–1974): Environmental Factors and Marketing Practices. European Journal of Marketing 7, 3: 155–165.

Drucker, P. (1958): Marketing and Economic Development. Journal of Marketing 22, 1: 252–259.

Dunn, Dan T., Jr. (1979): Agents and Distributing in the Middle East. Business Horizons 22, 5 (October): 69–78.

Duran, J. J. (1983): Country Risk Evaluation by International Financial Markets. Proceedings of the World Marketing Congress (ed. E. Kaynak, Halifax, Nova Scotia, Canada).

Economist (1983): Foreign Investment in Egypt. Open door, empty room (July 2): 64–65.

Eid, Nimr (1978): The Marketing Process with Special Reference to Lebanon, London: Longman Group Limited.

Eilts, Hermann F. (1982): Islamic Resurgence and American Business in the Middle East. In: The International Essays for Business Decision Makers. Edited by Mark B. Winchester, The Center for International Business: Dallas, TX, VI: 241–252.

El-Adly, Yousef A. (1980): The Effects of Inflation on Kuwaiti Corporate Financial Statements. Journal of Contemporary Business 9, 3: 109–122.

Elbashier, A. M. and J. R. Nicholls (1983): Export Marketing in the Middle East: The Importance of Cultural Differences. Journal of International Marketing 2, 1: 68–81.

Elbashier, A. M., and J. R. Nicholls (1983): Export Marketing to the Arab World: The Importance of Cultural Differences; Graham and Trotman, London.

El-Buruni, Massoud Y. (1980): Personal Value Systems of Libyan Managers: An Exploratory Study. Unpublished Doctoral Dissertation, Saint Louis University: 208–210.

El-Dirghami, A. F. (1979): The Impact of the Open-Door Policy on Marketing in the Public Sector Companies. Paper presented at the Conference on the Open-Door Policy and the Management of the Public Sector, Central Agency for Organization and Administration, Cairo, (May).

El-Ghazali, A. H. (1973): Planning for Economic Development: A Comparative Case of Indian and Egyptian Experiences, 1946–1972 (Cairo: The Modern Cairo Bookshop): 200.

El-Haddad, A. B. (1980): Marketing and Economic Growth: An Analysis of the Contribution of Marketing to Economic Growth in Developing Countries with Reference to Egypt. Ph. D. Thesis, Department of Marketing, Strathclyde University, Glasgow, Scotland, U.K.: 336–342.

Elliott House, Karen (1983): Modern Arabia. Wall Street Journal LXI, 163 (June 4): 15–16.

El Naggar, Fareed R. (1980): Middle Eastern Business Intensity and Market Growth (1970–1980); An Overview, Journal of Contemporary Business 9, 3: 71–84.

El-Sherbini, A. E. (1964): Some Basic Characteristics of Egyptian Market. National Institute of Management Development, Cairo, 5.

Elton, E. J., and M. J. Grumber (1981): Modern Portfolio Theory and Investment Analysis. New York: John Wiley & Sons.

Epstein, T. Scarlett (1982): Urban Food Marketing and Third World Rural Development, London: Croom Helm Publishers.

Erdilek, A. (1978): Institutional Arrangements in the Transfer of Foreign Industrial Technology to Turkey: Mission Findings and Suggestions. UNIDO Report for the Government of Turkey, Ankara, United Nations Development Program in Turkey.

Erdilek, A. (1982): Direct Foreign Investment in Turkish Manufacturing: An Analysis of the Conflicting Objectives and Frustrated Expectations of a Host Country, J. C. B. Mohr (Paul Siebeck), Tübingen.

Erdilek, A. (1984): International Technology Transfer in the Middle East and North Africa, Management Decision 22, 2: 45–49.

Eren, Nuri (1963): Turkey Today and Tomorrow: An Experiment in Westernization, New York: Frederic A. Praeger.

Etzioni, Amitai (1964): Modern Organizations, Englewood Cliffs, N. J.: Prentice-Hall, 106.

Export Trade (1981): Ticaret. Special Issue 2 (Fall): 8.

Fahey, Liam, and W. R. King (1977): Environmental Scanning for Corporate Planning. Business Horizons 20 (August): 61–71.

Fairlamb, David, and H. Sender (1983): How Good are Country Risk Forecasters? Dun's Business Month (May): 66–71.

Fayerweather, John (1983): Four Winning Strategies For the International Corporation. The Journal of Business Strategy 2, 1: 68–81.

Fazel, Mohammed, and Jan-Ole Ray (1977): Business Culture in the Middle East: The Case of Iran, Stockholm: Scandinavian Institute for Administrative Research.

Fazel, Mohammed, and Z. E. Shipchandler (1979): Understanding Iran's Business Environment. Baylor Business Studies 10, 2 (May–July): 61–72.

Focus on Saudi Business (1979): Middle East Economic Digest (October 19): 8.

Friedman, Kenneth (1979): Learning the Arabs' Silent Language. Psychology Today 13, 3 (August): 45, 47, 48, 50, 53–54.

Fuller, Edmund (1980): A Vision of Paradise, A Portrait of Arabia. Wall Street Journal (January 22): 18.

Gauldin, C. (1978): Self and Ideal Self-Images and Purchase Intentions. In: Proceedings of the Southern Marketing Association. Ed.: Franz, R. et al. New Orleans, (November).

Geyikdagi, M. Y. (1982): Risk Trends of U.S. Multinational and Domestic Firms, New York: Praeger.

Geyikdagi, M. Y. (1981): The Cost of Equity Capital and Risk of 28 U.S. Multinational Corporations vs. 28 U.S. Domestic Corporations: 1965–1978. Management International Review 21, 1: 89–94.

Geyikdagi, M. Y. (1984): Attitudes Towards Multinationlas: The Middle East in the World Context, Management Decision 22, 3: 14–21.

Gillis, Malcolm, and Ignatus Peprah (1981–82): State-Owned Enterprises in Developing Countries. The Wharton Magazine 6 (winter): 32–40.

Glaser, William A. (1971): Cross-National Comparisons of the Factory. Journal of Comparative Administration 3: 83–109.

Goldman, Arieh (1982): Adoption of Supermarket Shopping in a Developing Country: The Selective Adoption Phenomen. European Journal of Marketing 16, 1: 17–26.

Granner, Brian (1980): Cross-Cultural Adaptation In International Business. Journal of Contemporary Business 9, 3: 101–108.

Green, G., M. Novak, P. Sommerkamp, Keller, Ruber, and Andrew Szilagyi (1978): A Longitudinal Study of Leader Reward Behavior, Subordinate Expectancies, and Satisfaction. Personnel Psychology 21: 119–129.

Green, G., M. Novak, and P. Sommerkamp (1982): The Effects of Leader-Member Exchange and Job Design on Productivity and Satisfaction: Testing a Dual Attachment. Organizational Behavior and Human Performance 30: 109–134.

Gruneberg, Michael M. (1979): Understanding Job Satisfaction. New York: John Wiley and Sons.

Gupter, N., and T. A. Beehr (1972): Job Stress and Employee Behaviors. Organizational and Human Performance 7: 467–505.

Hackman, A. J. and G. Oldman (1975): Development of the Job Diagnostic Survey. Journal of Applied Psychology 60: 159–170.

Hafiz, Mohammed Ali (1980): Building on a Record of Achievement In Saudi Arabian Planning. Journal of Contemporary Business 9, 3: 65–70.

Haire, M., E. E. Ghiselli, and L. W. Porter (1966): Managerial Thinking: An International Study, New York: John Wiley & Sons, Inc.

Hall, Edward T. (1960): The Silent Language in Overseas Business. Harvard Business Review 38, 3 (May–June): 89–96.

Hamadi, Sania (1960): Temperament and Character of the Arabs. New York: Twayne Publishers.

Haner, F. T. (1980): Global Business: Strategy for the 1980's. New York: Praeger Publishers.

Hanna, Nessin (1977): Marketing Opportunities in Egypt: A Business Guide. R & E Research Associates Inc.

Harrell, Thomas W. (1971): Some Needs for Iranian Managers. Personnel Psychology 24: 477–479.

Hartshorn, J. E. (1962): Oil Companies and Governments. London: Faber and Faber, 301.

Havrylyshyn, Oli, and I. Alikhani (1982): Is There Cause For Export Optimism? An Inquiry into the Existence of a Second Generation of Successful Exporters. Review of World Economics 118: 651–663.

Hawkins, Robert S., N. Mintz, and M. Provissiers (1976): Government Takeovers of U.S. Foreign Affiliates. Journal of International Business Studies (Spring): 3–16.

Hibbert, E. P. (1979): The cultural dimension of marketing and the impact of industrialisation. European Research (January): 41–47.

Hiemenz, Ulrich (1983): Export Growth in Developing Asian Countries: Past Trends and Policy Issues. Review of World Economics 4: 119, 686–707.

Higgins, B. (1959): Economic Development. New York: W. W. Norton and Co., Inc., 82.

Higgins, Benjamin (1977): Economic Development and Cultural Change: Seamless Web or Patchwork Quilt? In: Manning Nash, ed.: Essays in Economic Development and Cultural Change. In: Honor of Bert F. Hoselitz, Supplement to Vol 25 of Economic Development and Cultural Change, Chicago University of Chicago Press, 99–122.

Himmetoglu, Bulent (1983): Personnel-Administration Practices of Turkish Industrial Firms. Studies of Management and Organizations 12: 73–81.

Horbon, J. D. (1980): Emphasis on Cultural Cross-Fertilization with Algeria's Technocrats. Business Quarterly 45, 4 (winter): 7–12.

Hudson, Michael C. (1977): Arab Politics. New York: Yale University Press.

Hulin, C. L. (1975): Effects of Changes in Job Satisfaction Levels on Employee Turnover, Journal of Applied Psychology 60: 329–333.

I.B.R.D. (1976): Appropriate Technology in World Bank Activities (July 19): 19.

Ikram, Khalid (1980): EGYPT Economic Management in a Period of Transition. Baltimore, Maryland: The John Hopkins University Press.

Information Canada (1970): Foreign Ownership and the Structure of Canadian Industry (Ottawa, Canada).

Isawi, C. P. (1963): Egypt in Revolution: An Economic Analysis. London: Oxford University Press, 51–52.

Jain, S. L. G. (1980): An Overview of Project Management in Mid-East. AACE Transactions, C.A.1 to C.A.6.

Jain, Subhash C. (1984): International Marketing Management. (Boston, Mass.: Kent Publishing).

James, Jeffrey (1983): Consumer Choice in the Third World. London: The Macmillan Press Limited.

James, L. R., and A. P. Jones (1980): Perceived Job Characteristics and Job Satisfaction: An Examination of Reciprocal Causation. Personnel Psychology 33: 97–135.

Johansson, Johny K. (1981): Japanese Export Management. Markneadstekniskt Centrum, Stockholm 16–18.

Jones, C. (1979): Formulating Plans for Joint Venture Companies in Saudi Arabia. In: Mark B. Winchester (ed.): The International Essays for Business Decision Makers, The Center For International Business, Houston, Texas, 162–169.

Jory, Ros (198): Banal in Beirut, Banned in Bahrain, International Advertiser (Jan/ Feb): 24–25.

Kaikati, Jack G. (1976): Doing Business in Iran: The Fastest Growing Import Market Between Europe and Japan. Atlanta Economic Review (September–October): 15–21.

Kaikati, Jack G. (1976): The Marketing Environment in Saudi Arabia. Akron Business and Economic Review (Summer): 5–13.

Kaikati, Jack G. (1978): The Arab Boycott-Middle East Business Dilemma. California Management Review 20, 3 (Spring): 32–46.

Kaikati, Jack G. (1979): Marketing Methods in the Middle East. In: Howard S. Gitlow and Edward W. Wheatley (eds.): Developments in Marketing Science 2: 103–107.

Kaikati, Jack G. (1979): Marketing Prices in Iran vis-a-vis Saudi-Arabia. Management International Review 19, 4: 31–37.

Kavcic, B., V. Rus, and Arnold S. Tannebaum (1971): Control, Participation and Effectiveness in Four Yugoslav Industrial Organizations. Administrative Science Quarterly 16: 74–86.

Kaynak, Erdener (1978): Difficulties of Undertaking Marketing Research in the Developing Countries. European Research 6, 6 (November): 251–9.

Kaynak, Erdener (1980): Government and Food Distribution in LDC,s: The Turkish Experience. Food Policy (May): 132–142.

Kaynak, Erdener, (1980): Transfer of Supermarketing Technology from Developed to Less-Developed Countries: The Case of Migros-Turk. The Finnish Journal of Business Economics 29, 1: 39–49.

Kaynak, Erdener (1981): Food Distribution Systems: Evolution in Latin America and the Middle East. Food Policy (May): 78–90.

Kaynak, Erdener (1982): Marketing in the Third World, Praeger Special Studies, New York, 5–12.

Kaynak, Erdener (1983): Market Potential Analysis for the Atlantic Canadian Products in the Arab Middle East. Paper presented at the 9th Annual Conference of the European International Business Association Conference, Norway December 18–20.

Kaynak, Erdener (1984): International Marketing Management. Praeger Special Studies, New York.

Kaynak, Erdener (1984): Marketing in the Middle East and North Africa. Management Decision 22, 1: 23–29.

Kaynak, Erdener, and S. Tamer Cavusgil (1982): The Evolution of Food Retailing Systems: Contrasting the Experience of Developed and Developing Countries. Journal of the Academy of Marketing Science 10, 3 (Summer): 249–269.

Kaynak, Erdener, and Ronald Savitt (1984): Comparative Marketing Systems. Praeger Special Studies, New York.

Keegan, Warren J. (1980): Multinational Marketing Management, (2nd ed.), Prentice-Hall Inc., Englewood Cliffs, New Jersey, 266.

Keller, Ruber, and Andrew Szilagyi (1978): A Longitudinal Study of Leader Reward Behavior, Subordinate Expectancies and Satisfaction. Personnel Psychology 21: 119–129.

Kelly, Joe, and Kamran Khozan (1980): Participative Management: Can It Work? Business Horizons 23: 74–79.

Kenis, Izzettin (1977): A Cross-Cultural Study of Personality and Leadership. Group and Organizational Studies 2: 49–60.

Kennedy, Charles R. (1981): Multinational Corporations, Political Risk Models and the Iranian Revolution. Working Paper # 81–10 (Austin: College of Business, University of Texas).

Khuri, Fuad I. (1968): The Etiquette of Bargaining in the Middle East. American Anthropologist 70, 4 (August): 698–700.

Kimball, John C. (1984): The Arabs 1984/85. Atlas and Almanac, The American Educational Trust.

Kindlegerger, C. P. (1958): Economic Development (New York: McGraw-Hill Book Co., Inc.): 107.

Kipnis, D. (1964): Mobility Expectations and Attitudes Toward Industrial Structure, Human Relations 17: 57–72.

Klat, Paul J. (1976): The Economic Outlook for the Arab Middle East. The Conference Board Record 13, 2 (February): 41–44 and 47.

Knudsen, Harold (1974): Explaining the National Propensity to Expropriate. An Ecological Approach, Journal of International Business Studies (Spring), 51–69.

Kobrin, Steven J. (1982): Managing Political Risk Assessment (Berkeley: University of California, Press).

Kobrin, Steven J., Baseh, S. Blank, and J. LaPalombara (1980): The Assessment of Non-Economic Environments by American Firms: A Preliminary Report. Journal of International Business Studies (Spring/Summer): 32–47.

Kostecki, M. M (1980): State Trading – A Major Factor in International Business. Centre for International Business Studies, H EC, University of Montreal, (November).

Kotler, P. (1973): The Major Tasks of Marketing Management. Journal of Marketing (October): 42–49.

Kraar, Louis (1977): The Super-Connector From Saudi Arabia. Fortune 98 (June): 109–116.

Kraar, Louis (1980): The Multinationals Get Smarter About Political Risks. Fortune (March 24): 80–98.

Kriesberg, M. (1970): Food Distribution Research for Developing Countries. Paper presented at the Food Distribution Research Society Annual Meeting, St. Louis, Missouri, (October 26).

Kurian, George Thomas (1982): Encyclopedia of the Third World. Revised Edition. 1. Facts on File, Inc.

Lauter, Geza P. (1969): Sociological-Cultural and Legal Factors Impeding Decentralization of Authority in Developing Countries. Academy of Management Journal 12: 367–378.

Lauter, Geza (1970): Environmental Constraints Impeding Managerial Performance in Developing Countries. Management International Review 10, 2–3: 45–52.

Lawler, E. E. (1973): Motivation in Work Organizations. Monterey, CA: Brooks and Cole.

Lee, J. A. (1979): Developing Managers in Developing Countries. International Business, David E. Ewing, ed.: Harvard Business Review Publication.

Leff, Nathaniel, H., and John U. Farley (1980): Advertising Expenditures in the Developing World. Journal of International Business Studies XI, 2 (Fall): 64–79.

Lenczowski, G. (1976): Middle East Oil in a Revolutionary Age. American Enterprise Institute for Public Policy Research, Washington, D. C.

Levitt, Theodore (1983): The Globalization of Markets Harvard Business Review 61, 3 (May–June): 92–102.

Levy, Marion J., Jr. (1966): Modernization of the Structure of Societies: A Setting for International Affairs. Princeton: Princeton University Press, 768.

Lewis, Bernard (1976): The Return of Islam, Commentary 61, 1 (January): 39–49.

Lewis, John W. (1969): The Social Limits of Politically Induced Changed. In: Chandler Morse, et al.: Modernization by Design: Social Change in the Twentieth Century, Ithaca: Cornell University Press.

Likert, R., and James G. Likert (1976): New Ways of Managing Conflict. New York: McGraw-Hill.

Lipmann, T. W. (1983): Saudis Say Windfall Ending But Stress New Opportunities for U.S. Businesses. Washington Post (15 May), Washington, D. C.

Littlefield, J. E. (1968): The Relationship of Marketing to Economic Development in Peru. The Southern Journal of Business 3, 3 (July): 1–14.

Looney, Robert E. (1982): Saudi Arabia's Islamic Growth Model. Journal of Economic Issues 16, 2 (June): 453–459.

Loutfi, M. (1975): Prospects for Development and Investment for Oil-producing Countries. In: J. D. Anthony (ed.): The Middle East: Oil, Politics and Development. American Enterprises Institute for Public Policy Research, Washington, D. C., 67–78.

Luqmani, Mushtaq, Quraeshi, Zahir A., and Linda Delene, (1980): Marketing in Islamic Countries: A Viewpoint, MSU Business Topics 28, 3 (Summer): 17–25.

Mabro, R., and S. Radwan (1976): The Industrialisation of Egypt 1939–1973: Policy and Performance (London: Oxford University Press), 74.

Mahmoud, Essam (1973): The Development of Labour Productivity in the Construction Industry. Published MBA Thesis. Ain Shams University, Cairo.

Mahmoud, E., and G. Rice (1983): A Managerial Procedure for Political Risk Forecasting. Proceedings of the World Marketing Congress (ed. E. Kaynak, Halifax, Nova Scotia, Canada).

Mahmoud, E., and G. Rice (1984): Marketing Problems in LDCs: The Case of Egypt. In: Kindra, G. S. (ed): Marketing in Developing Countries. (Bristol: Croom Helm Ltd.), 76–94.

Malone, Joe (1979): Dialogue in Durham. Middle East Economic Digest (October 5): 40.

Mann, R. C., and L. K. Williams (1962): Some effects of the Changing Work Environment in the Office. Journal of Social Issues 18: 90–101.

Mansfield, E. (1968): The Economics of Technological Change. W. W. Norton, New York.

Mason, John F. (1983): Saudi Arabia 1973–83: Ten Years of Progress, special survey sponsored by REDEC. Newsweek (May 30).

McConahay, Mary Jo (1979): Saudi's Reaffirm Faith in Yanbu Industrial Complex. Middle East Economic Digest (November 30): 5.

Mead, D. C. (1967): Growth and Structural Change in the Egyptian Economy (Homewood, Ill., Richard D. Irwin, Inc.).

Meade, R. D. (1967): An Experimental Study of Leadership in India. The Journal of Social Psychology 72: 35–44.

Meade, D., and J. O. Whittaker (1967): A Cross-Cultural Study of Authoritarianism. The Journal of Social Psychology 72: 35–44.

Meirc, S. A. (1977): A Summary Analysis of the Labor Movement in the Middle East and North Africa. Unpublished Report, Athens, Greece (January).

Meissner, Frank (1978): Rise of Third World Demands Marketing Be Stood On Its Head. Marketing News (October 6): 1 and 16.

Melikan, Levon H. (1956): Some Correlates of Authoritarianism in Two Cultural Groups. Journal of Psychology 42: 237–249.

Melikan, Levon H. (1959): Authoritarianism and Its Correlates in the Egyptian Culture and in the United States. Journal of Social Issues 15: 58.

Mendenhall, W., and J. E. Reinmuth (1974): Statistics for Management and Economics (2nd Ed.). North Scituate, Massachusetts: Duxbury Press.

Merton, R. K. (1976): Sociological Ambivalence and Other Essays (New York: Free Press).

Micallef, Joseph V. (1981): Political Risk Assessment. Columbia Journal of World Business (Summer): 48–52.

Michell, Paul (1979): Infrastructures and International Marketing Effectiveness. Columbia Journal of World Business (Spring): 91–101.

Middle East and African Economist (1982): XXXVI, 4: 27.

Middle East and African Economist (1982): XXXVI, 7, 8: 43.

Middle Eastern and North African Peoples and Cultures (1974): The New Encyclopaedia Britannica, Chicago: 12: 167–171.

Middle East Economic Digest (1981): Saudi Arabia: A Special Report (July): 7.

Mihcioglu, Cemal (1970): General Character of the Turkish Civil Service, The Turkish Administrators, A Cultural Survey. In: J. R. Hopper, and R. I. Levin, eds.: Public Administration Division. U.S. AID' Ankara, Turkey.

Mills. A. E. (1964): Environment and Size of Firm: A Study of International Trading in the Arab Middle East. The Journal of Management Studies 1, 1 (March): 68–80.

Morgan Guarantee Trust Company of New York (1978): Foreign Investors – Bullish on America (September).

Moustafa, Mohamed E. (1978): Pricing Strategy For Export Activity in Developing Nations. Journal of International Business Studies 9 (Spring/Summer): 1.

Moyer, R. (1965): Marketing in Economic Development. International Business Occasional Paper No. 1, Graduate School of Business Administration, Michigan University, East Lansing, Michigan, 1–53.

Mufson, S., and Y. M. Ibrahim (1982): Santa Fe International Thrives Since Kuwait Bought It a Year Ago. The Wall Street Journal (29 November), New York.

Muna, F. (1980): The Arab Executive (New York: St. Martin's Press).

Murrell, Kenneth L. (1979): A Cultural Analysis of the Egyptian Management Environment. In: Philip Harris and Gerald Meelin (eds.): Innovation in Global Consultation. Washington, D. C., International Consultants Foundation, 105–119.

Myall, Patrick (1979): Laws Unfriendly to Foreign, Funds, West Germany and the Middle East. Middle East Economic Digest Special Report (November), 21.

Naccache, G. (1961): in Al-Afkar (July): 14–16.

National Research Council (1978): A Background Review of the Relationships Between Technological Innovation and the Economy in Technology, Trade, and the U.S. Economy. National Academy of Sciences, Washington, D. C.

Negandhi, Anant R. (1983): Cross Cultural Management Research: Trend and Future Directions. Journal of International Business Studies 14: 17–27.

Nehrt, Lee C. (1970): The Political Climate for Private Foreign Investment (New York: Praeger Publishers).

Neubauer, Friedrich F., and N. B. Solomon (1977): A Managerial Approach to Environmental Assessment. Long Range Planning 10 (April): 13–20.

Nwokoye, Nonyelu G. (1981): Modern Marketing for Nigeria. London: The MacMillan Press.

O'Brien, P. K. (1966): The Revolution in Egypt's Economic System 1952–1965 (London: Oxford University Press): 13.

O'Sullivan, Edmund, and John Roberts (1981): Saudi-isation and the Private Sector, Middle East Economic Digest (24 July): 28.

Owen, Forrest F. (1977): Saudi Arabia: A Volatile – Paradoxical – Local Market. Advertising Age 48, Part 3 (July 11): 94–102.

Owen, R. (1976): Islam and Capitalism: A Critique of Rodenson Review of Middle East Studies 2.

Padolecchia, S. P. (1979): Marketing in the Developing World (New Delhi: Vikas Publishing House PVT Limited): 45.

Patai, Raphael (1973): The Arab Mind. Charles Scribner's Sons, New York.

Pateman, C. (1970): Participation and Democratic Theory (Cambridge: The University Press).

Pavitt, K. (1983): Technology Transfer Amongst the Industrially Advanced Countries: An Overview, Paper Presented at the US Social Science Research Council Conference on International Technology Transfer (2–3 June), New York.

Penrose, E. (1975): International Oil Companies and Governments in the Middle East. In: J. D. Anthony (ed.): The Middle East: Oil, Politics, and Development. American Enterprise Institute for Public Policy Research, Washington, D. C., 3–19.

Peretz, Don (1963): The Middle East Today. Holt, Rinehart and Winston, New York.

Pezeshkpur, Changiz (1978): Challenges to Management in the Arab World. Business Horizons 21: 47–55.

Porter, L. W., and E. E. Lawler (1968): Managerial Attitudes and Performance. Homewood, IL: Dorsey Press.

Porter, L. W., and R. M. Steers (1973): Organizational Work and Personnel Factors in Turnover and Absenteeism. Psychological Bulletin 80: 151–176.

Pras, B. (1980): La firme multinational face au risque. Paris: Presses Universitaires de France, 32–37.

Prasad, S. B. (1981): Managers' Attitudes in Brazil: Nationals vs Expatriates. Management International Review 21: 78–85.

Preston, Lee E. (1967): Marketing Organization in Arab Socialism. Journal of Marketing 31 (October): 1–7.

Pulakos, Elaine, and Neal Schmitt (1983): A Longitudinal Study of a Valence Model Approach for the Prediction of Job Satisfaction of New Employees. Journal of Applied Psychology 68: 307–312.

Rand, Edward J. (1976): Learning to Do Business in the Middle East. The Conference Board Record 13, 2 (February): 49–51.

Redding, S. G. (1982): Cultural Effects on the Marketing Process in Southeast Asia. Journal of the Market Research Society 24, 2 (April): 98–115.

Reuber, Grant, L. (1973): Private Foreign Investment in Development. Oxford: Clarendon Press, 16.

Rey, Ronald (1966): Labour Turnover as a Function of Workers Differences, Work Environment and Authoritarianism of Foreman. Journal of Applied Psychology 50: 497–500.

Rice, Gillian (1984): Marketing Management in Egypt. Management Decision 22, 4: 3–13.

Ritchie, J. B., and Raymond, E. Miles (1970): An Analysis of Quantity and Quality of Participation as Mediating Variables in the Participative Decision Making Process. Personnel Psychology 23: 347–359.

Ritchie, J. R., and R. J. LaBreque (1975): Marketing Research and Public Policy: A Functional Perspective. Journal of Marketing (July): 16.

Roberts, Karlene, R. Miles, and L. Blankenship (1968): Organizational Leadership, Satisfaction and Productivity: A Comparative Analysis. Academy of Management Journal 11: 401–414.

Robock, Stephen H. (1971): Political Risk: Identification and Assessment. Columbia Journal of World Business (July–August): 6–20.

Robock, Stephen H., and Kenneth Simmonds (1983): International Business and Multinational Enterprises (Homewood, Ill.: Richard D. Irwin).

Roche, Douglas (1980): Third World is the Developing Market. The Financial Post (July 26): 9.

Rodinson, R. (1974): Islam and Capitalism (English Edition, Harmondswroth, Middlesex: Penguin).

Roos, L. L., Jr., and N. P. Roos (1971): Managers of Modernization, Organization and Elietes in Turkey. Cambridge, Mass.: Harvard University Press.

Rostow, W. W. (1965): The Concept of National Market and Its Economic Growth Implications. In Bennett, PD (ed.): Marketing and Economic Development. American Marketing Association Proceedings (Fall): 11–19.

Rousseau, D. (1978): Relationship of Work to Nonwork. Journal of Applied Psychology 63: 513–517.

Roy, D. (1977): Management Education and Training in the Arab World. International Review of Administrative Science XLIII: 221–228.

Rugh, William (1973): Emergence of a New Middle Class in Saudi Arabia. Middle East Journal 27 (winter): 16.

Rugman, A. M. (1979): International Diversification and the Multinational Enterprise. Lexington, Massachusetts: Lexington Books.

Rush, Harold, M. F. (1971): Behavioral Science: Concepts and Management Application. The Conference Board.

Saddik. S. M. (1969): Marketing in the Wool Textile, Textile Machinery, and Clothing Industries. PhD Thesis, Bradford University, Bradford, England.

Saddik, S. M. (1973): An Analysis of the Status of Marketing in Egypt. European Journal of Marketing (Summer): 77–81.

Said, Edward W. (1978): Orientalism. Pantheon Books, New York.

Salacuse, Jeswald W. (1980): Arab Capital and Middle Eastern Development Finance. Journal of World Trade Law 14, 4 (July–August): 283–309.

Samli A. Coskun (1972): Market Potentials Can be Determined at the International Level. Australian Journal of Market Research (August–November): 85–92.

Samli, A. C. (1977): An Approach For Estimating Market Potential in East Europe. Journal of International Business Studies 8, 2 (Fall/Winter): 49–53.

Samli, A. C. and J. I. Hirsch (1979): Sino-American Marketing Prospects: Potential and Barriers. In: The Proceedings of the Academy of International Business Asia Pacific Dimensions of International Business Conference, Honolulu, Hawaii (December): 476–484.

Samli, A.: Market Potentials Can be Determined at the International Level. Australian Journal of Market Research (August–November): 85–92.

Sarwar, Muhammad (1981): The Holy Quran's Arabic Text and English Translation. New York: Islamic Seminary.

Saudi Arabia: A Costly Plan For Rapid Growth (1980): Business Week. 2630 (March 31): 52, 54 and 59.

Savage, Alan H. (1978): Planning and Control Problems in Developing Countries. Managerial Planning, 17–23.

Sawiris, S. B. (1971): Planning Economic Development in Underdeveloped Countries with Special Reference to Egypt. Unpublished PhD Dissertation, University Libre De Bruxelles, 346–347.

Sayigh, Y. A. (1975): Oil in Developmental and Political Strategy: An Arab View in the Middle East. Oil, Politics, and Development, 37–44.

Schwadran, B. (1977): Middle East Oil: Issues and Problems. Schenkman Publishing Co., Cambridge, Mass.

Schwartz, E. Brantley (1977): Marketing in the Middle East. CMC Monograph 8, Princeton, New Jersey, 48.

Scrivener, Robert C. (1979): International Markets or Die. The Business Quarterly 44, 2 (Summer): 72–75.

Searby, Daniel M. (1976): Doing Business in the Middle East: Speeding Up Project Development in Egypt. In Mark B. Winchester (ed.): The International Trade Conference of the Southwest, Dallas, Texas, 8–14.

Searby, Daniel M. (1976): Doing Business in the Mideast: The Game is Rigged. Harvard Business Review 54, 1 (January–February): 56–64.

Severiens, J. T. (1970–80): Foreign Investment in Egypt: What Are the Dividends of Peace? Middle East Review 12, 2 (Winter): 45–55.

Shapiro, Alan C. (1981): Managing Political Risk: A Policy Approach. Columbia Journal of World Business (Fall): 32–39.

Sherbini, Abdel Aziz (1968): Import-Oriented Marketing Mechanisms. MSU Business Topics (Spring): 70–73.

Sherbiny, Naiem, A. (1975): Arab Oil and International Business: Future Implications. Journal of Business Administration 7, 1: 103–117.

Shilling, Nancy A. (1977): Arab Market: The Opportunities and Obstacles. Advertising Age 48 (July 11): 68–70 and 72.

Shilling, Nancy A. (1977): The Agent in the Arab World. Dallas: Intercrescent Publishing Company.

Shuaib, Shuaib A. (1980): Some Aspects of Accounting Regulation in Kuwait. Journal of Contemporary Business 9, 3: 85–99.

Shuptrine, F. K., and F. A. Osmanski, (1975): Marketing's Changing Role: Expanding or Contracting. Journal of Marketing (April): 58–66.

Simiar, Farhad (1983): Major Causes of Joint-Venture Failures in the Middle East: The Case of Iran. Management International Review 23, 1: 58–68.

Simon, Jeffrey D. (1982): Political Risk Assessment: Post Trends and Future Prospects. Columbia Journal of World Business (Fall): 62–71.

Sinclair, Stuart (1982): The State of the Third World in 1982. In: Third World Economic Handbook. Euromonitor Publications Limited, London, 3–6 and 133–136.

Sinclair, Stuart (1982): Third World Economic Handbook. Euromonitor Publications Limited, London, 12.

Singer, H. W. (1950): The Distribution of Gains between Industry and Borrowing Countries. American Economic Review (May).

Skinner, Wickham C. (1964): A Test Case in Turkey. California Management Review 6: 53–66.

Slater, A. G. (1977): International Logistics Strategies. Management Decision 15, 4: 380–395.

Stanley M. T. (1981): Capital Structure and Cost Capital for the Multinational Firm. Journal of International Business Studies (Spring/Summer) XII: 1.

Steers, R. M. (1977): Antecedents and Outcomes of Organizational Commitment. Administrative Science Quarterly 22: 46–56.

Stephens, D. B. (1981): Cultural Variations in Leadership Style: A Methodological Experience in Comparing Managers in the U.S. and Peruvian Textile Industries. Management International Review 21: 47–55.

Stessin, Lawrence (1973): Culture Shock and the American Business Overseas. Exchange 9: 1.

Stevens, Christopher (1979): Food Aid and the Developing World. London: Croom Helm Publishers.

Steward, F. (1979): International Technology Transfer: Issues and Options. Staff Working Paper, 344, The World Bank, Washington D. C.

Stewart, Charles F. (1961): The Changing Middle East Market. Journal of Marketing 25 (January): 47–51.

Stogdill, Ralph (1974): Handbook of Leadership. New York: The Free Press.

Stonequist, E. (1973): The Marginal Man: A Study in Personality and Culture Conflict (New York: Charles Scribner's Sons).

Strauss, Georgia (1974): Job Satisfaction, Motivation and Job Redesign. Berkeley California Institute of Industrial Relations: University of California, Reprint no. 390.

Szyliowicz, Joseph S. (1980): The Prospects For Scientific and Technological Development in Saudi Arabia. Journal of Contemporary Business 9, 3: 41–58.

Taher, Abdul Hadi (1980): The Potential For Increased Arab Ownership of Transportation Facilities. Journal of Contemporary Business 9, 3: 59–63.

Tannenbaum, A. S., S. Mozina, J. Jerovsek, and R. Likert (1970): Testing A Management Style. European Business 27: 60–68.

Tanner, James and John Close (1979): Saudis Allowing Higher Oil Level to Remain. The Wall Street Journal (September 27): 3.

Teece, D. J. (1977): Technology Transfer by Multinational Firms: The Resource Cost of Transferring Technological Know-How. The Economic Journal 87: 242–261.

Teece, D. J. (1981): The Market for Know-how and the Efficient International Transfer of Technology. Stanford University Graduate School of Business Research Paper, 608.

Telephone Engineer and Management (1982): When in Saudi-Arabia – Interco Adapts Quickly to Local Customs 86, 11 (June 1): 60–61.

Terpstra, Vern (1981): On Marketing Appropriate Products in Developing Countries. Journal of International Marketing 1, 3:3.

Terrill, William A. (1965): Management Organization and Methods in Turkey. Human Organization 24: 96–104.

The Boston Consulting Group (1970): Prospectives on Experience. Boston, Massachusetts.

The Europe Year Book, 1982: A World Survey (1982): London, England: Europa Publications Limited.

Thomas, L. Kean, and Bill McDonald (1978): Job Satisfaction and Life Satisfaction: An Empirical Evaluation of Their Interrelationship. Journal of Applied Psychology 63: 530–532.

Thomas, Philip S. (1980): Environmental Scanning: The State of the Arts, Long Range Planning (Summer): 19–25.

Thomson, John R. (1979): Middle East Distribution Advertising Age 48, 28 (July 11): 80, 82–83.

Thomson, John R. (1983): Marketing in the Arab World. Advertising Age's Focus (January–March), no page number.

Tinnin, David B. (1980): The Saudis Awaken to Their Vulnerability. Fortune 101, 5 (March 10): 48–56.

Tosi, H., J. Hunter, T. J. R. Chesser, and S. Caroll (1976): How Real Are Changes Induced by Management by Objectives. Administrative Science Quarterly 21: 276–306.

Tsurumi, Yoshihiro (1972): R & D Factors and Exports of Manufactured Goods from Japan in The Product Life Cycle and International Trade. Edited by Louis T. Wells, Jr., Harvard University Press, Boston, Massachusetts, 162: 178.

Tuncalp, Secil, and Ugur Yavas (1983): Supermarkets Gaining Rapid Acceptance in Saudi Arabia. Marketing News (February 4): 5.

Turner, Jack H. (1982): Petro Bodies: Asian Workers in Saudi Arabia, in The International Essays for Business Decision Makers. Edited by Mark B. Winchester: The Center for International Business: Dallas, TX, VI: 253–264.

Üçüncü Beş Yıllık Kalkınma Planı 1973–1977 (1973): Third Five-Year Development Plan 1973–1977. State Planning Organization Ankara, Turkey, 64.

UNIDO (1977): National Approaches to the Acquisition of Technology, United Nations, New York.

United Nations (1978): Transnational Corporation in World Developments: A Reexamination (New York: United Nations).

United Nations (1982): Yearbook of International Trade Statistics. 1. Trade by Country. New York: United Nations.

United Nations (1983): Statistical Yearbook (1981). New York: United Nations.

Upshaw, Douglas N. (1976): Organizing to Sell Middle East Markets. The Conference Board Record 13, 2 (February): 6, 46–48.

U.S. Department of Commerce (1981): Marketing in Egypt. Overseas Business Reports (December).

Vassiliou, G. (1980): Marketing in the Middle East. Graham & Trotman, London.

Vernon, Raymond (1966): International Investment and International Trade in the Product Cycle. Quarterly Journal of Economics 80 (May): 199.

Vernon, Raymond (1977): The Strain on National Objectives: The Developing Countries. In: Storm Over the Multinationals. Harvard University Press, Cambridge, Mass.: 139–173.

Vroom, V. H. (1976): Leadership. In: Handbook of Industrial and Organizational Psychology. Marvin D. Dunnette (ed.), Chicago: Rand McNally College Publishing Company.

Vroom, V. H., and P. W. Yetton (1973): Leadership and Decision-Making. Pittsburgh: The University of Pittsburgh Press.

Vukmir, Branko, (1933). Selling Through Agents: The Law in Three Middle East Markets. International Trade Forum 19, 3 (July–September): 4–7 and 30–31.

Wahby, Mohammed (1979): Islamic Revival. Middle East Economic Digest (November 23): 4.

Wahby, Mohammed (1979): The Arabs and Their Image in the West. Middle East Economic Digest (October 5): 15.

Wall Street Journal (1982): GM Runs Into a Middle East Crisis It's Too Hot and Dusty in Baghdad (February 23): 37.

Walmsley, J. (1979): Joint Ventures in Saudi Arabia. Graham & Trotman, London.

Watt, W. M. (1961): Islam and Integration of Society. Evanston: Northwestern University Press.

Weigand, Robert E. (1968): The Arab League Boycott of Israel. MSU Business Topics (Spring): 74–80.

Wells, Louis T. (1968): A Product Life Cycle for International Trade? Journal of Marketing 32 (July): 4.

Wells, Louis T. (1975): Social Cost/Benefit Analysis for MNCs. Harvard Business Review (March–April): 40–47.

Williams, L. K., W. K. Whyte, and C. S. Green (1966): Do Cultural Differences Affect Worker's Attitudes? Industrial Relations 5: 105–117.

Williams, Simon (1965): Negotiating Investment in Emerging Countries. Harvard Business Review 43, 1 (January–February): 89–99.

Wind, Yoram, and S. P. Douglas (1972): International Market Segmentation. Journal of Marketing 6, 1: 17–25.

Wood, G. E., and N. A. Jianakoplos: Coordinated International Economic Expansion: Are Convoys or Locomotives the Answer? In: D. A. Anderson, M. Luqmani, and Z. A. Quraeshi, eds.: International Business 1979. A Selection of Current Readings, East Lansing, Michigan: Michigan State University.

World Business Weekly (1981): Cairo's Telephone System Improves (February): 19.

World's Apart? Islam vs. Washington (1979): Many Experts Doubt It's as Simple as That Wall Street Journal (December 21). 19.

Wright, Peter (1981): Doing Business in Islamic Markets. Harvard Business Review 59 (January–February): 35–40.

Yaprak, Attila, and K. T. Sheldon (1984): Political Risk Management. In: Multinational Firms: An Integrative Approach, Management Decision 22: 6, forthcoming.

Yavas, Ugur, and Erdener Kaynak (1980): Current Status of Marketing Research in Developing Countries: Problems and Opportunities. Journal of International Marketing and Marketing Research 5, 2 (June): 79–89.

Yavas, Ugur, and Secil Tuncalp (1982): The Changing Patterns of Shopping. Saudi Business (December 18–24): 24–26.

Yavas, Ugur, and Secil Tuncalp (1983): Expatriate Shoppers and How They Compare (March 5–11): 17–21.

Yavas, Ugur, and Secil Tuncalp (1983): Grocery Shopping Patterns in Saudi Arabia: Prospects for the Diffusion of Supermarkets. Der Markt 87: 131–137.

Yavas, Ugur, and Secil Tuncalp (1984): Perceived Risk in Grocery Outlet Selection: A Case Study in Saudi Arabia. European Journal of Marketing 17: 4.

Yavas, Ugur, Erdener Kaynak, and Eser Borak (1981): Modern Retailing Institutions in Developing Countries: Determinants of Supermarket Patronage in Istanbul, Turkey. Journal of Business Research 9, 4 (December): 367–379.

Yavas, Ugur, Erdener Kaynak and Eser Borak (1982): Food Shopping Orientations in Turkey: Some Lessons for Policy Makers. Food Policy (May): 133–140.

Yearbook of National Accounts Statistic – 1979: Volume II – International Tables – United Nations (1980). New York: United Nations, 185–305.

Young, George B. (1977): A Market Making Up For Lost Time. Industrial Marketing 62 (July): 74–76.

Zahra, S. A. (1980): Egyptian Management at the Cross-Roads. Management International Review 20: 3.

Zif, Jehiel (1980): Opening International Borders: A Methodolgy to Assess Business Opportunities and Societal Effects. Journal of Contemporary Business 9, 3: 21–30.

The Editor

ERDENER KAYNAK is Professor of Marketing and Chairman, Department of Business Administration, Mount Saint Vincent University, Halifax, Nova Scotia, Canada. He holds a B. Econ. degree from the University of Istanbul, an M. A. in Marketing from the University of Lancaster, and a Ph. D. in Marketing Management from the Cranfield Institute of Technology. He has taught at Hacettepe University in Ankara, Turkey and Acadia University in Wolfville, Nova Scotia, Canada. Furthermore, he has conducted post-doctoral research studies at Michigan State University, U.S.A., University of Lund, Sweden, University of Stirling, Scotland, and the Chinese University of Hong Kong and has lectured and held executive training programs in Europe, North America, the Middle East, Latin America, and the Far East. He is the founder and president of a Halifax-based company, Cross-Cultural Marketing Services Incorporated.

Dr. Kaynak has served as a consultant to business as well as a number of Canadian and international organizations. He has been the recipient of a number of research scholarships and distinctions; most notably Fulbright Post-Doctoral Research Scholar, Turkish Government Scholarship, Fellow of the Salzburg Seminar in American Studies, British Council Fellowship, Swedish Institute Research Scholarship and German Academic Exchange Service Scholarship. Dr. Kaynak is a Board of Governor and Director of International Progroms with the Academy of Marketing Science. He has published some sixty articles in refereed scholarly journals including the Journal of Macromarketing, Journal of Business Research, Journal of Advertising Research, Journal of the Academy of Marketing Science, European Journal of Marketing, International Journal of Physical Distribution and Materials Administration, European Management Journal, Management International Review, European Research, International Journal of Marketing and Marketing Research, International Journal of Advertising and many others. He is the author of three books published by Praeger Publishers Inc. of New York, one in *Marketing in the Third World,* the second one in *Comparative Marketing Systems* co-authored with Ronald Savitt of Michigan State University and the third one in *International Marketing Management.* In addition to this, he has read papers and chaired sessions in more than a dozen countries at over 40 conferences. He is on the Editorial Review Board of the Journal of the Academy of Marketing Science, Management Decision, a regional editor for the Middle East of the Journal of Enterprise Management and North American Editorial Board member of the Journal of International Marketing and Marketing Research, Journal of International Advertising, International Marketing Review and the Service Industries Journal. He prepared a major series on industry and commerce in the Middle East which was published by *Management Decision* during 1984. He was the organizer and chairman of three international congresses: one on tourism, one on housing development, and a World Marketing Congress, devoted to Managing the International Marketing Function: Creative Challenges of the Eighties.

The Authors

Riad A. Ajami is Associate Professor of International Business Policy, College of Administrative Science, The Ohio State University. During the 1983–84 academic year Dr. Ajami was a Visiting Sholar at Harvard Center for International Affairs of Harvard University, Boston, U.S.A.

Abbas J. Ali is Assistant Professor of Management in the School of Business and Management at Saginaw Valley State College, Michigan, U.S.A.

Lyn S. Amine is Associate Professor of Marketing, Department of Marketing, College of Business and Economics of the University of Wisconsin – Whitewater, Wisconsin, U.S.A.

S. Tamer Cavusgil is Professor of Marketing, Director of Business Research Centre, Department of Marketing, Bradley University, Peoria, Illinois, U.S.A.

Adel I. El-Ansary is Professor and Chairman of Business Administration at the School of Government and Business Administration of the George Washington University, Washington, D.C., U.S.A.

Asim Erdilek is Associate Professor of Economics, Department of Economics, Case Western Reserve University, Cleveland, Ohio, U.S.A.

Awad El-Haddad is Assistant Professor of Marketing, Faculty of Management Sciences, King Faisal University, Al-Ahsa, Saudi Arabia.

Necla V. Geyikdagi is a Free Lance Consultant and Researcher in Economics in New York, New York, U.S.A.

M. Yasar Geyikdagi is Professor of International Business and Finance, Department of Business Administration, State University of New York, College at Old Westbury, Long Island, U.S.A.

Metin Gürol (late) was Associate Professor of Marketing, Department of Marketing, Saint Joseph's University, Philadelphia, Pennsylvania, U.S.A.

Essam Mahmoud is Associate Professor of Management, College of Business and Economics, West Virginia University, Morgantown, West Virginia, U.S.A.

Lance Masters is Associate Professor of International Business at California State College, San Bernardino, California, U.S.A.

Y. Nabil Razzouk is Assistant Professor of International Business at California State College, San Bernardino, California, U.S.A.

Gillian Rice is Assistant Professor of Marketing, Department of Marketing, College of Business and Economics, West Virginia University, Morgantown, West Virginia, U.S.A.

Paul Swiercz is Assistant Professor of Management and Chairman of the Department of Management/Marketing at Saginaw Valley State College, Michigan, U.S.A.

Attila Yaprak is Associate Professor of Marketing, School of Business Administration, Wayne State University, Detroit, Michigan, U.S.A.

Ugur Yücelt is Associate Professor of Management, Division of Business and Management, The Pennsylvania State University, Capitol Campus, Middletown, Pennsylvania, U.S.A.

Author Index

Subject Index

financial evaluation procedure 72
Ford 172
Foreign Capital Investment Code 235
   Investment Capital Committee 235
Fortune 79
France 77, 82, 155, 166

GAIFZ (the General Authority for Investment and Free Zones) 220, 221
GATT 87
general customer characteristics 38, 39
General Electric 8, 42, 46
General Foods Corporation 118
geocentric attitudes 17
Germany 77, 82, 117, 166, 203
Ghana 59
government-financed development
   projects market 32
government ownership 4
Gillette 8, 173
Greece 155
growing stage countries 34, 35
Gulf Cooperation Council (GCC) 98
Gulf States 34, 94, 107, 110, 153

hypothetical grouping of Arab markets
   36

I.B.R.D. 46
import-substitution oriented 93
Indonesia 21, 59, 110
Information Canada 62
institutionalization 71
institutionalized firms 64
intermediate stage countries 34, 35
International Harvester 172
International Technology Transfer
   (ITT) 11, 85, 88, 94
Iran 15, 57, 59, 72, 76, 93, 94, 98 113,
   163, 176
Iraq 6, 35, 49, 76, 83, 93, 94, 98, 110,
   163
Islam 29, 104, 136
Islamic Polity 147
Israel 163, 166
Italy 77, 82

Japan 77, 82, 116, 209, 210
Japanese multinationals 55
John Deere 172
Johnson & Johnson 40
Jordan 35, 76, 93, 110, 163

Klenex 37
Koranic law 166
Kraft 8
Kuwait 6, 11, 19, 21, 24, 25, 34, 41, 93,
   94, 95, 98, 107, 110, 111, 163
Kuwait Foreign Trading Contracting
   and Investment Company 25
Kuwait Fund 25
Kuwait Petroleum Corporation (KPC)
   94, 95, 235
Kuwait Real Estate Investment Corporation 25

labour-intensive countries 93, 110
Leadership Decision Style Index 142
   Scale 142
Lebanon 7, 76, 93, 110, 153, 163, 241
Libya 59, 76, 93, 98, 107, 176
Libyan manager 138
Likert System Theory 115
literary heritage 155

macro political risk 59
macro segment 38
Maghreb 163
management style
   benevolent-authoritarian 13, 114
   consultative 13, 114
   exploitative-authoritarian 13, 114
   participative 13, 114
managerial gap 44
Marcona Mining Company 70
market commonalities 164
market index 78
Mauritania 21, 25
Mecca 166
Medina 166
Merck 66

de Gruyter Studies in Organization

An international series by internationally known authors presenting current research in organization.

Editorial Board: *Michael Aiken,* USA (University of Wisconsin) · *Franco Ferraresi,* Italy (University Torino) · *David J. Hickson,* Great Britain (University Bradford) · *Alfred Kieser,* Federal Republic of Germany (University Mannheim) · *Cornelis J. Lammers,* The Netherlands (University Leiden) · *Johan Olson,* Norway (University Bergen) · *Jean-Claude Thoenig,* France (INSEAD, Fontainebleau)

The Japanese Industrial System
By *Charles J. McMillan*
2nd revised edition
1985. 15,5 x 23 cm. XII, 356 pages. Cloth DM 88,-.
ISBN 3 11 010410 5

Political Management
Redefining the Public Sphere
By *Hall Thomas Wilson*
1984. 15,5 x 23 cm. X, 316 pages. Cloth DM 98,-.
ISBN 3 11 009902 0

Limits to Bureaucratic Growth
By *Marshall W. Meyer* in Association with *William Stevenson* and *Stephen Webster*
1985. 15,5 x 23 cm. X, 228 pages. Cloth DM 88,-.
ISBN 3 11 009865 2

Guidance, Control and Evaluation in the Public Sector
Edited by *F. X. Kaufmann, G. Majone, V. Ostrom*
1985. 17 x 24 cm. XIV, 830 pages. Cloth DM 198,-.
ISBN 3 11 009707 9

The American Samurai
Blending American and Japanese Managerial Practice
By *Jon P. Alston*
1986. 15,5 x 23 cm. Approx. 390 pages. Cloth approx. DM 98,-.
ISBN 3 11 010619 1

Forthcoming Title:
Management in China
By *Oiva Laaksonen*
1986. 15,5 x 23 cm. Approx. 290 pages. Cloth approx. DM 88,-.
ISBN 3 11 009958 6

Prices are subject to change without notice

WALTER DE GRUYTER · BERLIN · NEW YORK

ORGANIZATION STUDIES

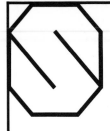

An international multidisciplinary journal devoted to the study of organizations, organizing and the organized in, and between societies

Editor-in-Chief: David J. Hickson, University of Bradford

Co-Editor: Alfred Kieser, Mannheim

Managing Editor: Susan van der Werff

Organization Studies is a supranational journal, based neither on any one nation nor on collaboration between any particular nations. Its aim is to present diverse theoretical and empirical research from all nations, spanning a broad view of organizations and organizing. Its current Editorial Board is drawn from thirteen nations, and its contributors are world-wide.

O. S. is published in English because that language is the most widely read in this field of research. But manuscripts in other languages can be reviewed in those languages prior to translation. O. S. reviews books published in languages other than English to bring them before its international readership, and News and Notes cover conferences and research in many countries.

O. S. has published papers by authors from sociology, political science, management and public administration, psychology and economics. Some among the range of titles are listed overleaf. O. S. is not only about the study of "the organization", though that is central. It is also about the processes of organizing people, whether in business, public services, or public administration and government; and it is about the response of "the organized". It is not only about the contemporary scene, especially differences around the world, but also about the historical developments which have led to that scene.

Subscription rates 1986

Per volume of four issues. Libraries and institutions **DM 118,–** / approx. US $ 43.70. Individuals (except FRG and Switzerland) **DM 59,–** / approx. US $ 21.85 (DM-prices are definitive, $-prices are approximate and subject to fluctuations in the exchange rate).

Published in collaboration with the European Group for Organizational Studies (EGOS) and the Maison des Sciences de l'Homme, Paris by

WALTER DE GRUYTER · BERLIN · NEW YORK

Verlag Walter de Gruyter & Co., Genthiner Straße 13, D-1000 Berlin 30, Tel.: (0 30) 2 60 05-0
Walter de Gruyter, Inc., 200 Saw Mill River Road, Hawthorne, N. Y. 10532, Tel.: (914) 747-0110